CW00548190

# TWO MEN
## ✳ IN A BOAT ✳
# Rowing Two Rivers

# TWO MEN

## ❋ IN A BOAT ❋

## Rowing Two Rivers

*In the Watery Footsteps of*
*Captain Horatio Hornblower RN*

Martin Andrew

First published in the UK in July 2021 by
Journey Books, an imprint of Bradt Guides Ltd
31a High Street, Chesham, Buckinghamshire, HP5 1BW, England

www.bradtguides.com

ISBN: 9781784779986

British Library Cataloguing in Publication Data
A catalogue record for this book is available from the British Library

**Photos**
All photos © Martin Andrew
*Front cover Flying Colours 71* beached at Sully-sur-Loire
*Back cover Flying Colours 71* at Blois on the river Loire

**Maps** Martin Andrew

Digital conversion by www.dataworks.co.in
Printed in the UK by Jellyfish Print Solutions

To find out more about our Journey Books imprint, visit www.bradtguides.com/journeybooks

# Acknowledgements

This book is dedicated first and foremost to my wife Jill who has been a constant source of encouragement but has had lots to worry about, given my accident-prone nature.

Special thanks to my oldest friend and fellow Hornblower fan, Richard Robinson, who has read and reread drafts and contributed numerous suggestions and amendments. He is of course my fellow rower, the 'Richard' of the text and always good company. A few of the photographs are his and I am grateful for their use.

My brother Nigel Andrew, author of the much-acclaimed *The Mother of Beauty* (Thorntree Press 2019) on the 17th-century golden age of church monuments, also read the text in draft and made many helpful suggestions.

All four of us share a love of historic architecture and art and history.

# Contents

**Introduction** .................................................................................viii

**PART I: THE RIVER SEVERN**

**1**   The Two Men's Boat, the Loire Unravels .................................2

**2**   Upper Arley to Wales where We Dip Oars at Last................13

**3**   A Long Day's Rowing from Wales to Shrewsbury ...............23

**4**   In Shrewsbury and Onwards to Shrewsbury Weir..............33

**5**   A Rough Landing at Atcham Bridge ....................................43

**6**   Rowing Past Wroxeter ..........................................................50

**7**   Buildwas Abbey and Supper in Ironbridge..........................59

**8**   The Darbys of Coalbrookdale ..............................................70

**9**   Through Ironbridge Gorge Past Swimming
        Firefighters and Coalport.....................................................76

**10**   On Past Bridgnorth .............................................................87

**11**   Quatford, Collieries and Back to Upper Arley ....................94

**12**   Back to the Severn: Bridgnorth and on to Bewdley...........103

**13**   Bewdley, Ribbesford and on to Stourport...........................112

**14**   Rowing to Holt Fleet in the Rain........................................121

**15**   With Swans and Sculls to Worcester...................................132

**16**   A Glamping Night and Worcester ......................................143

**17**   Down to Upton-upon-Severn .............................................152

**18**   Rippling to Ripple and Tewkesbury ...................................159

**19**   Journey's End and the Tidal Severn Abandoned ...............169

**20**   Homage to Paddy Leigh Fermor at Dumbleton ...............176

## PART II: THE RIVER LOIRE

| 21 | To the Loire at Nevers, June 2017 ........................................ 183 |
| 22 | No Château de Graçay and on to the Iron Town |
| | of Fourchambault ........................................................ 192 |
| 23 | La Charité-sur-Loire, la Fille Ainée de Cluny .................... 200 |
| 24 | The Wine Country of Sancerre ........................................... 208 |
| 25 | Portage and an Involuntary Dip at Ousson-sur-Loire ......... 216 |
| 26 | Briare's Aqueduct and Gien .............................................. 225 |
| 27 | Caillard's Revenge ............................................................ 233 |
| 28 | A Fruitless Search for a Lost Boat .................................... 241 |
| 29 | Back to Gien with a New Boat, October 2018 .................... 247 |
| 30 | Sully, St Benoît-sur-Loire and on to Jargeau ...................... 257 |
| 31 | Joan of Arc at Jargeau and the Canal d'Orléans ................ 266 |
| 32 | The Maid at Orléans ........................................................ 274 |
| 33 | The Happy Return, May 2019 ........................................... 281 |
| 34 | Rowing Back to Beaugency ............................................... 286 |
| 35 | Nuclear Portage and Madame de Pompadour ..................... 293 |
| 36 | Entre Deux Châteaux: Menars to |
| | Chaumont-sur-Loire ...................................................... 298 |
| 37 | Royal Amboise ................................................................. 305 |
| 38 | Doing Justice to Blois ...................................................... 315 |
| 39 | A Happy Return Postponed .............................................. 321 |

**Bibliography:** A Selection of the Books Referred to
and Used in this Book ................................................................. 328

# Introduction

As Richard and I hauled our ten-foot aluminium rowing boat, evocatively named *Flying Colours 70*, as fast as possible across tern-rich sandbanks in the shadow of the great fourteen-arched bridge at Nevers, our plans to recreate Captain Horatio Hornblower RN's 1811 escape down the river Loire finally sprang to life. Obviously, we did not have (or need) the Comte de Graçay's oxen to haul us to the water's edge. We were keen to wet our keel in the Loire but these sandbanks and islands are home to nesting terns, the islets with numerous 'keep off' notices. To add verisimilitude to the idea of 'escape' a lot of official-looking French functionaries had appeared as if from nowhere about fifty metres away as we dragged the boat towards the water. They gathered round pickups and tractor-hauled mowing machines looking pretty purposeful, one or two fully rigged as bureaucrats so in our imaginations we feared a watered-down Caillard-like intervention.

Across what seemed an interminably long 'beach', the sun blazing down and the temperature at least thirty degrees, we sweated and strained to drag the boat through the soft sand to the river and finally managed to launch and clamber aboard, the functionaries and labourers looking on but not intervening. Perhaps their natural officiousness had melted away in the heat. It was nine o'clock in the morning and as I rowed, Richard waved nonchalantly to them, passing beyond their gaze once through the very much post-Hornblower railway bridge.

*****

This June day in 2017 was the culmination of two years of intermittent preparation that included the unexpected bonus of rowing down much of the River Severn in 2016 before we finally got the Loire and the 'full Hornblower'. It all started in April 2015 when, apropos of nothing at all that I could see, Richard said: 'Have you read any Hornblower recently, because I've got an idea?' I always get nervous when Richard has an idea.

At the time we were walking in the Mani, that wild area in southern mainland Greece that occupies the middle finger of the three that jut into the sea from the Peloponnese. This is the Greece where Patrick Leigh Fermor and his wife Joan lived and built their house at Kalamitsi, just south of Kardamyli and a few miles from Stoupa above which Richard has a place in the hills. At that moment we were walking out onto sun-baked and blindingly white Cape Tigani past circular, long-abandoned, stone-edged salt pans towards the implacably hostile cape rising from its rock-strewn peninsula. Incredibly, a town had grown up and sweltered here, Byzantine and Frankish but now merely low ruins. Tigani is Greek for frying pan which seemed an entirely appropriate name.

Richard expanded on his idea. 'You remember *Flying Colours*?' I certainly did for when I was young this was one of an immensely popular series of novels about the British navy set in Napoleonic times. Interest revived a few years ago for a new generation with a TV series starring the splendidly named and very Welsh actor Ioan Gruffudd as our hero, Horatio Hornblower. My father introduced me to the novels in the late 1950s and had been a fan of Forester since before the war: very much a similar story with Richard and his father.

*Flying Colours* had been published in 1938 and although I had not read it since my twenties I began to get an inkling of what Richard was thinking. Our hero, Hornblower, having been a prisoner of the French after a naval battle, was being sent by coach in the depths of winter from Spain to Paris, escorted by soldiers under a particularly unpleasant functionary, Colonel Jean-Baptiste Caillard, an imperial aide-de-camp. Also in the coach were Hornblower's first lieutenant, William Bush, and his coxswain, Brown, and it was evident Hornblower was headed for certain execution by Napoleon as an example to all. To complicate any escape plan, Bush had lost his foot in the battle and was confined to a stretcher, unable to walk. In a snowstorm the coach got bogged down, poised perilously near the banks of a river. This was the river Loire and Hornblower and Brown overpowered the detestable Caillard and they and Bush escaped. I recalled that the river featured large and along the way was a near-drowning and a long, long haul on oars.

These Hornblower novels set in the British navy's golden age are all wooden walls, hearts of oak, broadsides of cannon, and streams of lethal splinters the size of spears in the heart of battle. Wonderful they are and at their centre is our uncertain, constantly self-doubting hero. After their escape they steal a rowing boat, near-drown, winter in a château owned by a friendly anti-Napoleon count, build a new rowing boat and escape down the Loire from near Nevers to the sea at Nantes.

That in a nutshell was what had inspired Richard. We would row the Loire next year, in 2016. I pointed out we had no boat but he would research this so our current lack would be no obstacle. He also pointed out that the Loire is a well-known and well-organised river with kayaks and equipment for hire as well as numerous guidebooks for the keen paddler.

But I had not heard of people rowing it. Well, not since Hornblower, that is. For although C S Forester and his wife Kathleen had voyaged along some of the Loire in 1928 they had used a fifteen-foot dinghy with a grimly unreliable motor, a trip that obviously provided the idea for *Flying Colours* published ten years later.

'It's a very long river,' I said.

'I've thought of that too: we set off from as near the likely spot where Hornblower launched into the river or from Nevers itself and see how far we get in the time we have available.'

This was easy enough for a retired man to say with a wife used to his disappearing for weeks on end to colourful locations such as Colombia, Iran, Japan, Bulgaria, Jordan or Greece's Mount Athos. Not so easy for an envious me: still working and not free to up sticks whenever I felt like it.

'In a week to ten days we could probably get as far as Orléans,' I suggested.

That seemed a reasonable ambition and we started building our castles in the air as we worked our way back off Tigani and its sun-bleached, stone-covered isthmus. Paddy Leigh Fermor had seen Tigani's salt pans still in use in the 1950s. I feel entitled to use the shortened version of his name as he encouraged it and Richard was a member of the now-defunct Patrick Leigh Fermor Society. We toiled up to Agitria, a white-painted Byzantine church in the lee of massive, overhanging cliffs and caves where Paddy had reported that, amazingly, the salt workers lived.

# PART I

# THE RIVER SEVERN

# 1

# The Two Men's Boat, the Loire Unravels

Our Tigani talk had been the previous year and back in England we decided that the following May would be good as the Loire would probably be over its winter swelling but the water level not too low. Later on it could well be shallower and likely to involve many potentially embarrassing groundings, portaging and carrying the boat over sand and shingle banks.

To prepare for the trip I bought a guide to the Loire entitled *La Loire vue du fleuve* by a Jean-François Souchard. Although aimed at kayak and canoe it has a detailed guide to the whole river: exciting reading and the stuff of dreams. In that small way our preparation was off to a promising start and of course I reread *Flying Colours* and C Northcote Parkinson's book, *The Life and Times of Horatio Hornblower*, which weaves a full and possibly too detailed biography of our hero. For once and rather unexpectedly Northcote Parkinson is brief, giving over a meagre three pages to the escape in 1810 and the long voyage down the Loire in 1811.

I had bought the Loire guide as an earnest of our intent but bigger fish were meanwhile being fried by Richard who was researching the right boat: it had to be light enough for us to carry but sturdy enough to survive groundings and fast water. Aluminium seemed the best bet. He telephoned a few weeks later:

'It's a Marine Ally 10M made in the Czech Republic: seems ideal.'

'Ten metres long?' I queried. The thought of portaging a vessel over thirty feet long did not appeal.

'No, it's ten feet, not metres.' I felt slightly foolish and somehow rather pleased that in the Czech Republic now at the heart of a metric world they chose feet as a dimension (you can tell that because the metric version of the boat's ten-feet length in their handbook is an awkward 3.08m).

'How heavy?'

'A mere forty-one kilos! And its draught is about four inches unladen so ideal for manhandling over sandbanks and anything else the Loire can throw at us. It's also unsinkable with polystyrene foam under the seats. The good news is they've got one in their showroom and yard so we can go and have a look.'

All this was sounding interesting of course and I asked to which harbour or seaside location we would head. Richard replied that it was at Welwyn Garden City in landlocked Hertfordshire and the boatyard was called Barnet Marine, an equally landlocked location. Apparently, the firm had started in Barnet as a camping shop with a bit of chandlery thrown in, soon changing solely to small boats and all that goes with them before upping anchor to Welwyn Garden City.

Richard came up from his Exmoor farmhouse to my Buckinghamshire home and we drove over to Welwyn. Weaving our way into the industrial estates east of the railway that bisects Welwyn Garden City, we reached the premises of Barnet Marine, the East Coast Main Line trains thundering past beyond a thin screen of scrubby trees and a metal fence. Upstairs it was an Aladdin's cave of boating: rubber dinghies, life jackets, winches, pumps, ropes and everything you could think of and hope for in the world of small boats. Richard emerged from his bargaining with an extra rowlock, three oars thrown in and the deposit paid. It was agreed that I would pick up the boat, pay the balance and roof-rack it back to Haddenham and my garden.

A couple of months later I set off for Welwyn Garden City. Strange to say, I've never driven with an upside-down boat on a car roof so I was a bit apprehensive, particularly as it turned out to be wider amidships than the roof-rack bars I had borrowed from Richard. The Barnet Marine guys lashed a baulk of timber to the rear bar and supplemented our webbing straps with numerous of their own. I set off for home, the boat strapped to within an inch of its life and no movement possible in any direction.

Once the boat was off the car roof and in my back garden with the help of a kayaking neighbour (his car registration number K8 NOE, confirming his keenness), I thought it an admirable addition to the garden. It has to be admitted that my wife did not share this view of the brand-new, shiny aluminium boat. I pointed out the delightful *eau de nil* paint colour of the interior. All, I'm sorry to say, to no avail and it was made clear that after this and any other rowing jaunts the boat went back to Richard's farmyard. I said it could be set up with the bows in the air and serve as a garden seat: the sort of thing you see in fishing harbours and fisherman's (and incoming second-homers') cottages all along the coast. No dice.

Having weathered my wife Jill's various Jerome K Jerome-style jokes about two men in a boat instead of three and there being no dog, for various reasons of no interest to the reader it became very difficult to get away to France. The upshot was that any hope of French river rowing, disappeared when I returned from Greece in April 2016. I had been walking in the Mani again with Richard and my brother.

While there we had visited Paddy and Joan Leigh Fermor's villa at Kalamitsi days before its contents were supposed to be crated up and sent somewhere while the villa was restored. In fine Greek style nothing in fact happened for another two years.

I steeled myself and rang Richard, having made the decision to abandon the Loire for the time being in discussion with Jill.

'I don't want the project to disappear: merely postpone the Loire until next year. I'm sorry …' Perhaps overeagerly I continued: 'We can still have a trial run and get the boat's keel christened on an English river. I think I can get away for five or six days. That should be enough to give us time on whatever river we choose. I'll investigate.'

*****

Following a bit of thought I emailed Richard to suggest the River Dart as being near to him in Devon, as well as putting forward the rivers Severn, Thames and Trent as more long-distance alternatives. I rather fancied the Trent myself as my mother came from Gainsborough, one of the possible sites for George Eliot's St Ogg's in *The Mill on the Floss*, and she (my mother) had lived in a house called St Ogg's near the Old Hall before World War II. I had also enjoyed Tom Fort's TV programme rowing the river in a punt, the *Trent Otter*. I hadn't then read his book about it, *Downstream: Across England in a Punt*, and only found it in a bookshop a couple of days before we set out on our Severn trip and had it in my rucksack. But I'm a bit ahead of myself here. Richard did not fancy the Trent at all and said the Dart was too short, too tidal and he wanted to go further afield than his own backyard.

That left a field of two, the Thames and the Severn. Each of these mighty rivers had a connection with our hero, Richard reminding me that Hornblower, a newly promoted captain, had been in Gloucester on the banks of the Severn to meet his Uncle Jonathan according to Northcote Parkinson. Hornblower was with his first wife, the heavily pregnant Maria, and his infant son Horatio. Forester used her delicate condition as something of a pretext to write a tour-de-force description of a canal and river voyage. A stagecoach conveniently being considered too jolty and violent for Maria's journey to London, this inland voyage is described in *Hornblower and the Atropos*, the novel starting east of Gloucester on the Thames and Severn Canal. A drunken bargeman is injured and Hornblower steps up, as he is desperate to get to London to take command of the *Atropos*, even 'legging' through the two-mile-long Sapperton Tunnel before steering the seventy-foot passage boat all the way along the Thames to London from the canal's junction upstream of Lechlade.

Forester's writing covering this canal and river voyage has a pace and authenticity that bowls the reader along. Indeed, he had first-hand knowledge of it for as he remarked in his *The Hornblower Companion* published in 1964: '*Hornblower's biographer happened to have had extensive experience on the rivers and canals of England as well as in other countries. Long before such travel once more became fashionable he captained a boat from London to Llangollen and back again.*' His crew, he wrote, on that occasion were his infant son and his wife, obviously giving him the idea for Hornblower's canal voyage, also undertaken with a baby son and wife on board.

The fictional Hornblower had thus impinged on both the Severn and Thames and whichever we chose would have some sort of connection. If we rowed the latter, we would be following his route, but of course there was more to the choice than that. In my researches I found you needed a licence to row all the Thames but on the Severn only below Stourport, the Thames one bought from the Environment Agency and the (rather cheaper) Severn one from the Canal & River Trust. In fact, we both rather preferred the Severn, for I suppose *Three Men in A Boat* had somewhat queered the pitch for writing about a rowing expedition on the Thames.

This superb comic novel cum travelogue would be impossible to emulate and, in any case, the three men rowed upstream to Oxford from Kingston which seems like unnecessarily hard work and downstream only from Oxford as far as Pangbourne (in the rain) before abandoning the trip. We would go with the flow, whichever river we chose. I did point out that the three men didn't actually get further upstream than Oxford so if we chose the Thames we could start somewhere far upstream, say Lechlade, and not cross their path until Oxford, still accompanied by the fictional ghost of Horatio Hornblower. We were not seduced by Jerome's advocacy of rowing against the current as he rather undermined it by making it clear it only applied when he was steering and Tom Fort, for example, more sensibly rowed the Trent downstream.

Deciding to reproduce Hornblower's exploits on the Loire meant rowing only, a choice that had the fortuitous result that we would see more of the river and its life than we would have done in a kayak or canoe. Kayaks seem to require more in the way of paddle action whereas in a boat you can hope to idle in the current. The rowing boat necessary to reproduce Hornblower's *Flying Colours* exploits had the happy outcome of a style that gave a different perspective on a river and one that did not mean one of us looking at the other's back in a two-man kayak with comments shouted over the shoulder or across the water in single-seater kayaks. In a rowing boat the oarsman faces the steersman: ideal for conversation.

Some years ago I had read the aptly named Brian Waters' two wonderful anecdotal books *Severn Tide*, published in 1947, and *Severn Stream*, following in 1949, and was pleased to find that Tom Fort also admired them. Waters was a local lad having been born in Tewkesbury on the banks of the Severn in December 1906. Mind you, I was under no illusion that Waters described anything other than a long-gone world of salmon fishing using nets suspended between coracles, coal-mining villages or eel fishing using handmade 'putcheons'. Not to mention a world in which fact-checking never got in the way of a good story.

These books, though, can still inform and enrich the experience of visiting places along the River Severn. No Pevsner county volume is likely to tell you the tale of Sir Walter de Balun whose cross-legged effigy lies in Upper Arley church. He was to go on crusade to the Holy Land immediately after marrying Yseult or Isolde, a daughter of the Earl of March. They married in Southampton from where this crusade was to set sail but he unwisely took part in a joust immediately after or even during the wedding feast and was fatally wounded, his marriage unconsummated and his wife a widow within hours of the ceremony. She had the effigy made with his legs crossed as a sign that he had been on crusade despite not even boarding ship for the Holy Land, although having taken the vow made him technically at least a crusader. Pevsner's *Buildings of England* volume for Worcestershire is less anecdotal and drier, noting that the fine limestone effigy is reputed to be this Sir Walter who died in 1288 but takes the view that the effigy appears by the style of the armour to be of about 1340. Brian Waters' version is the more romantic; whether entirely accurate it matters not a jot. The books are full of this sort of interest as well as the eccentric countrymen and women, fishermen, innkeepers, craftsmen and boat people found along the length of this great river.

Richard agreed the Severn it would be, so I investigated the licence which turned out mainly to cover the cost of going through the locks below Stourport. Our solitary rowing boat was often the sole occupant of one of these vast locks, usually accompanied by a shouted conversation with the lock-keeper peering down from far above us before the gates opened and we rowed off downstream. We had originally assumed we would have to 'portage', that is lift the boat out of the water and carry it past locks or weirs, fearing our humble vessel would be beneath the dignity of the toweringly high lock pounds and their keepers. We could not have been more wrong and the locks proved to be great fun and something of a welcome novelty amid their normal fare of vast river-cruise ships, narrowboats, and ballast barges. The lock-keepers seemed keen to know what we were up to and why, although the Loire aspect was a bit tricky to explain and I am not sure many were convinced by our answers.

Rowing downstream was the only way to go of course as the Severn has quite a strong current: only the super-fit or someone with an outboard motor would try and fight its currents upstream. I did try at one point on our trip, my arms a blur as we just about maintained our position. Books on the Severn describe the sinew-bursting strain of hauling the Severn trows (the Severn's almost flat-bottomed, single-masted cargo-carrying barges) upstream: six to eight men harnessed like horses, their noses close to the ground scrabbling for purchase on the path as they fought the current. One horrified writer noted that the difference between these sweat-soaked men and horses lay only in the fact that the horses didn't fill the air with foul oaths and prodigious grunting. Clearly, upstream a non-starter then.

Since we had decided to row the Severn far upstream from Bewdley, I decided to buy a licence just in case and a week's permit was inexpensive. While all this was under consideration, I fitted the third rowlock to the rear transom, neatly in the centre, intending this to be used for steering the boat and as a single paddle sweep guiding it in the current: a deluded pride in symmetry. A couple of days later Richard rang to point out that on the centre line the steersman would have to be sitting off-centre and this would upset the balance of such a light boat. He thinks of these things, so I removed it and fitted it further across towards the port side of the transom. Problem solved, leaving just a couple of redundant holes.

Richard and I had been looking at maps and information to see how far up the Severn above Bewdley we could start with five or so days at our disposal. Obviously, we would need to leave one car at the finish. Somewhere around or upstream of Bewdley seemed a reasonably achievable distance downstream. Once we had agreed a starting date, Richard booked bed and breakfast at Worralls Grove, conveniently close to the river in Upper Arley, coincidentally a village with a certain resonance for me as will become clear in the next chapter. Accommodation sorted, we agreed we wished to start in Wales where the Severn is named *Hafren*. Initially, I looked at a launch deep within Wales at, say, Welshpool or even further upriver, seduced by the siren voice of Brian Waters' *Severn Stream* and his lively tales of Newtown and its inhabitants.

On the web, though, there were many canoeists critical of the Severn upstream of the border, listing numerous obstructions and problems. A glance at the OS 1:50000 map also showed the river meandering wildly and apparently purposelessly as it sought to get past Breidden Hill, an outlier from Long Mountain above Welshpool. Perhaps the Welsh stretches of the river could be left as a future option.

Brian Waters devoted several pages to Melverley, the first village in England near where the Afon Vyrnwy reaches the Severn, but we settled for Crew Green, the last village in Wales before the Severn flows into Shropshire and England. Richard had a half-memory of having stayed in Crew Green with his wife Vicky some years before but could not remember where. Still, it seemed a reasonable basis for a search as we hoped we would find somewhere to leave the car at a friendly B & B, a caravan site or a farm. Admittedly, a slightly risky approach but we usually take Mr Micawber's view that something will turn up.

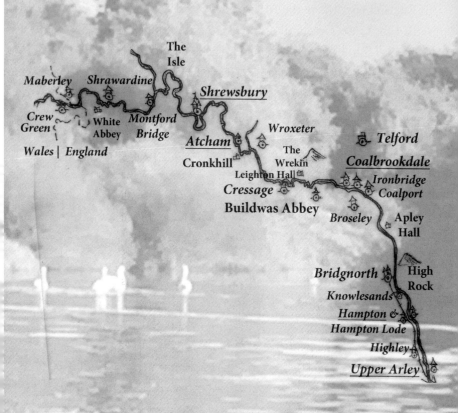

The Isle

Maberley  Shrawardine

*Shrewsbury*

Crew
Green    White    Montford
         Abbey    Bridge

Wales | England

*Atcham*                Wroxeter

Cronkhill                          *Telford*

                    The      *Coalbrookdale*
                    Wrekin
          Leighton Hall          Ironbridge
      *Cressage*                  Coalport

      Buildwas Abbey      *Broseley*    Apley
                                        Hall

                          *Bridgnorth*    High
                                          Rock
                    *Knowlesands*
                    *Hampton &*
                    *Hampton Lode*
                        *Highley*
                    *Upper Arley*

# Map 1: The River Severn
# Between Crew Green, Wales,
# and Upper Arley

*Note: Places underlined are the locations of the hotels and pubs where we stayed the night*

# 2

# Upper Arley to Wales where We Dip Oars at Last

This may seem a long preamble with no oars dipped in the water, but with 'messing about in boats' it is the preparation that seems to matter just as much. You only have to visit any haven for small boats to see chatting, painting, scraping, restoring, polishing, rigging repairs and every conceivable activity with little apparent urgency to get a boat into the water. In our case the preparations and reasons for rowing the Severn are quicker and easier to relate. Perhaps not in as comic a way as in Jerome K Jerome's *Three Men In a Boat*, whose protagonists and Montmorency the dog finally cast off at the end of five long chapters. In his underrated sequel *Three Men on the Bummel* it is also well into the book, about a third in fact, and at the beginning of Chapter Six before they land at Hamburg and mount their bicycles to head for the Black Forest. This preamble lets the reader off lightly with only the occasional diversionary anecdote and it will also become clear why Paddy Leigh Fermor has been mentioned.

However, we are not there yet for Richard had to drive up from Devon to Upper Arley and I transported the boat there. It turned out that he had surreptitiously put an electric outboard motor in his boot. Did he fear that we would bottle out of rowing? The weather was warm and sunny with fluffy, high clouds as I set off for Worcestershire, the sleek aluminium boat upside-down atop the car, secured by only two straps whereas the lads at Barnet Marine had used half a dozen. My chosen route avoided major towns to reach the Wyre Forest where I descended eastwards off the main road via narrow winding lanes of great delight to Arley Station on the Severn Valley Railway, some eighty feet above the riverbank. Richard had suggested we meet in the station car park at Upper Arley but the station was closed: its white gates firmly padlocked, so I drove on to a car park by the river. Ah: the village of Upper Arley and, more to the point, our B & B were on the opposite bank, the river spanned only by a footbridge.

That problem could wait for the autumn sun was warm, the river grey-blue and flowing merrily, its surface rippled by a lively current. Mothers and their children were out walking their dogs alongside the river, several spaniels plunging in and out of the shallows. Toddlers were promised ice creams in the café on the Upper Arley side of the river as a bribe to get them to walk without being carried. Sounded good to me but we were all in for disappointment: the post office and Riverside Tearooms were closed.

I walked to the footbridge and stood in its centre admiring the picture-book beauty of the village on the east bank with its many-arched brick causeway behind a 'beach'. Beyond rose the densely treed grounds of demolished Arley House, now a well-known arboretum. I looked down at the river and tried to imagine how we would row it, feeling a bit uncertain, my limited experience being of the boating lake variety.

Looking upstream I saw that the road from the station direction headed down to the riverbank while on the Upper Arley bank was what was obviously the landing point opposite for a now-defunct ferry. This is where what looks like a dry publication that I've had on my bookshelves for years, in fact since I was first interested in geology and fossil hunting, comes into its own. Published in Worcester in 1964 it is snappily titled *The River Severn between Upper Arley (Worcs.) and Gloucester: Its general geology, navigation, bygone fords and alluvial deposits* and is by a Linsdall Richardson FRSE, FGS.

For years it had sat beside those superb Institute of Geological Sciences volumes of the British Regional Geology that I could actually afford as a teenager and had accumulated in the 1960s. They were published in a pre-inflationary era when the price was even printed on the cover (5/- for the Wealden District volume, for example). Upper Arley and the Wyre Forest are in the Central England volume and Linsdall Richardson features frequently in its references and bibliography. First published in 1936, my 1975 third edition reprint of Central England had cost the princely sum of 40p and replaced a long fallen apart 1950s edition. The upper reaches of the Severn towards Crew Green are covered by the North Wales volume (my 1961 reprint 6/-). As you may have guessed geology and fossil hunting had been a hobby in my youth and Richard and I had hunted them in places ranging from the carboniferous limestone of the Peak District to the Bracklesham Beds in Sussex.

By pure chance on his part Richard had chosen a bed and breakfast in Upper Arley of Linsdall Richardson's title. Richardson, a prolific writer on geology, particularly that of Worcestershire, the Cotswolds and central England, appears to have had a particular interest in springs and wells, producing studies of them for various counties. He was awarded the prestigious Lyell Medal in 1937 by the Geological Society of London. No geological lightweight then, but of particular interest to me for this trip was the section on bygone fords, ferries and bridges (rather than, I have to confess, the boreholes that he covered in great detail).

Later on Richard wondered whether Sir Lewis Leigh Fermor, Paddy Leigh Fermor's remote but distinguished geologist father, knew Linsdall Richardson: it seemed highly likely. Perhaps he was on leave in England when the Lyell Medal was presented and Sir Lewis was after all Director of the Geological Survey of India from 1932. Perhaps they met later when Lewis, back in England, became a Vice President of the Geological Society in 1945 or when Lewis was elected President of the Bristol Naturalists' Society that same year and right in the heart of Linsdall country.

For Upper Arley, Richardson records that the river here was known to be wadeable at low water. This however he loftily dismisses: *'so far as the writer is aware, there is no record of this fact in script or print'*. He then quotes the earliest known sources for a ferry here (the 1320s) that also refer to the Wyre Forest I had driven through half an hour ago. This ferry had a long life when owned by the lord of the manor, until in 1931 he gave it to the county council which was fine until the 1960s when the ferry, having lost money for years, was replaced by the

1971 footbridge. Old photographs of the various ferry boats survive, mainly from later years when it had a sturdy mast-like post supporting a stout cable that crossed the river and was attached to further posts on each bank about 200 yards upstream. Sounds a hazardous process, depending on the current and a rudder to swing the boat across the river and indeed many lives had been lost over the years for the Severn can be highly treacherous.

My musings or rather daydreaming were interrupted by the arrival of Richard. He had worked his way through Bewdley to descend the same lane to discover that our B & B could only be reached via the road bridges at either Bewdley or Bridgnorth, about eleven miles or so by road instead of a quarter of a mile via the footbridge. We discussed leaving our cars on the right bank in the car park but that would not work as the B & B had agreed that we could park one there to be collected after we had finished our watery journey. With Richard suitably discomfited and brows furrowed in apologetic mode we crossed the footbridge, and had a quick walk around the village. No refreshment still, so we continued along the road past the former ferry point and followed it uphill with our 'Pevsner' volume in hand. This was the somewhat bulky 2007 edition of *The Buildings of England: Worcestershire*, one of the series of county architectural history volumes started by the indefatigable Sir Nikolaus Pevsner in the 1950s. As a German Jew he had been forced to resign from his teaching post at Göttingen university in 1933 by the Nazi regime. He came to England and Germany's loss was very much our gain. The first county volumes were slim Pelican paperbacks at 2/6 (12.5 pence) each but are now £40 or so and spectacularly expanded.

Pevsner died in 1983 but when I was working at London's Courtauld Institute of Art in the 1970s I always made sure that I ran the projectors whenever he came to lecture: I was also a postgraduate student and working there in the slide library. Remember slides? We kept projectors just for him in the basement at Portman Square, one a splendid brass and teak machine converted to electricity in the 1950s complete with cloth-braided wires. His slides were pre-war three-inch glass ones, some in neat wooden frames and many with the building in a central circle, the surrounds blacked out. Several generations of architectural historians and tourists owe a great debt of gratitude to Pevsner and I have no doubt they always carry the relevant county volume on their travels.

Uphill we reached the church and from the churchyard gate it showed little sign of Norman architecture, built in well-mellowed pinkish-red sandstone much patched with local buff stone. The nave porch, south chapel and chancel crusty with battlements, we paused to look at the views to the south and they were indeed fine. The arboretum trees in the grounds of the now demolished mansion blocked westerly views for this is yet another parish church located close to the site of a manor house.

Fortunately, the church was unlocked and inside we could see that the nave south wall is partly Norman but the rest of the church is later, mostly 14th century. The effigy of the knight we particularly wanted to see is rather good, although set on a Victorian tomb chest. Here he lies in his armour, a long surcoat, his crossed legs resting on a rather surprised-looking lion. From what I know of effigies and armour it certainly seemed mid-14th rather than late-13th century whatever Brian Waters might have thought. Time was marching on and we needed to head for the B & B.

*****

Recrossing the footbridge our short convoy proceeded into the Wyre Forest, crossing the river at Bewdley. From Bellman's Cross we turned left towards Upper Arley and left again just before the village onto a long drive, initially between undulating fields, then remnants of apple orchards. Ahead was the B & B, Worralls Grove. It was either a former farmhouse or a miller's house, set beside a small watermill powered by a stream that debouches into the Severn. Beyond this stream Eymore Wood, a dense belt of woodland, runs inland for over a mile alongside the stream cum parish boundary. Set above the river you can look across its shining, fast-flowing waters to see Severn Valley Railway steam trains puffing along purposefully, steam rising in pulsing clouds. Inside Worralls Grove there was evidence of a 17th-century timber-framing that had been encased in 18th and 19th-century brick. The gable window of our room at the head of the stairs looked out to steeply sloping former orchards amid whose few surviving and decidedly gnarled apple trees sheep contentedly grazed. Richard, being Richard, had brought a bottle of Malmsey which is as good for drinking as for drowning 15th-century dukes. Richard said he had bought it for the now-postponed Loire trip because of its connections to the Royal Navy's golden age of the Hornblower novels. On their long sea voyages or blockading Toulon or Brest most wines would be exposed to heat and movement that would transform (ruin) their flavour. To counter this, spirits and heat were added to ensure it remained suitable for an officer's dinner table. Although the Loire naval link was gone for the moment the full bottle remained so we asked the owner Amanda to get some glasses and have a drink with us if she could spare the time. She could and we learned how she and her partner Rob had come to set up the B & B in 2012. Worralls Grove had apparently won a round of Channel 4's *Three in a Bed*, a

TV programme that pits B & Bs against each other. For supper she suggested the Bellmans Cross Inn back at the main road junction. After a phone call to reserve us a table she was whisked away in her partner's bright red Ferrari: quite a stylish exit. The Bellmans Cross Inn turned out to be a 19th-century brick building decked out both inside and out with timber-framing of a decidedly un-Tudor form and design. All a bit disconcerting to an architectural historian like me but the food was good and the pub welcoming. A few glasses of excellent wine, and we drove back to Worralls Grove well contented.

*****

Next morning, breakfast was fully up to expectation: bacon for me is a key test of quality, for Richard it is coffee and it certainly passed muster for him and his, in my view, unnecessarily fastidious taste buds. Saying our farewells and leaving Richard's car at Worralls Grove we headed via the Shrewsbury bypass to Wales, land of my great-grandmother but generally speaking not Richard's cup of tea.

Approaching Crew Green, it was time for Richard's memory banks to be interrogated. Initially without success, we ended up winding towards Kempster's Hill before admitting defeat. After a couple of passes through the village, more of a hamlet, its centre mostly modern housing, I suggested we try Seven Oaks Holiday Home Park east of the village. Perhaps we would be allowed to park and launch the boat from its riverbank. No such luck, the chap in the office looked us up and down and presumably thought we would lower the tone of his what he at least regarded as upmarket mobile-home park. He even left his office to point back towards Crew Green in case we did not get the message and suggested Brook House Farm which apparently did B & B.

After a couple of unsuccessful passes up and down the main road we finally located Brook House Farm, somewhat embarrassingly close to the holiday home park. Driving into its yard Richard recognised it immediately as the farm where he and Vicky had stayed. We located Julia, the owner, amid the outhouses, and she was as friendly as he remembered. It was no problem at all to leave the car for a few days so we said we would stay the night in a week or so, if she had a room. When she found out that I knew about planning matters she regaled us with an extended saga of her difficulties with enforcement and planning in general. I won't say more but I could not see why one of her problems, a traditional wooden caravan in a nearby field, could have led to so many planning problems and enforcement notices. Eventually, somewhat to our relief she suggested that she stop talking so that we could get on the river before lunchtime.

She pointed out a track heading towards the river and at a pond bearing right through a gate into a field where there was a sort of beach that might be suitable but asked us to be careful not to let any sheep escape into the launch field through the gate. This proved slightly trickier than anticipated, so Richard manned the gate, opening it just enough to let the car through but not the decidedly inquisitive sheep. I checked the map to make sure the launch was in Wales. It was and the border followed the bank for a mile until Wales headed south, no doubt to Richard's relief.

The boat and our gear unloaded, Richard repeated the gate procedure for me to drive the car back to the farm's parking area. Back by the river, upstream we could see a steel lattice-girder bridge crossing the river. It had been built as a railway bridge in 1947 but given a second life as a road bridge when the line closed in 1962. A branch of the Shropshire and Montgomeryshire Light Railway, it had opened in 1911 as one of the famous Colonel Stephens' shoestring light railways. Before this the line had a chequered history of closures and bankruptcies as the cumbersomely named Potteries, Shropshire and North Wales Railway ('Potts' for short). The beach, more a muddy riverside shelf, was a good enough place to get the boat into the river. We finally launched at 11.45am, me at the oars, grinning with the sheer pleasure of at last starting our picaresque river adventure.

# 3

# A Long Day's Rowing from Wales to Shrewsbury

The river was glassily calm for the first couple of miles and its course fairly serpentine, the clouds white and high, the calm occasionally ruffled by breezes, the water reflecting an intense blue sky. After about half a mile we swapped roles and shortly the Welsh bank became English. Two and a half miles from our launching point a pub was marked on the map, the Royal Hill, an inn to which Brian Waters devotes many enthusiastic pages, much of it about coracles, salmon and a real character of a former landlord named Griff Phillips, including a photograph of Griff sitting in his coracle near the Royal Hill. Waters

was walking the riverbank and wrote that you '*seldom catch the reflection of a human face, until at Royal Hill a Severn punt proclaims the ferry. This is the only ferry, and almost the only punt, remaining on the river above Shrewsbury.*'

No ferry now and nowhere to land for a pint, we changed rowers again and I rowed for two and a half miles until according to the map we were opposite

White Abbey and the remains of Alberbury Priory. In fact, these are one and the same, White Abbey Farm incorporating the remains of a priory founded in 1221. Brian Waters informed us that the priory '*was dissolved long before the reformation by Henry VI who closed this and other such houses (including Deerhurst along the Severn) on account of their subjugation to French monasteries*'. He continues that '*even after five centuries of change one enters this building, so similar to a hundred other farmhouses one has known, with a sense of shock to find that the chapel is now a kitchen.*' Again, there was nowhere to land, a problem that beset our first long day of rowing.

The river bore sharply north-east at a poplar copse and along the left bank cattle grazed slopes criss-crossed by the paths they had made to drink or stand in the water watching boats pass. Come to think of it they probably watched us with surprise for unlike in Brian Waters' day we were the only river traffic: no coracles, punts, eel trappers, fishermen or others. Indeed, about the only people we saw before we reached the curiously named Shrawardine were a couple of picnickers and they were on the riverbank leaning against their big Kawasaki motorcycles.

The river was now less tranquil on the surface and the boughs of fallen trees lay in the margins or formed obstructions in midstream where slipstreams of water swirled where they broke surface or eddies whirled where they did not. Willows overhung the river in places; sometimes there were no trees close to the river where cow pasture came up to the steep riverbanks. The current, though, was not strong enough for us to make much progress with the steering oar alone so we rowed most of the time, a fairly easy stroke rate as we basked in the sunshine.

We followed a group of nine swans that kept well ahead of us for most of the afternoon, usually between fifty and a hundred yards distant, but we never closed on them. One or two occasionally rose in the water and lazily flapped their wings, their progress looking completely relaxed and effortless. Shortly after this we passed between the stone abutments of a long-demolished 'Potts' railway bridge; sole survivors as the piers in the riverbed had been demolished back in 1962. Round the bend the banks were more treed and turning southwards the wind no longer blew along the river so the surface was less ruffled, except where the breeze slipped through the trees or the water powered across the frequent underwater obstacles. Richard shipped the oars and I put the steering oar into the water and we drifted gently towards Shrawardine, the name apparently Anglo-Saxon and meaning 'sheriff's defensive enclosure'.

This village had an active Civil War, having been held for King Charles. There are remains of a castle, largely slighted in 1645 by Parliamentary troops following its capture while the Royalist commander, Sir William Vaughan, had pulled down the church and vicarage. According to Brian Waters the 'Lion of Shrawardine' '*withstood a five-day siege before the fortress was gutted by fire*'. He added that the stones of the church, the castle and the vicarage '*were shipped downstream to Shrewsbury for the building of the old Welsh Bridge, Frankwell Quay, and the rebuilding of Shrewsbury Castle*'. It struck us as an unfeasibly large quantity of stone to salvage, as Shrawardine's church had also been rebuilt in stone in 1649.

I saw a moored boat ahead and set Richard rowing towards it to investigate, hoping for a landing place. It was a punt with three village-hall style plastic chairs in line-ahead mode, presumably for fishing in comfort, and was tied up at a very small landing stage cum fishing station. The bows vanished noisily into adjacent reeds and Richard leapt ashore, putting a couple of turns around the mooring post. As this was a private garden with no way into the village, discretion seemed the better part of valour and we re-embarked somewhat sheepishly, me now at the oars, and rowed on. A more lively river turned east and ran relatively straight for nearly two miles, followed by a loop past a wooded island near Montford village. On this part of the route a barn owl flitted through a riverside copse and there were buzzards, kites and a heron. We almost caught up with the swans that seemed to have been waiting for us before resuming their stately progress downstream.

I had noticed an inn marked on the OS map near Montford Bridge and, as it was now nearly three o'clock in the afternoon, we were a bit peckish, not to mention distinctly thirsty. We were approaching the modern bridge carrying the A5 across the river, beyond which was the old Holyhead Road bridge built by Thomas Telford. Richard spotted a likely landing place where we could scramble up the bank and secure the boat just below the modern bridge: it was far from ideal and merely a notch in the bank with a tiny area of mud but we were helped by a woman walking her friendly and bouncy spaniel along the riverbank who caught our thrown rope and held the boat while we scrambled ashore. After ten miles of rowing we had at last managed to land.

\*\*\*\*\*

Atop the bank we chatted to the dog walker as I made a fuss of her dog, Richard customarily ignoring it; he not being particularly noted as dog-friendly by dogs, friends or family. We left everything in the boat: rowlocks, oars and packs. I was somewhat uneasy at this but Richard was confident that no-one would take anything, presumably on 'code of the river fraternity' grounds, if such a thing exists. Once I had got used to this I relaxed and indeed, apart from when we tied up in Worcester, we always left everything in the boat and merely shipped the oars. Trust your fellow man (and woman) until proved otherwise as my father used to say, and by and large he was rarely disappointed.

We walked through the campsite near the old bridge to find the pub, the Wingfield Arms, closed and no sign of a shop, garage or other possible source of sustenance. We walked across Telford's bridge and saw the old toll-keeper's cottage, whitewashed stone with an octagonal two-storey core, one of his standard designs for the Holyhead Road. Near it we asked another dog walker whether she knew anywhere for refreshment within walking distance. She said there was a café and toilets servicing the A5 near the new bridge (it will probably always be known as 'new' by locals). We headed back through the campsite, across a field and over a post and wire fence onto what turned out to be the access road to the services and followed this under the A5 and up to the Montford Bridge Café.

By now it was ten to four in the afternoon and we made the unwelcome discovery that no hot food or even a sandwich was served after 3.30pm. We perforce made do with a very welcome cafetière of coffee and a slice of excellent fruit cake, several bikers also eating and gossiping there. We bought bottles of much-needed water and were amused by signage at the toilets depicting a stick man and woman with their legs crossed.

*****

Sort of refuelled we headed back to the boat and paused to admire the reddish-pink sandstone of Thomas Telford's Holyhead Road Bridge, its road a continuation of Roman Watling Street that ran from Kent to Shrewsbury (or rather its nearby predecessor, Wroxeter). The whole of the road from Shrewsbury to Holyhead had been greatly improved and realigned by Telford. Part of these works included the Montford Bridge and Brian Waters tells us it cost '*only £5,800*', this relative cheapness a result of quarrying the sandstone from Ness Cliff, five miles further along the Holyhead Road, not to mention his use of convicts from Shrewsbury Prison, also designed and built by him. This was more enlightened than it reads, for he had discussed the idea with the great penal reformer John Howard who was convinced healthy outdoor work would be better for convicts than being shut up in their cells. Howard had met Telford and they discussed how to design Shrewsbury Prison's layout in a more enlightened way than previous gaols. Telford put Howard's advice into practice and also used parties of convicts for his archaeological excavations of Wroxeter's Roman town beyond Atcham.

Thomas Telford was a fine example of the 18th and 19th-century men that made Britain's industrial revolution. To me and Richard he is an engineering hero as great as Isambard Kingdom Brunel and, like George Stephenson, he was of humble origin and largely self-taught, the orphaned son of an Eskdale shepherd and, like many other great engineers, a Scot. He was a man of parts as well as being an engineer, architect, canal and road builder and something of a poet in his own right. He was a friend of Robert Southey who groaningly nicknamed him the 'Colossus of Roads'. By the time he died in 1834 he had placed an indelible stamp on the civil engineering of Britain. You only have to row through Montford Bridge to see how much more he was than just a civil engineer: he had an instinctive eye for line. So great is his reputation that one book on the Severn even attributes to him the design of the Victoria Bridge that carries the Severn Valley Railway across the Severn downstream of Upper Arley, despite his having died over a quarter of a century before it reached the drawing board.

Montford Bridge of the early 1790s was Telford's first following his appointment as Shropshire's County Surveyor of Bridges. This fine structure, its central arch slightly wider, is best seen from the river as its elegant arches and fine pinkish-red ashlar now support a 1960s widened concrete road deck so Telford's parapets are no more. These changes to meet the demands of modern motoring did it no aesthetic favours and ironically it proved unnecessary as the nearby modern road bridge took the A5 traffic elsewhere and this brutal treatment could have been avoided.

Montford Bridge was the only one between Crew Green and Shrewsbury, a distance of over twenty miles, until joined by the nearby modern road bridge, and as such was our first. When in the river in a rowing boat embankments or high banks and riverside scrub conceal views, so bridges assume greater significance than on terra firma. Telford's bridge replaced a timber one of 1637 that had been swept away by floodwater in the 1690s, itself replacing a succession of timber and stone ones from the 13th century onwards. The earlier bridges were on a slightly different alignment, the earlier Wingfield

Arms pub aligned on this rather than Telford's. Rebuilding appears the norm along the tempestuous River Severn; over the centuries not only a notorious flooder of fields and towns but also a prodigious serial destroyer of bridges

Bridge fabric frequently records repairs following flood damage, rebuilding where the river was in extremis, decay-accelerated collapse or the scars of the history. Each seems to have had this history of renewal and rebuilding, although we ourselves were rowing in calmer waters and normal water levels. In a similar way to parish churches, bridges are a deeper record of the river and the communities it passes through than the frequently renewed and flood-scoured banks. Crossing rivers has always had significance for settlements and for strategic importance. Control of bridges was often critical in wartime and, moreover, their destruction very effectively cut communications. This became very striking on the Loire when we finally got there for that wide river and its crossings were a vital element in resisting the German advances in 1940 and, conversely, German resistance to Allied advances from the south in 1944, many being bombed or deliberately blown up twice in four years. It is striking also how dependent riverside communities were on ferry boats of all shapes and sizes but easy to seize and destroy: the dash to capture bridges to obstruct the enemy or to get your own troops across is a leitmotif of history. For those on a river, bridges help make sense of its history, besides giving the rower targets and markers of fluvial progress.

As often as not there were remnants of earlier bridges to be seen, particularly on the Loire so we could to some extent read their history in the fabric, including re-use of parts of earlier stone piers and abutments, or the remains of old piers left just breaking the surface of the water near replacement bridges. From Horatius defending Rome in Macauley's poem to the film *A Bridge Too Far,* the role of bridges has been crucial. Incidentally, were the real-life Horatio Nelson and the fictional Horatio Hornblower named after the Roman bridge defender? It was certainly a popular name in the 18th and early 19th centuries, no doubt the product of a Classical education.

We rowed under Telford's bridge and Richard, as is his normal practice, aimed for the central arch: never quite sure what point he is making, though. According to Waters this stretch of the Severn *'flows away from the bridge, and is joined by the Winding (*River*) Perry before encircling the Isle, where the Severn twists for five and a half miles around a low hill, before returning to within less than three hundred yards of its upper course'.* He added that coracles were usually carried across this narrow isthmus. This stretch is certainly taxing because so little progress is made towards Shrewsbury.

That was still to come for as we passed Mytton we saw our first kingfisher of the trip, an iridescent blue flash amid the overhanging trees. At Isle Grange neck I took over the oars and rowed onward around this enormously long loop. We had left Montford Bridge in sunshine but by the time we were passing Fitz, a small village with a Georgian church, it was raining. The shower only lasted twenty minutes and a subsequent rainbow emerged high in the sky as the low evening sun emerged and rain clouds parted. This stretch of sandy riverbank was peppered with sand-martin nesting burrows.

After six miles or so and opposite Berwick House, we again changed over and Richard rowed on, the sun now setting and cloud building up. We were still over three miles short of Shrewsbury but there seemed no alternative to rowing on into the gathering gloom. We had not previously given a moment's thought to rowing in the dark and by the time we passed Shelton it was fully dark. Hereabouts we met our first boat, a single scull looming out of the darkness perilously close, the rower sporting a head torch. I remembered that my mobile phone had a built-in torch so I used it whenever we heard boats approaching. It was much needed for as we neared Shrewsbury we encountered an extraordinary number of keen scullers training in the dark.

For a while there had been lights emanating from habitations on the right bank, although the river looped away from it. At last we reached houses and street lights on the left bank and with them the outskirts of Shrewsbury, and sufficient illumination to show us a quay where we could land, a slipway at its left-hand end. I steered to it and with something of a sense of relief we landed at Benbow Quay at just before 8.00pm.

# 4

# In Shrewsbury and Onwards to Shrewsbury Weir

Benbow Quay was in fact not in use but we tied up to conveniently placed looping chains that hung from sheet piles, positioning the boat so that it could not be seen by passers-by on the road above for we were leaving the oars on board. At the top of the somewhat overgrown slipway the gates were firmly padlocked, so we climbed the railings, emerging to the surprise of people strolling along the riverside walk with its benches and trees, presumably paid for by Benbow Quay, the modern housing development opposite.

Richard got his phone out and trawled the web to find us a hotel. Amazingly, there were rooms available even at this very short notice, so we booked the Shrewsbury Hotel, near the Welsh Bridge, further along the riverfront. Seeing the Welsh Bridge gave me a chance to remind Richard that Shrewsbury had been the main town of Powys in ancient times, according to Gerald of Wales in *The Journey through Wales* (visiting it in 1188). He reported that before the English pushed west and until the 8th century the town was named 'Pengwern' (the head of the alder grove). The Lords of Powys had their palace (a grandiose name for a no doubt humbler structure) where the castle now sits, the memory still raw to an Anglo-Welshman several centuries later. I was warming to my theme of Welsh loss but Richard was unimpressed, so we hefted our backpacks and walked to the hotel, booking in at about

8.30pm. 'Would we like to eat at the hotel?' Not surprisingly, we chose this easy option, satisfied with our day's rowing but disappointed that there had been so few chances of getting off the river in our twenty-two miles rowed since launching in Wales.

*****

During breakfast in the hotel, we were amazed by the number of presumably hardened 'regulars' coming in to set about numerous pints of beer with considerable gusto. At 9.00am, leaving our bags with the hotel, the *Shropshire* Pevsner volume in hand, we set off to explore Shrewsbury. Initially, things were disappointing in the area south of the hotel. By the 1930s much of this area had become squalid slums and was cleared for car parks and a bus station, but amid it sits one of the town's best timber-framed buildings spared the demolition gangs: Rowley's House, and Rowley's Mansion. The former was originally a very large late 16th-century brewhouse for William Rowley, a local brewer and draper whose 1618 Mansion was attached and built in then-expensive brick: both now superbly restored as a museum and university centre.

Ahead uphill the rather wonderful and elegant Market Hall tower dominates the view. This 240-foot-high brick tower with its needle pinnacle built in the 1960s is the sole redeeming element to an ugly modern concrete replacement for a Victorian predecessor. The tower fits remarkably well into a rich historic townscape of church towers and old buildings. Apparently, the older market hall was in the way of the highway planners. Pevsner described it as '*the chief Victorian contribution to public architecture in the town*': not sure whether this was praise or not.

Shrewsbury away from the riverside soon regained its historic character. It grew up within a loop of the River Severn, creating an easily defensible isthmus no more than 300 yards across and in medieval times guarded by a castle. From early times two bridges crossed the river into the town, Welsh Bridge from the west and English Bridge from the east. Our old friend Brian Waters comments delightfully that *'the twisted ribbon of river almost ties a bow where the ancient town of Salop is confined to a hill shaped like an upturned coracle that someone has dented with his foot'*.

The building of Roger de Montgomery Earl of Shrewsbury's late-11th-century castle followed the customarily ruthless Norman approach: demolishing fifty-one houses of a large and thriving Anglo-Saxon town big enough even then to have had six parish churches. Roger also founded Shrewsbury Abbey to the east of English Bridge, its Norman nave surviving as the parish church of Holy Cross. The town's wealth came from the wool trade, and many fine 16th and 17th-century timber-framed houses survive from this period. Another bout of prosperity in the 18th century added brick Georgian town houses and refrontings to older ones.

Our hero, Thomas Telford, was also busy in the town, for example, at Old St Chad's Church, which promptly collapsed after his advice had been ignored. Being thus proved spectacularly right, though, made his reputation. His Holyhead Road also passed through the town, heading north-west towards Wales. He carefully restored the superb St Mary's Church in the 1790s and converted part of the castle into a dwelling for the MP, his patron Sir William Pulteney of Bath fame, and supervised the building of the town's new gaol.

Uphill past the Market Hall and into the town's core where much more historic fabric and character survives, we turned into the Square which is dominated by the Old Market House, a rugged building of the 1590s in local Grinshill sandstone, its upper floor carried on robust arches and sturdy Tuscan columns. Its north-east elevation has a somewhat provincial statue of the Black Prince and below this a plaque giving a remarkably precise date for the building. '*The XV day of June was this building begonn William Jones and Thomas Charlton Gent then bayliffes and was erected and covered* [roofed] *in their time*'. Immediately below the plaque is a small date '*1596*'.

At the High Street end of the square is a statue of Clive of India, a Shropshire lad born at Styche near Market Drayton who had been MP for Shrewsbury and its mayor in 1762. I had to choose my photo of the Old Market House with care for the bland and insulting Princess House occupies the Square's long fourth side: a 1970s offering wholly unworthy of its location. Peering out from behind the Old Market House is the pedimented Music Hall built in the 1830s as public assembly rooms and hosting a craft and schools fair.

Continuing our tour of the medieval heart of the town, we walked along streets named after the trades practised in each such as Butcher Row, Fish Street, Milk Street and the less obvious Grope Lane, this last being the town's red-light district so to speak. Seeing a bookshop, I bought OS Explorer maps covering Shrewsbury and Ironbridge, my 1:50000 OS map not at large enough a scale to sufficiently 'read' the scenery through which we were rowing.

We reached the very fine St Mary's Church on the east side of, unsurprisingly, St Mary's Street that has sufficient surviving Norman work to appeal to the both of us and was built in the mid-12th century. The west tower in red sandstone has three Norman lower storeys while the transepts and south porch are also Norman. Beside the tower entrance doorway, a stone plaque informed us of an attempt to 'fly' across the river from the spire top that failed spectacularly and fatally in 1739. Robert Cadman was a steeplejack who had been involved in repairing the spire but was also a well-known tightrope walker. Fatally for him, an assistant over-tightened the rope and it broke before he reached the river. He plunged to his death, to the horror of his wife and thousands of spectators, and is buried in St Mary's churchyard.

Inside the church the nave is light and airy, the early 13th-century Gothic arcades still round-arched but elegantly moulded and with fine stiff-leaf capitals above equally elegant and slender piers which are as good as similar work at Wells Cathedral. There is also a superb collection of stained glass including the great east window's 14th-century Tree of Jesse, relocated from Shrewsbury's long-demolished Greyfriars church. One monument in particular caught our eye. This is to Admiral John Benbow who died in 1702 of wounds received in the Battle of Cartagena off the Caribbean coast of what is now Colombia. A local boy, reputedly from Coton Hill in Shrewsbury, his stirring naval feats spawned numerous songs and inns and taverns were named in his honour, in real life as well as in *Treasure Island*. Oddly, the fine wall memorial dates from about 1840, long after his death, and shows a ship of the line in full sail. The inscription rather gives the game away stating that his '*heroic exploits long rendered him the boast of the British navy and still point him out as the Nelson of his times*'. We had coincidentally landed near where he may have been born for Coton Hill is near Benbow Quay.

The former vestry north of the chancel is now a café so we ordered coffees, and to accompany them Richard had a massive slice of coffee and walnut cake and I a substantial fruit scone. We munched contentedly looking across at some fine 17th-century Flemish stained-glass roundels set in the north window, a café a cut above many. We left the church at eleven o'clock and descended St Mary's Water Lane, through the 13th-century Water Gate archway to the riverside walk and then crossed English Bridge to visit Holy Cross or Shrewsbury Abbey on the east side of the river, Richard having not seen it before. Its Norman nave, mostly dating from about 1100, survives, being given a second life as a parish church after Henry VIII's Dissolution of the Monasteries, the transepts and choir all demolished. In the 1880s a rather good new chancel and transepts were added to the surviving nave, designed by John Loughborough Pearson, an excellent choice and a sympathetic architect whose design complemented and enhanced the church. His son, Frank, added the current nave clerestory, a successful effort in the Neo-Norman style. It has to be said that the 14th century treated the building in some good ways and some bad. The oddest was the removal of three bays of nave arcade to make way for the large west tower inserted in their stead.

The church was well worth the visit but as it was near midday we headed back across English Bridge to the hotel. Our backpacks collected and farewells said, we headed along the riverbank to Benbow Quay pleased that we had seen the admiral's memorial in St Mary's Church.

*****

Having looked around Shrewsbury as landlubbers we were very much looking forward to seeing it from the water. All was well with the boat and the small 'red duster' on its short metal flagpole fluttered proudly at the stern. We were afloat again by half past twelve to row the two miles of river that loop around the town, in the process moving the boat a mere 300 yards nearer Atcham as the crow flies. Richard suggested that he row so I could take photographs.

The river was glassy and reflected an intense blue sky laced with high fluffy clouds, the bridge arches complete circles in the unruffled water. A perfect afternoon's weather for rowing with a series of bridges to look forward to before we left town: something of a contrast to yesterday's single bridge. First was Frankwell Bridge, a 1979 cable-stayed, fashionable single-pylon footbridge that links a car park and the council offices to the modern Riverside Shopping Centre (no great architectural triumph). Soon we rowed past our hotel and the very large concrete sculpture known as Quantum Leap, a sort of ribbed skeleton arch on the riverside path erected to celebrate the bicentenary of Charles Darwin's 1809 birth in the town (another illustrious Salopian). It's over forty feet high so you can't miss it and astonishingly cost more than Anthony Gormley's celebrated, bigger and better Angel of the North.

Then we were through the rather dull but remarkably unaltered five-arched Welsh Bridge, built in the 1790s in Grinshill sandstone to replace a medieval one, this time not by Telford. From here the town moves away from the river and curves round Quarry Park. This was, as the name suggests, where red sandstone was quarried in medieval times but became a Georgian public park below the town walls; an illusion of a rural stretch, a double avenue of trees following the curve of the river. On the right bank The Boathouse pub has coracles propped against the riverside wall (Brian Waters would have been delighted) and then the river continues beneath a suspension bridge, Porthill Bridge, and past Shrewsbury School and its large 1921 boathouse. Kingsland Bridge of 1882 was next, an iron-arched toll bridge for cars, cycles and pedestrians, its arch carrying a suspended deck, a design first used in cast iron in 1796 by Thomas Telford at Buildwas. We passed beneath it and a similar footbridge, Greyfriars Bridge of 1880, and rounding the next bend English Bridge came into view. This bridge is altogether more exciting than the rather stolid Welsh Bridge designed by 'local boy' John Gwynn in the 1770s to replace a medieval one.

Admittedly, English Bridge was rebuilt in the 1920s, its 'hump' flattened and the roadway widened but with most of the original Grinshill stone re-used. The central of its seven arches has a pediment above a rather good sculpted head of a bearded Neptune on the arch keystone set against his crossed trident and spear. We rowed through a central arch flanked by giant, somewhat anatomically incorrect fish-scaled stone 'dolphins' squatting on its cutwaters. The next bridge, less architecturally refined in grey-painted iron, carries the railway across the river onto the neck of the town's isthmus. There are massive, positively Piranesian, octagonal 1840s iron piers that conceal an 1830s stone arched railway bridge, now inconsiderately sandwiched by iron and steel bridges added for extra railway tracks.

Rounding the bend beyond the railway bridges we passed under Castle Bridge, a pre-stressed concrete footbridge of 1951, Britain's first. Richard used to work in a 1960s office building on London's High Holborn. This building had also used pre-stressed cables set in concrete to span a new road beneath, Proctor Street. He was told by the structural engineers that demolishing the building would be tricky as releasing the tension of the cables within their concrete overcoats would probably fire the upper five storeys of suddenly deconstructed building hundreds of feet into the air, descending to devastate the whole of Holborn and Kingsway.

Immediately past this bridge, we heard the roar of fast water and a quick look at the map showed there was a weir across the whole width of the river: no chance of rowing that, judging by the prodigious volumes of water rushing over it. Our very first 'portage' carrying the boat loomed. We ghosted on, keeping close to the wall of the left bank's promenade and within about forty yards of the weir eased towards steps up to the promenade. Richard went for a recce and returned to say that we could relaunch below the weir where concrete steps led down to the riverbank. Although fenced and gated for water authority use only, we ignored this for after all they had ignored boats in building their continuous weir.

We unloaded the packs, unshipped the oars and hauled the boat out of the water which proved remarkably easy with two of us. There were a fair number of people strolling about, so we were pleased to avoid mishap. We carried backpacks and oars to the water authority gate to lighten the boat and reduce it to its forty-one kilos empty weight and returned for the boat. We hefted it over the gate, down the steps and back into the water. Our audience dispersed and, reloaded and re-oared, we rowed away: our first portage completed without a hitch.

# 5

# A Rough Landing
# at Atcham Bridge

Not far beyond the weir the river bore north-north-east, the start of another sweeping loop, suburbs of Shrewsbury accompanying us on both sides. We rowed alongside a long tree-clad island and then under Telford Way Bridge, a 1964 concrete one, again of pre-stressed type and yet another commemoration of our hero. Shrewsbury at last left behind, the tree-flanked river bent eastwards, initially accompanied by two kingfishers flashing along amid overhanging trees. Two more bridges carried the A49 above us and, the long loop completed, the river turned south. Ahead, fifteen swans across the whole of the river idled along while beyond them was what looked like a more interesting bridge.

As we approached this railway bridge the curve of the river meant we saw only a great stone pier in the centre of the river and half the span of a metal arch to each side. Nearer, it was evident that the spans were cast iron and helpfully the left arch has a maker's plate: '*Cast at Coalbrookdale Foundry 1848*', a place we were aiming to get to in a day or two. A more prestigious shield-shaped iron plaque on the central pier told us who built the bridge: '*Hammond and Murray Contractor 1848*'. Through the bridge a similar shield on its south side named the designer: '*William Baker Esq. Engineer 1848*', the suffix 'Esq.' showing he regarded himself a gentleman and a cut above mere contractors and foundrymen. Baker was indeed an illustrious civil engineer specialising in railways and he and Victorian bridge makers, engineers and designers were proud of their use of the latest materials and technology, usually helpfully dating their work.

A little beyond the bridge a rock-formed weir stretched across the river, less of a problem towards the left bank. The rocks were mostly just below the surface but we ground onto them and got stuck fast. Rocking the boat shifted us a bit and vigorous rowing on my part, Richard pushing against the rocks with the steering oar, succeeded in freeing us and we bounced or 'shot' the weir. We wondered if this was the remnant of Preston's fish-weir mentioned by Brian Waters that had survived into the early-20th century.

Beyond, the left bank was treeless with cattle standing in the shallows watching us with bovine incuriosity. Soon, a tiny fishing stage and mature trees indicated Ferry House and the site of the defunct Preston Ferry. In the Middle Ages it had belonged to Haughmond Abbey whose ruins lie a couple of miles north. We saw two more kingfishers as Richard took over the oars beneath the Shrewsbury A5 bypass bridge. On the last stretch towards Atcham the B4380 was audible on the right bank as it ran parallel to the river, invisible behind riverbank willow and alder scrub. Prior to Shrewsbury's bypass it had been part of Telford's London to Holyhead road.

*****

When we reached the 1920s Atcham Bridge, the Georgian one beyond it, we looked for somewhere to land. Richard spotted a precipitous but just about feasible spot on the bank beneath the Georgian bridge. With difficulty he almost managed to scramble up the nettle-infested slope with the painter but it had been rendered slick and muddy by the recent rain and he fell back onto the boat, near-capsizing it. I managed to fling myself across to right the boat, also contorting to keep my phone and wallet pocket above the river water as it flooded into the boat: we were both soaked, Richard wetter by far. Laughing uncontrollably and again stumbling into the river to add insult to injury and ensuring we were as wet as possible, we finally got to the top of the bank, slipping and sliding all the while and vigorously attacked

by what seemed unnecessarily
virulent nettles and thornily
spiteful brambles. The painter
tied to a tree, we had to go down
the bank again to get our packs
that had been kept above the
worst of the water by the rowing
bench amidships. We left the

boat with its bows on the bank but the stern full of dark and muddy
river, our empty water bottles bobbing about in the murk. We landed
thus, all dignity lost, at five o'clock.

Water streaming from us, we headed towards the pretty smart-
looking Mytton and Mermaid Hotel. We went in to see if they had
a room available. We made muddy puddles on the cream-coloured
hall carpet but the receptionist was completely unruffled and booked
us into the Attingham Suite (sounded and was quite posh) and for
dinner. She waved away our apologies and seemed quite amused by
our attempts to get out of the river. We squelched upstairs to change
into dry clothes and have a shower. Again, a cream carpet suffered and
we hoped that a bit of judicious foot-scuffing next morning might
improve matters.

Apparently, what had been the Talbot Hotel closed in late-
Victorian times but was reopened with its present name in the 1930s by
the great architect Clough Williams-Ellis, the builder of Portmeirion
village on the coast of Gwynedd. The hotel had served the London to
Holyhead road as a coaching inn and much trade came from visitors
to Attingham Hall for it faces its main gateway and lodges. We walked
out to look at this Classical composition, a triumphal arch extended
to screen the lodges, and also admired the hotel itself, a fine Georgian

three-storey brick façade with stately sash windows below a hipped tiled roof, predating 1780s Attingham Hall by twenty or so years.

We asked why the Talbot had been renamed the Mytton and Mermaid. Apparently, the funeral cortège of 'Mad Jack' Mytton had stopped here in 1834 on its way from debtors' prison in London to his ancestral home of Halston Hall near Oswestry that he had gambled away during a rakehell life. No-one on duty seemed to know where the mermaid in the hotel's name came from and I'm sure there have been no confirmed sightings in the Severn below Atcham Bridge.

From the hotel the old London to Holyhead road bridge largely screens its ferroconcrete 1929 replacement: elegant and fine but not a patch on John Gwynn's seven-arched stone bridge of about 1770 and one of his finest designs. This is a view emphatically endorsed by Brian Waters who wrote: '*of the thirty-four road bridges spanning the Severn, the eighteenth-century bridge built by John Gwynne is still the masterpiece*'. Now a footbridge, we walked out onto it and watched a heron wading and fishing in the river beneath before going back past the hotel to look at the exterior of the locked red sandstone St Eata's Church. We repaired to the hotel for an excellent dinner, washed down with good white wine. Back in our room, as a nightcap we followed up with a couple of glasses of unctuously dark Oloroso sherry that I happened to have in my backpack.

*****

On Thursday morning the dome of the sky was a deep blue, a few low clouds fringing the horizon. It looked promising after yesterday's cloudy later afternoon and evening, not to mention the two periods of rain. Over an excellent breakfast we consulted our trusty Pevsner's *Shropshire* to see what was of interest along the river below Atcham.

Three major sites leapt out at us: Wroxeter, the remains of a walled Roman town, Buildwas Abbey and Ironbridge. We particularly fancied Wroxeter as Thomas Telford (who else?) had been among the first to excavate it in the 1780s. He methodically recorded what was found, almost in an archaeologically modern manner, and exposed some of the ruins of Roman Viroconium: truly a man of parts. This was in an age when as often as not archaeology was treated as a sort of spectator sport. A luncheon party of gentlemen would set a gang of labourers to dig through a dozen ancient burial mounds or tumuli in search of bones, jewels, swords, watching from behind tables groaning with cold meats and game pies.

After breakfast we peered over the bank at the boat, still tilted and half-full of muddy water. The empty plastic water bottles floating in the boat would serve to bail it. Deferring this tedious task, we paid up and thanked the hotel, apologising again for the muddy marks on the hall, staircase and bedroom carpets (we had laboriously cleaned the non-carpeted bathroom floor on our knees). Leaving our packs on a bench, we visited St Eata's Church. Guidebooks and Pevsner all make much of its unique dedication, particularly as Eata was a 7th-century Bishop of Hexham, then Lindisfarne, both a long, long way away and in a different Anglo-Saxon kingdom.

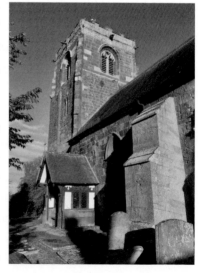

The mainly pinkish-red sandstone of the church was bathed in golden early morning sunshine, its situation by the river delightful. The nave and lower tower are Norman, the rest later medieval, the porch timber-framed and dated '*1665*'. The west doorway into the tower is c1200, still round-arched but with five colonettes supporting it that give a convincing perspective impression of great depth to what is in fact a relatively shallow arch. One paler stone block beside the priest's door into the chancel was used by generations of Atcham folk to sharpen their scythes and billhooks, eleven deep side-by-side grooves worn into it. The church incorporates Roman stone salvaged from Viroconium/Wroxeter, two miles away as the crow flies but over three via the serpentine windings of the Severn hereabouts.

The important Anglo-Norman historian Orderic Vitalis was christened here. Reading medieval history at the University of London in the 1960s, his *Historia Ecclesiastica* was a key medieval Latin text with which I wrestled (what a long time ago it all seems). Fortunately, it was easier to read than Classical Latin, being less pure and, thank goodness, more akin in grammatical structure to French. Collecting our packs, we descended the riverbank and managed with great care to reach the boat without further mishap. We tipped as much of the water out as we could, finishing the job baling with the tiny water bottles, and cast off.

# 6

# Rowing Past Wroxeter

A little downstream of Atcham I paused on the oars so we could look back at the south side of Gwynn's superb bridge, bathed golden in the sunshine with the darker shadows of bank trees adding to a sharply etched effect. After a southward stretch, the river bore east and we saw a white building behind us, the bank here for once unobscured by continuous trees.

I recognised it as John Nash's most celebrated villa, Cronkhill, which I'm afraid we hadn't spotted on the map at breakfast, possibly focusing on Wroxeter further downstream. Built in 1802 it is a splendidly Italianate composition verging towards Cottage Orné and the first such in England. Standing on the edge of slightly higher flood-proof ground, framed by a backdrop

of mature trees, it was built for Francis Walford, Lord Berwick of Attingham Park's estate agent (that is the man who ran the estate not a sharp-suited purveyor of houses). From the river it is small and villa-like with a circular tower and at the left a wing with a colonnaded loggia serving as a terrace to the first floor, all covered in bright white stucco. Trees screen brick service ranges thus contriving to make the stucco parts appear a small villa straight from a 17th-century Poussin or Lorraine painting. A delightful picturesque composition, all the better for seeing it from the river.

After Cronkhill, the river winding eastwards towards Wroxeter, we ran aground once again but got free of the gravel without getting out of the boat. Our hopes of landing at Wroxeter proved over-optimistic and we had to row on, a green woodpecker darting in and out of the trees on the island screening the village. There had been a ford at the south end of the island which survived in some shape or form into the later 19th century, remarkably long-lived as it had been a ford on the Roman road from Abergavenny to Wroxeter. Brian Waters informed us that '*two columns from the forum stand at the gateway of Wroxeter church, another is the garden roller at the Cound Lodge Inn*'. Constructive recycling indeed.

The river again began heading south as we ran aground twice in the mile downstream from Wroxeter, once with Richard having to get out to haul the boat free, firmly telling me not to assist with the oars as the gravel merely frayed the ends of the wooden blades. Just before it bore east, it was filled from bank to bank by upwards of a hundred Brent geese accompanied by numerous gulls bobbing up and down on the water. They dispersed as we passed and then the river was forced south at Eyton Rock, its riverside ridge draped in tall, mature trees, narrowing the river and we sped through before it widened and again slowed down.

There was a pub sign on the map at Cound where there had once been a ferry. If we could land, we would have a drink and check whether the garden roller using a column from Roman Viroconium was still there. Tantalisingly, we could see the pub, now renamed The Riverside Inn, a Georgian painted brick coaching inn whose main front unexpectedly faces the river, its rear the main road. The reason is simple, the road formerly ran between it and the river. All frightfully interesting no doubt, but there was nowhere to land on these steep banks. We changed oarsman and decided to press on to Cressage where a pub was also marked on the map.

The left bank hereabouts is shown on the OS map as having a race course, in fact a point-to-point and '*a superb old course*' but we could see nothing of this from our lowly position below the steep banks. Still, at least we could see kingfishers that racegoers could not. The river turned sharply south-east and we rowed alongside river-cut sandstone cliffs, no more than fifty feet high but heavily treed. There were clear signs of old quarrying activity, the stone no doubt loaded directly into barges for use at sites up and down the river. Here many of the trees were perfectly and brightly reflected in the smooth surface of the river or shattered and distorted in eddies and wind-ruffled stretches, more kingfishers added further touches of bright colour.

Around the next bend we saw Cressage Bridge which nowadays carries a B road across the river rather than the main road to Shrewsbury. From a distance it looks like any of the other Georgian stone bridges along the River Severn, its arches perhaps less ornamented but with cutwaters and balustraded parapets. In fact, it is modern, built in ferroconcrete in 1913, the local cement giving it a yellowish limestone hue. According to Brian Waters it replaced the last of the old wooden trestle bridges and was until then a toll bridge (1d per '*foot passenger*') and he concedes '*it possesses a grace seldom achieved by bridges of the present* [20th] *century*'. However elegant, it had replaced the 1799 timber bridge by, of course, Thomas Telford, at that time living in Shrewsbury.

Again, there were few options for landing but I steered towards a fence under the left of the three arches and Richard, shipping the oars, grabbing hold tied the boat to it. A steep scramble up the bank followed, aided by the fence, which separated a field of grazing sheep from the scrubby underside of the bridge. We emerged onto the road via the Severn Way long-distance footpath stile close to the end of the bridge balustrade, and about seven miles downstream from Atcham.

*****

Standing on Cressage Bridge about a third of a mile from the village centre we paused to look down at the river and up to the hills. To the north-east the striking tree-clad peak of the Wrekin rises to 1300 feet out of the rolling countryside. An outlier of the ancient rock of the Long Mynd to the south-west, the Wrekin had a large Iron Age hill fort at its summit, an ideal location for dominating the surrounding

country. Modernity has impinged with telecoms and TV masts, erected to much popular disquiet at the time, being in the Shropshire Hills Area of Outstanding Natural Beauty. From the bridge the Wrekin, Brian Waters' *'chief glory of Shropshire'*, looks a dark-green tree-clad cone and it is no wonder many think it an extinct volcano. It has a somewhat brooding presence, the trees giving it a blurred outline, Housman's *'forest fleece'*. Telford, in all likelihood on a brief excursion from the construction of Cressage Bridge, climbed it and recommended others to do so for the superb views obtainable from its summit ridge. Brian Waters comments on its changing moods in different weathers and considers this view from near the bridge *'the finest view along the Severn where the Wrekin, two miles away, looms above the arch of the bridge spanning the river'*.

Looking north-west we saw a brick and concrete World War II pillbox squatting in its large field by the river, part of a defensive line to protect the Severn bridges. However, we felt that if the Panzers had reached here the game would surely have been up. Turning eastwards we could see the pink cooling towers and tall chimney of the Ironbridge Power Station about four miles away. We would be rowing past that in due course but it is striking that the colour is 'vernacular' in that the cement used for them was coloured to match local sandstones. They are still enormous, of course, but this simple colour change suggested by the landscape architect Kenneth Booth was an effective attempt to blend them into the landscape.

Setting off for Cressage, we were looking forward to a pint and a little something for lunch. The first house on the right is all that is left of a Victorian Severn Valley Railway station. Standing by the Celtic-cross war memorial on its triangular road island hemmed in by paviours, benches and signs, we saw the pub: The Eagles. Closed and boarded up! Perhaps there would be a shop or garage in the village so first we walked along Harley Road past the parish church, an unimpressive early Victorian one relocated above flood level, its medieval predecessor nearer the river continually damaged by the Severn's winter flooding.

No shops along this road, although a few rather good 'black and white' 17th-century timber-framed cottages. Retracing our steps to the deserted pub we turned east into Sheinton Road, the other 'main street' of the village. Again a few older houses and cottages and we walked on past a junction, The Moors, which seemed to offer only modern estate houses. We reached the village school, a collection of prefab buildings, and at last saw someone to ask. He told us there was a shop in The Moors at its far end, helpfully named The Village Shop. Its Indian shopkeeper welcomed us but there was little of culinary excitement. We bought wafer-thin sandwiches: a chicken and bacon mayo for me, Richard opting for tuna mayo (we never did discern any trace of mayonnaise, though). We ate on the bench by the war memorial before heading back to the bridge.

*****

Relaunching without incident, Richard rowed while I looked back at the bridge briefly bathed in sunshine, its concrete glowing pale honey. The river now trended eastwards in a series of winding loops, more kingfishers and at times views of the power station cooling towers. Looking down at the map I spotted a woodland hangar named Tarts Rough. Before either of us could start making feeble jokes we hit suitably rough water and rapids opposite the wood. A gravel beach blocked two-thirds of the river and we were 'flashed' through and spun around to face back upstream before we knew what was happening and lashed by willow branches into the bargain. Was that vigorous stretch of water what was meant by the 'rough' in Tarts Rough, we wondered? Obviously not, as it is apparently a tautological place name, the most well-known example being the River Avon in which the British (Old Welsh) for river is '*afon*'. The tart in the name is Anglo-Saxon for rough, hence 'rough rough'.

Tarts Rough and other woodland forms the west boundary to Leighton Hall's parkland beside the riverbank. The Hall itself is well back from the river and its high banks hid the ground floor from us so all we could see was the top half of a late 18th-century block, dormers in its roof and a forest of chimneys receding into the distance. It was set amid magnificent specimen parkland trees that also entirely hid the nearby parish church, the river merely a parkland feature. We drifted by, sand-martin nest holes pockmarking the riverbank. Beyond a wooded right-hand boundary, the river twisted and turned through two loops, the banks largely treeless, and the fields beyond cattle-grazed.

The river narrowed as we approached Buildwas, 'mouth' of the Ironbridge Gorge whose sides rise 300 feet from the river. Buildwas Abbey is not seen from the river and as Brian Waters puts it over-excitedly '*trees rob one of the most beautiful ruins north of the Mediterranean of its riparian setting*'. He then gets truly fanciful stating that after the fall of Rome man '*fought and grovelled in the dust*'. He amplifies: '*It is not through letters that he regained his heritage for the works of the pen-men were known to few, but it was by means of the columned pillar and the rounded arch that he fought his way back to that frame of mind we call civilization*'. He was setting high expectations for the ruined abbey.

Ahead was the modern Buildwas Bridge, as usual the latest in a succession, the original being medieval stone washed away in the Great Flood of February 1795, the frozen river melting abruptly and

the waters rising a devastating twenty feet. Telford had undertaken repairs to the bridge in the early 1790s as Shropshire County Surveyor but after the floods he abandoned stone and designed only the second iron bridge across the Severn, the world-famous Iron Bridge being the first. The latter has a very high, fully semicircular arch and Telford thought that Abraham Darby and the contractors had in a delightfully pithy comment not *'disentangled their minds from the form of a stone arch'.* In truth, the Iron Bridge uses timber technology rather than stone with tusk tenons, dovetails and mortise and tenon joints, all in wrought or cast iron. Telford had the idea of a shallower and stronger arch and although thirty feet longer its weight in iron was half that of the Iron Bridge. Opened in 1796, sadly it was not there for us to admire being replaced in 1905 and again in 1992 by the current steel one (the photograph above obviously predates 1905).

However, before we went under this bridge we had to land on the steep and wooded right bank to get at Buildwas Abbey. I spotted a fishing station, the usual three-foot-square mini-quay, and directed Richard towards it but there were mudbanks and gravel and swirling eddies so I climbed out of the boat and dragged it to shore, Richard using the oars as paddles in the strong current. Once on the fishing station I tied the boat to a tree, its bows pointing upstream as the water swirled past. Richard climbed out of the boat onto the fishing quay and we had landed after a winding five-mile row from Cressage and our nugatory lunch.

# 7

# Buildwas Abbey and Supper in Ironbridge

Without the map we would have rowed straight past for, as Brian Waters reported, there is no clue that a ruined abbey lies hereabouts. The riverbank rose steeply, heavily treed with many fine limes, beech, oaks and tall conifers as well as the usual sycamore scrub, saplings and the like. Scrambling up we emerged in a rather neglected-looking car park, a many-gabled stone-built house beyond. Autumn leaves strewed the car park unswept, evidently no-one was home. This is Abbey House, a complex building with parts of the medieval abbot's lodgings and the monks' infirmary incorporated within its enlargement into a Tudor country house for the Lord of Powis who acquired the site after the abbey had been dissolved.

We assumed that the building was 'between occupants' which suited us perfectly as we had arrived uninvited from the riverbank into its private grounds. The house looked decidedly Victorian and mock-medieval but its west end incorporates a medieval arcade of five pointed arches, now serving as a screen linking the house to a 16th-century former dovecote. Later in Ironbridge, locals told us that for thirty years or so it had been the social club for Buildwas Power Station but had closed in 2015 a year before the power station's final closure. I suppose we should have noticed the pink cooling towers were without steam adding a *'perpetual cloud to the landscape'*.

We skirted to the right of Abbey House across a field to see how we could get into the abbey to admire Brian Waters' much-praised ruins. In the field was a brick pigsty. Nothing remarkable about that in itself but the low walls enclosing the pig runs re-used medieval stone salvaged from the abbey of quite unnecessarily grand dimensions: pampered pigs indeed. We scaled the metal fence enclosing the abbey as it was not open to the public that day. Not really trespassing as I am a paid-up member of English Heritage, the abbey ruins' custodians.

It was a Savignac abbey founded in 1135 by the Bishop of Chester, Roger de Clinton, and most of what we saw dated from the 1150s after the Savignac orders had merged with the Cistercians. Largely complete by 1190 it is architecturally remarkably and unusually coherent. It looks peaceful now but suffered numerous Welsh raids, the worst being a spectacular one in 1350 when raiders carried off the abbot and the monks as well as their booty. Later, the great Owain Glyndŵr's followers arrived in 1406 from Powis and sacked the abbey pretty thoroughly. Glyndŵr had conquered most of Wales after 1400, driving out and defeating the English on numerous occasions, and even establishing a Welsh Parliament at Machynlleth. To a Welshman this was the Last War of Independence, to the English of course mere rebellion. The 'rebels' defied the might of England for over a decade but at least Owain did not suffer the same gruesome fate as David III (or Dafydd ap Gruffydd) the last Prince of Wales. Captured by Edward I he was tried for treason by a kangaroo-court Parliament summoned to Shrewsbury in September 1283.

Dafydd's execution was brutal: a hanging, drawing and quartering relished by that singularly brutal English king, the 'Hammer of the Scots': a cruelly well-earned nickname. Later, Edward inflicted the same barbarous punishment on Scotland's great hero, William

Wallace, who also had Welsh blood: Edward had a reprehensible attitude to his Celtic neighbours. Yesterday in Shrewsbury we had seen a bronze plaque recording the execution location at the corner of St Mary's Street. The more fortunate Owain merely melted away into the Welsh hills and was never seen again. The abbey's final raid was by Henry VIII's commissioners who closed the abbey and expelled the monks once and for all. The Welsh, though, had the last laugh for the abbey was granted to the Lord of Powis, a more respectable descendant of the 14th-century raiders.

Richard joined me and we walked along the nave, roofless but with both main arcades intact. The stone used was a hard buff-coloured sandstone quarried at nearby Broseley and it has weathered remarkably well: after all the church has been roofless for centuries. 18th-century prints show it far more romantic and picturesquely ivy-clad: no manicured English Heritage lawns then. It was on an 18th-century tourist itinerary that in those days could combine the melancholy of a ruined monastery with visits to the blast furnaces of

Coalbrookdale which lit the night skies into a lurid red and orange inferno. Difficult now to grasp how exciting the Industrial Revolution was in the 18th century. Who would now want to combine a visit to the ruins of Margam Abbey with Port Talbot steelworks?

Buildwas was a Cistercian house, a monastic order that, at least in its early years, practised an austere lifestyle within equally austere architecture. To the modern eye, used to unpainted stonework in churches, we appreciate the purity of architectural forms: the arches, columns and capitals. Now the stonework has settled into the mellowness that comes with centuries of weather: the austerity

of the original whitewashed spaces tempered by the beauty of the stone. Brian Waters waxed lyrically but obscurely that Buildwas' secret is that '*one sees the internal structure of the church, naked and unadorned, in the fullness of light*', continuing: '*As it stands in its arrested fall it remains a fabric almost in the process of being built as in decay*'.

Not all is roofless and the chapter house where the monks met for running the monastery is intact. Its stone-vaulted roof is carried on four columns and surviving medieval floor tiles have been re-used here, many decorated with patterns such as *fleur-de-lys*, crosses and foliage. An impressive space made the more striking in scale through its floor being set below the cloister pavement. Not an unusual medieval architectural device, I know, used for example at Dryburgh Abbey in the Scottish borders.

Back at Abbey House, we descended through the woods towards where we thought the boat was but our aim was off and we had to walk parallel to the bank until we saw the marks of our ascent from the river. Back in the boat we cast off and watched two kingfishers within overhanging branches, one actually staying perched on a branch long enough for us to admire its brilliantly coloured feathers. The river was lively in the 'rapids' beneath Buildwas Bridge. I glanced to my right and was amazed to see an otter swimming alongside, obviously fishing as it kept diving and reappearing. It kept pace with the boat for a while before diving one last time.

*****

Shortly afterwards, we rowed past the power stations on the south or right bank, one of its large buildings close to the bank. It looked remarkably similar to one of those Art Deco factories strung out along London's Great West Road and it does date from that period, being built around 1930. It housed the cooling water intakes whose enormous decaying extraction pipes vanish into the river.

Opposite on the left bank and behind the 1932 steel bridge built to access the power station is the site of a truly spectacular 1773 landslip and Brian Waters describes a shocking sequence of events. First a crack in the ground was noticed with '*a field of oats heaving and rolling like the waves of the sea. Though the morning was calm, trees were waving as though in a gale. The river which was in flood, became storm-wracked and appeared to flow backwards. Then a chasm appeared, and eighteen acres of land with trees and hedges came moving down to the river with a great noise.*' Eighteen acres! This massive landslip was blamed on an earthquake but recent research suggests rain saturation of queasy subsoils and strata combined with unusually high river levels.

A pair of swans idling across the river ahead, we approached the next bridge, a 1963 concrete one built to access Ironbridge B whose four elegant but vast pink cooling towers rear above bankside trees. Their effect was carefully modulated as they are set in a curving line to respond to the river's bends. Overtaking the swans for once, a better prospect came into view: a cast-iron single-span railway bridge, its abutments invisible amid the dense trees lining the riverbanks. Before reaching the bridge itself static caravans lined the left bank. Nearby a couple of boats were tricked out as pirate ships with stubby masts, nets of 'rigging', Jolly Roger flags at the mastheads and one with a skeleton hanging at its yardarm (not real, I hasten to add). The boats were painted black and presumably associated with the campsite or The Meadows pub on the bank, no doubt offering 'pirate cruises'.

The Albert Edward railway bridge is (or was) an exact twin of the 1861 Victoria Bridge near Upper Arley crossed by the Severn Valley Railway's steam-hauled trains. Being cast at the nearby Coalbrookdale Company it only had a mile or so to travel upstream in its component parts while the Victoria Bridge went downstream in barges. Named after Queen Victoria's eldest son, the wayward 'Bertie' who became

King as Edward VII, like Victoria Bridge it has a 200-foot span, and is ornamented with cast nameplates: the ones at the apex carrying the bridge's name and date '*1863*', the engineer's name '*John Fowler*' and other plates naming the contractors and the Coalbrookdale Company. Sadly, its deck and balustrades did not survive the construction of the power station as it was feared that the coal traffic would impose

unacceptable stress, so in 1933 a structural steel deck replaced the upper works. Fowler's brick abutments, though, are intact and pretty impressive, their quoins rusticated and in contrasting yellow brick. Rowing beneath we could admire the ironwork with its row of four cast-iron supporting arches.

Through the bridge we could see the pinnacled tower to Ironbridge Church and buildings lining the road through the gorge. Richard started looking for somewhere to land and, rounding a bend, we saw what looked like an old quay with a muddy shingle beach. We grounded on the beach and pulled the boat alongside the quay, tied up and took stock. We had landed near the mouth of the Coal Brook that gave Coalbrookdale its name and where its former wharves and warehouses occupy the riverbank between it and Ironbridge itself.

*****

We were within sight of a world-famous iron bridge, for once not designed and built by Telford. This was where it would be no exaggeration to claim that Britain's 18th-century Industrial

Revolution began: in the Ironbridge Gorge. Here the Severn cut a gorge to expose rich seams of coal, sandstone, ironstone and fuller's earth, while a cloak of dense woodland stretched in both directions to provide pit props and charcoal to fire the furnaces. There had been mining here since the earlier Middle Ages, much of it undertaken by religious houses such as Buildwas Abbey. It is difficult to visualise the gorge in its industrial pomp, now once again heavily treed, the houses tranquil in the warm light of the setting sun.

We were also landing within the boundaries of Telford, a new town named after that heroic and indefatigable architect, civil engineer, canal and bridge builder. With a disappointing modern centre, it incorporates the River Severn's Gorge as it flows through Coalbrookdale, Ironbridge and Coalport. This had not originally been the case when an uninspiringly named 'Dawley New Town' had first been designated in 1963. In 1968 it was enlarged to take in the river and dreary names were canvassed for the enlarged town including 'Wrekin Forest City' or the more obscure but romantic-sounding 'Dawleyoak'. The then Government Minister, Anthony Greenwood, who had proposed the enlargements rebuffed all options and suggested 'Telford'. It shows how far by the 1960s the great Telford had faded from Shropshire memory as outrage burst out all round (nowadays it would have been a Twitterstorm). Who was this Scotsman and what right had he to be commemorated in deepest Salop? The minister pointed out that Thomas Telford had made a very major contribution to Shropshire and stuck to his guns. No doubt the grumbling continued but to many the name was a just tribute to the 'Colossus of Roads' and we hope Telford residents are now justifiably proud.

By chance we had landed at the quay where the Coalbrookdale Company loaded its barges. The quayside was criss-crossed with railway tracks, some retaining locally cast iron rails. One of the four-wheeled flatbed wagons used for loading and unloading is preserved, its wheels secured by iron pegs through the axle as in timber technology. It is safe within the wharfage building, which resembles more a Gothic Revival school than an industrial warehouse, its offices crusty with battlements, turrets and leaded-light windows. This curious building of 1834 has a new life as The Museum of the Gorge.

The quay and warehouse are actually in between Coalbrookdale to the west and Ironbridge proper to the east. The area is known as The Wharfage, a jumble of inns, gabled warehouses, cottages and smarter detached houses. In short, the usual sociable, cheek-by-jowl jumble of earlier phases of the 18th-century industrial revolution before successful iron masters moved to posher houses away from smoke, smells and bustle. There are even the remains of a substantial limekiln, sandwiched between The Malthouse and The Swan Taphouse.

The first thing, though, was to secure a bed for the night and we had landed in front of The Swan Taphouse, one of The Wharfage's 18th-century inns. We hoisted our packs and climbed the steps from the wharf, an encouraging '*B & B*' on the signboard. Inside, the barman, Tom, tall enough to be a rugby second-row forward at six-foot-eight, welcomed us and there were two single rooms available. We gratefully booked them, retiring to change into different clothes for the evening.

Back in the bar over a Peroni we asked Tom and a fellow drinker, Lawrence, about the power stations and Ironbridge. Lawrence told us that the power station had finally closed the previous week, apparently well beyond the scheduled date: he did not seem surprised at this. Tom suggested we leave the oars in his office which seemed eminently sensible, given the boat's somewhat public mooring place. Having done this, he suggested supper at La Casita tapas bar in the centre of Ironbridge.

We headed east along the Gorge pausing to read the information board by the limekilns that had been in production from about 1760 until 1870, using limestone quarried from the hills immediately behind. The better stone was used for building, the poor and friable for making lime mortar or fertiliser for the fields. Up New Road, the parish church of Ironbridge, St Luke, dating from the 1830s is, frankly, more picturesque from a distance. Mostly brick-built, its tower plays an important role in views along the gorge and there are expansive views from behind the locally cast churchyard railings across the town to wooded slopes beyond.

From the church we worked our way down to the High Street via long flights of steps, to emerge near the market square where the north side is occupied by The Tontine Hotel of 1783, to its right the former market hall, now with shops behind its five ground-storey arches, and the former Butter Market, its four arches now blocked and in use as a hairdresser's and a chemist. This area is the heart of the late 18th-century town while opposite of course is the famous Iron Bridge, so we walked out onto it in the gathering twilight. What a splendid view looking upstream! The bank on our left heavily wooded, trees in full leaf, and to the right the buildings of The Wharfage following the sweep of the river. The Museum of the Gorge buildings closed the vista with trees in the park behind, a dense black sylvan backdrop.

La Casita tapas bar near the bridge is in a surprisingly modest two-storey late-eighteenth-century building, dwarfed amid the grander ones of the Market Square and High Street. We ate upstairs and talked to the patroness, a lively lass with a dense mane of flowing chestnut-brown hair and a ready wit. Following a good range of freshly cooked tapas and Spanish white wine we left very cheerful and it was so convivial a meal I cannot for the life of me remember what we ate. Returning to The Swan Taphouse we had another drink in the bar and retired to polish off a bit more of my bottle of Oloroso to keep the Spanish theme going. I went to my room, Richard no doubt a bit relieved to have a night free of my (alleged) snoring.

# 8

# The Darbys of Coalbrookdale

Over a somewhat leisurely breakfast in The Swan Taphouse I asked Tom whether the motorbike parked outside was his. It was and while Richard glazed over, we discussed the finer points of various motorbikes, including many I had owned and ridden over the years. Breakfast passed enjoyably for me at least, although accompanied by an instant coffee, something of an anathema to Richard.

Mind you, we found that by staying at The Swan we had again crossed the path of Thomas Telford for we later learned that The Swan had been used for occasional meetings not only by Telford, but by other luminaries of the Industrial Revolution including the great Broseley ironmaster John Wilkinson who had subscribed to the Iron Bridge, insisting it be built in iron, and Richard Trevithick. Presumably, they met with Abraham Darby III here to discuss business and projects over a pint of ale or claret and a locally made Broseley clay pipe.

Looking forward to an industrial archaeology feast, at nine o'clock we set off to walk into the steep-sided valley of the Coal Brook, once flowing black through near-surface coal seams. A map outside the Museum of the Gorge showed us that there were numerous forges, furnaces and their accompanying header ponds along the course of the Brook. We turned up Dale Road into the crowded former beating heart of the 18th-century industrial revolution. Initially, it was disappointing for there was virtually no trace of the Lower Forge and its 400-foot-long pool: it had been filled in by 1900 while modern housing occupied the site of the forge itself. In the early days the brook was sufficiently vigorous to turn a number of waterwheels to power forges in that era of charcoal-based iron smelting.

The arrival of the first of three generations of the Darby family transformed iron smelting and the valley, although none of the Darbys made old bones. Abraham I had initially been a brass founder but by 1705 he had moved on to working with iron, arriving in Coalbrookdale from Bristol in 1708 to develop coal and coke-powered furnaces. His son, Abraham II, refined this, solely using coke, and brought in big steam engines to recycle the water to keep waterwheels turning day and night to drive the furnace bellows, as well as casting the first iron rails and flanged wheels. His son, Abraham III, rebuilt the Coalbrookdale Ironworks and of course cast the Iron Bridge that transformed the Severn valley and the world, and like so many 18th-century entrepreneurs, the Darbys were Nonconformist, in their case Quakers.

Amazingly, the Darby family and the Coalbrookdale Company initially made their money from casting three-legged cooking pots. As Brian Waters says, '*There was one in every peasant home, and when the trade declined the export market continued with India and Africa.*' So far so good, but he goes on to say they were used in cannibal feasts: not a suitable anecdote for current sensitivities. In any case it is the rather more glamorous higher-end ironwork for which the company is rightly remembered: Boulton and Watt steam engines built under licence, rails, architectural castings, lamp posts and bridges. Intriguingly, in 1787 they even produced an early steam-powered railway locomotive designed for iron wagon-way tracks by William Reynolds. Well ahead of its time, the steam locomotive killed a man during its firing-up and a local jury promised huge fines for any further attempts at such Devil's work.

The works attracted many engineers and the like, including the great Cornish steam pioneer Richard Trevithick. In 1802 the high-pressure boiler and engine for his celebrated early steam locomotive were made at the Coalbrookdale Ironworks, other parts in Bridgnorth further downstream. Another visitor was Jonathan Hornblower who, with his brother Josiah, built Newcomen steam engines for the tin mines of Cornwall. Bearing in mind our Loire plans it was interesting to cross the trail of a real Hornblower in Coalbrookdale.

As I wrote earlier, Coalbrookdale and Ironbridge were also very much on the 18th-century tourist trail or to put it rather more elegantly the British Grand Tour. The excitement of new industry meant there were numerous artists producing prints for sale to the tourist. The most famous depiction is by an artist born in Strasbourg, the splendidly named Philip James de Loutherbourg who had settled in London in the 1770s. His memorable and dramatic 1801 oil painting *Coalbrookdale by Night* shows the sky lit up by the leaping flaming glow of the furnaces making the clouds of smoke above them luridly red and orange. As the furnaces were fed and working continuously, the best effects for visitors were of course at night and the painting splendidly evokes the heady excitement of the Industrial Revolution. I could enthuse for many pages but we were still at the foot of the Coal Brook valley so we pressed on. Beyond a whopping 1911 Queen Anne-style primary school, suburban houses line Dale Road ending at a surviving 17th-century timber-framed cottage with what on closer examination turned out to be locally cast iron chimney pots. Next we passed the site of Middle Forge, circles in the grass marking the site of the blast furnaces.

Round the bend, a steep-sided valley was the site of the former Upper Forge Pool. It is now occupied by Aga-Rayburn's

Coalbrookdale Foundry: iron casting is still alive and flourishing. Strangely moving in a Britain where so many historic factory sites sit

derelict and windswept. Beyond this is one of the finest, most important and superbly curated industrial museums in the country. The Museum of Iron occupies the old Coalbrookdale Iron Works established in 1709. Past an ornate Queen Victoria's Diamond Jubilee street lamp cast at Coalbrookdale (where else?), we descended to enter the museum via the Great Warehouse of 1838, a clock tower added later to give it greater architectural heft.

Once in the main yard, we looked northwards, the view flanked on the left by the arches of an 1860s railway viaduct and on the right by the Long Warehouse, mostly late Victorian, the upper two floors carried on an open arcade of cast-iron columns. The north side terminated by a mass of jumbled old brickwork with at its centre a modern triangular-section building lit by a south wall entirely of glass. It resembles a 1960s style of church and could be seen as a shrine dedicated to the Industrial Revolution, for it houses the Old Furnace

where in 1709 Abraham Darby I first smelted iron using coke. Some of the furnace structure is 17th century so, like a great cathedral, it is built on older foundations and crypts. Picked out in white on some of the ironwork are cast dates, the earliest '*1638*', surviving from charcoal-smelting days and around the corner above another 17th-century date are two bars with '*Abraham Darby 1777*' cast on each. Like a fringe of side chapels on either side of the Old Furnace's enclosing building are other structures in varying states of survival: a snapper furnace and a waterwheel pit, for example, and behind them all rears the high brick walling of the dam that held back the great Upper Furnace Pool, substantial enough to carry factory tramways.

The whole thing is utterly awe-inspiring and the yard in which we stood was itself once covered in buildings. Distributed on the grass and gravel of this yard, apart from parked cars, are examples of ironwork products, including a stretch of tramway track and a complete cast-iron Classical cornice lintel that must have weighed several tons and been devilish complex to cast.

As our main aim was to row the river, we had to tear ourselves away from Coalbrookdale, limiting ourselves to an hour's visit. But not before pausing in the bookshop in the Great Warehouse to buy a take-away coffee and talk to the friendly museum staff. We told them we thought this one of the best-presented museums we had ever visited. The coffee was important to our morale as well, for the dry acrid taste of breakfast's instant coffee still lingered. We said our farewells and set off back down the dale, sipping our coffees.

# 9

# Through Ironbridge Gorge Past Swimming Firefighters and Coalport

Back at The Swan, we collected our packs and the oars and said our farewells. We got the boat ready under the admiring gaze of a Sikh family feeding nearby ducks, the father taking photographs (of us, not the ducks). We relaunched just before eleven o'clock into a river in its gorge where the current flowed strong and the breeze ruffled the water, giving us an unjustifiably strong conviction of speed. We were looking

forward to rowing beneath the celebrated Iron Bridge upon which we had stood the previous evening. The right bank had a number of wooden fishing stations, one occupied by an angler in a snappy white baseball cap. On this stretch through the gorge the river seems fringed by washed-down boulders of varying sizes forming natural craggy embankments, the boulders seemingly larger once past Ironbridge.

Ahead we could see the arch of the Iron Bridge and, as we neared it, a solitary and tiny figure walked across to bring home the scale of the thing and its breathtaking daring as a world first. The lower stonework screened by tree branches, the elegant cast-iron arches and the flanking Gothic ogee-arched side panels were now fully visible, painted an elegant but fading blue-grey. At the apex the arch is slender and the road deck also, so the whole thing has an ethereal quality: a worthy centrepiece for the Ironbridge Gorge World Heritage Site.

It was built for the go-ahead Abraham Darby III who was fed up with the Benthall Ferry despite part-owning it. The ferry carried iron ore and pig iron as well as people but its capacity was clearly limited. The ever-impatient and bustling Darby saw a bridge as the solution, probably for two reasons: pure transport capacity needs and equally significantly as an advertisement for his cast iron. With the benefit of hindsight of course we know it was a success, but at the time its unproven technology and a span of 120 feet by a single arch was an astonishing declaration of confidence. Construction started after a successful petition to Parliament in 1776. The ferryboat had a brief twilit monopoly transporting timber, draft horses and other requirements for its nemesis; even so the ferry limped on until 1904, probably because there was also a toll charge for crossing the bridge, foot-passengers charged a halfpenny each, oddly the same rate for a calf, pig, sheep or lamb, while an ox or cow was a whole penny. There

were no exemptions, not even for the military or the Royal Family, according to the painted toll board.

Work started in 1777 to the designs of the architect Thomas Farnolls Pritchard who had originally been a Shrewsbury joiner. He died before work was properly under way and Abraham Darby III took over and, despite a crisis of confidence and even thoughts of stone, brick or timber alternatives, cast iron won out and it was finished by autumn 1779, although formally opened only on New Year's Day 1781. Richard felt this interval of over a year uncharacteristic of Abraham Darby's dynamic approach but no doubt there were sound reasons or perhaps, as Richard surmised, it was informally in use as soon as complete. Brian Waters describes the arch as '*a perfect semicircle, surrounded by a spider's web of struts and girders, giving an oriental effect*'. The ironwork weighed '*three hundred and seventy-eight and a half tons*' and '*was erected in three months without the least obstruction to the navigation of the river or any loss of life*' and it was made from '*cold cast iron, a very pure iron, extremely hard, and showing a remarkable resistance to corrosion*'. Over 1700 separate cast-iron pieces were assembled largely using carpentry-style joints (Farnolls influenced, presumably), thus combining the new material with traditional timber techniques. So remarkable was it that a 1784 visitor, John Byng, described it as *'one of the wonders of the world'*. Despite this accolade in 1956 the county council proposed its demolition!

We speculated on the reaction to this *'spider's web of struts and girders'* from contemporaries used to massive stone or brick bridges, particularly given the Severn's habit of destroying bridges. What chance for such a delicate structure? Fourteen years later it survived its first major test, the Great Flood of 1795, and was the only one along the river not damaged. The bridge had a profound effect on Thomas Telford who took to iron bridges and aqueducts like a duck to water.

The bridge is, to use a much-abused epithet, 'iconic', a word justified both as the first major use of cast iron for such a grand structure and because for many years it was the secular icon of the Ironbridge Gorge Museum until replaced recently by an ever-whizzy marketing industry.

As we drifted slowly beneath the five iron arches that support the bridge deck, we looked upwards, our necks craning and remarkably the structure still looked diaphanous. We could now read the proud inscription on the nearest arch ironwork: *'This bridge was cast at Coalbrookdale and was erected in the year MDCCLXXIX'*. Then we were through, but still looking back at the bridge, spellbound by such elegant civil engineering. Not that the profession was so named until an aged Telford (who else?) was elected founding president of the Institution of Civil Engineers.

We were quite lucky to see the bridge un-scaffolded as in 2017 a major restoration programme got under way, led by English Heritage, and much of the bridge vanished from public view behind scaffolding to emerge repainted in its original red-brown (red oxide) colour. I hope our enthusiasm not excessive but Richard and I approach all this from different directions, Richard as a professional engineer and me as a historian and architectural historian. However, we both share a great interest in industrial history for my grandfather, Cecil Daniel Andrew, was an engineer of some distinction and was, according to my grandmother at least, one of Sir Henry Fowler's chief assistants at the London Midland Railway in the 1920s. Our fathers were both engineers and Richard's paternal grandfather a railway man.

Beyond the bridge the wind no longer ruffled the surface but soon enough the water got lively so careful rowing was needed to avoid gravelly shallows, eddies over large riverbed boulders and submerged tree parts. We passed truly massive boulders on the right bank carpeted in lurid yellow-green mosses while evidence of higher river levels was in purple plastic detritus trapped in willow scrub some eight feet above the river.

Ahead the calm surface gave way to rough water across the whole river's width. We approached with caution and could see a weir of some sort with less turbulent water nearer the left bank. I steered us towards that, hoping for a gap in the weir at the foot of a stone embankment wall rising sheer from the river. Going to the left of Salmon Bar proved sound but even so we barely scraped over, the bottom of the boat grinding noisily. A lively and rocky ride, the pale sunlight dancing and flickering across the ripples, took us to Jackfield Bridge, Richard hitting one oar or the other on gravel or submerged boulders. We had been warned by Brian Waters that '*the fall in the*

*Severn between Jackfield and Coalport is very rapid, and the stream is swifter here than anywhere else along the English Severn'.* How very true. The Bridge is a 1994 asymmetrical cable-stay type similar to but heavier duty than Shrewsbury's. An earlier one had replaced a ferry, Adam's Ferry, named after a 17th-century ferryman Adam Crumpton.

*****

Beyond Jackfield Bridge I turned the boat sideways for Richard to look at what I could see. I couldn't make sense of it: lots of yellow heads bobbing about in the river and spread across it from bank to bank. Was this a sponsored swim, a bathing club or an 'incident'? We were soon close enough to realise this was some sort of training and men were now gathering in the water by the left bank for instruction. They had crossed from the Jackfield bank where a large red and black rubber dinghy was moored with a parked fire engine behind it: West Midlands Fire Service.

As this was an active exercise we would be in the way as we headed towards what looked pretty impressive rapids: presumably turbulent enough for training purposes. We rowed slowly on as the firefighters climbed out of the water. A shouted conversation with their instructor suggested we land a few yards further down the bank but well above

what now appeared a vigorous mass of white water and rocks. Richard threw up the painter and one of the firemen caught it to guide us into the 'cove', which was rather a grand name for a minor indentation amid the jumbled rocks of the left bank. We leapt out of the boat and tied up.

This stretch of river had a glacis or sloping embankment of bare boulders on the right bank which narrowed the river to about sixty feet, rather than the more usual hundred feet or so. That along with the clusters of boulders within the river itself combined to greatly speed the river as it descended abruptly between narrowed banks, producing a genuine stretch of 'white water'. It seemed to offer either another portage-training opportunity or a lively challenge to our rowing skills. I knew which option Richard would take while I had fears of a mortally embarrassing capsize, leading to a genuine rescue and red-faced coverage in a local paper. 'Fear not,' said Richard, 'Vicky and I made it onto French south-west television when we grounded our boat near Bordeaux.' Not sure whether that was reassuring, but tamely portaging past the hundred-yard stretch of white-water rapids would hardly be fun. Richard suggested we empty the boat of our packs, mobile phones, seats and any other lumber so if the worst came to the worst we would lose only our dignity.

In any case we wanted to watch the exercise as one by one the men waded out in hi-vis jackets over black waterproof gear, each with a backpack and wearing their yellow helmets. Once out in the middle, each man lay back in the water and, feet first, shot through the boiling water steering with his circling arms to keep away from the rocks. The first one waded out near our tied-up boat and set off, the instructor telling the others to watch: I presume the more experienced going first. 'Watch what he does. Go with the flow and get into your defensive

position, use your arms to keep you away from that bank and you'll go nicely down the stream and negotiate the obstacles.' With that, HMS Fireman was gone, feet together as the 'bows' of a human boat.

We watched. 'Here he comes. Is he doing the right route?' Richard opined that it was not the one he would have chosen, then I said: 'OK so far, is he going to be spun sideways?' The fireman reached the most violent white water and Richard decided. 'Right, so that's the one. That's the line we should follow.' We noted particular hotspots that might cause problems and by the time we had watched all the human boats run the rapids we had agreed the best line for the boat.

The firemen moved along the bank beyond the rapids for debriefing as I believe such post-event analyses are termed. We emptied the boat, placing everything higher up the bank, Richard perhaps fearing a freak ten-foot wave. We boarded, Richard at the steering oar. 'Row out to the middle and keep rowing until I tell you to stop, then we should whizz through just on my oar. I'll keep us on line and you keep the oars out of the water, unless I tell you.' Rowing out, stern first, I turned and was told to keep the line by following the direction of his hand ('if you can manage that for once'), and then ship oars. As we shot downstream into the deeper 'V' between racing water towards the first really vigorous white-water swirl the steering oar shot out of its rowlock and we crabbed sideways before Richard by sheer force got the bows pointing downstream away from semi-submerged rocks. We shot into and through the next big drop, firemen giving us the thumbs up, and we were in calmer water.

Apart from a mid-water crisis with Richard laughing maniacally as he steered like a gondolier, the rocking and bobbing boat had made it, although perilously close to various nasty-looking rocks. I took up the oars again and we beached. More chat, kit collected and we were back on the water around midday. Downstream, the river was lively and round the next bend we bounced across further rock-strewn rapids, the boat grazing the gravel and opposite The Half Moon pub graunching across yet more rapids.

The next bridge came into view, a steel-framed footbridge funded as a World War I Memorial to the dead of Coalport and Jackfield. It replaced Tuckies Ferry that in 1799 had overturned with forty-one people on board, mostly workers at John Rose's china works, twenty-eight drowning.

Through the bridge, the water still lively, we passed the brick buildings of the Coalport China Works, now partly the Coalport China Museum, other parts a youth hostel. The factory grew up where the Shropshire Canal reached the Severn in 1792, the Coalport porcelain works opening shortly after and closing in 1926. According to Brian Waters this closure was caused when an importunate trade union official demanded to see the company books and accounts. The owner Charles Brough '*an elderly irritable man, irritated beyond his temper by external interference in the management of his exclusive business, finally closed his works. The machinery and the goodwill were taken over by a firm in the Potteries*'. As he adds, '*only the shapely kilns on the riverbank stand as a memorial to the skill and workmanship that made the name of Coalport known in every continent*'. The gloss is slightly scuffed by

Brian Waters having spent the previous page discussing large-scale pilfering by the workers. The riverside buildings looked late 19th century and we could see one of the bottle kilns immediately behind. However, we were not intending to land as we had both visited in the past.

Just beyond the factory buildings a rocky reef jutted halfway across the river forcing us to race past beside the left bank. Another stretch of near-the-surface rocks and gravel ridges, rapids and shallows followed, taking us almost to the more elegant and historic Coalport bridge. Like many crossings of this turbulent river, it had a chequered history, first built in 1777 in timber on stone piers and commemorated in the name of the pub just beyond, the 'Woodbridge Inn'. Formerly the 'Ferry Inn', oddly it acquired the current name in the 20th century long after the bridge had been rebuilt in iron following the Great Flood of 1795 (and again rebuilt in 1818 in a sturdier form). We paused on the oars to look more closely. The 1777 sandstone piers with their cutwaters survive, supporting later brick piers. Compared with the Iron Bridge it seems a more minimal structure, the only real enrichments the balustrades and at the bridge apex a fan-like feature inscribed '*Coalport Bridge*' and '*1818*'.

Contemplating The Woodbridge Inn for lunch was brief for there was nowhere to land. As we rowed on, I asked Richard about his boat, the *At Last*, which he had mentioned running aground on the Garonne and making it onto French TV. Needless to say, the French made a meal of the discomfiture of *les rosbifs*: tagging the item

'Trafalgar Revenge'. This boat was a forty-six-foot-long Clyde-built larch-on-oak gentleman's sailing boat built in 1929 for cruising the Scottish Isles. There was a Severn connection as he had bought it in 1991 from near Stourport (he couldn't remember where), taking it down a flooded Severn to the Worcester canal basin to repair and live in while he worked in Bristol. It was a beast to handle as a previous owner had had the bright idea of converting it from a single centrally located screw or propeller to twin screws rendering the rudder an ineffective steering mechanism: a nasty baptism of fire in a flooded Severn with a current of about eight knots.

Three months later Richard ventured downstream from Worcester in the dark, deliberately grounding on a mudbank at the mouth of the Avon to await the tide before running up to Bristol. The massive Bristol lock gates were opened just for him and he moored beyond Brunel's SS *Great Britain*. A couple of years later in 1994, another quite exciting voyage saw him sail to Falmouth. He and his wife Vicky and two friends crossed to Bordeaux, en route towing a becalmed yacht into port. The televised grounding incident took place on the tidal Garonne not far from Bordeaux. Richard then asked me whether he had ever told me about his adventures in a dugout canoe in Amazonia. Well, no, but that would be for another time.

# 10

# On Past Bridgnorth

Brian Waters noted that the '*Severn is a beautifully wooded river, and nowhere more so than below Coalport, where the remaining shreds of the forest of Morfe embower the meadow lands*'. Beautifully put, but we were not out of the gorge yet and the river would continue vigorously beset by shallows and gravel ridges for a good few miles yet, but more enjoyable rowing than above Shrewsbury and better training for the Loire. Ahead of us four swans bobbed in the rough water and as usual effortlessly kept ahead until Bridgnorth where they paused to usher us past.

Approaching the next bridge we hit more rapids, ground out on gravel ridges and bounced past rocks, all concealed just below the water whose bed shelved at an alarming rate: one moment with three or four feet below the keel, the next rearing up to within inches of the surface, the boat scraping and/or being stopped. This time we managed to force ourselves off the gravel by dint of rocking the boat and shoving with the oars. I did detect what I thought an expression of annoyance occasionally flit across the Robinson visage: perhaps I was choosing the wrong line to steer.

A dull bridge across to unglamorous Coalport Sewage Works marked where the river turned south to escape the gorge. This did not mean the water became flat and dull. Round the next bend it narrowed with an islet on the left and vigorous rough water in the narrowed main river. We assumed this was a remnant of Severn

Navigation, boats following the channel or 'barge gutter' between the 'bylet' and the bank, the main river unnavigable. We grounded pretty decisively in its shoals and no amount of rocking and shoving would free us. Richard climbed out, or rather mostly left the boat, keeping one leg in, the other in the water. He managed to free us and get the rest of him back in as we were swept onwards.

Gradually, the steepness of the right or west bank eased as we rowed a long sweeping bend, the left bank climbing upwards from the river 150 heavily wooded feet. The right bank was now occupied by a long meadow and for once treeless, sheep grazing to the water's edge. Beyond woods marked the course of the old railway line. While Richard rowed, I changed Explorer maps to cover the next stretch of our voyage.

Ahead the river edged away from the right bank, leaving a gravelly beach occupying half its width where it was joined by the Dean Brook. It merged just above the beach so we assumed its added water, however

slight, sufficiently diverted the main current away from the bank to produce a silting shoal. We grounded before bouncing merrily round the bend, the swans seeming to pause to see how we handled the challenge before continuing their effortless way downstream.

Past the woods on the left we saw another bridge, the swans passing stately and elegant beneath its white-painted metalwork. The steep bank was now on the right, while on the left the hills retreated and large fields were glimpsed beyond riverbank trees and scrub. This was Apley Hall's former parkland and the 1905 bridge had been built by the then owners to replace a ferry dating back to the 15th century. This metal suspension bridge with criss-cross latticework to balustrades and piers looked identical to the 1922 Port Hill Bridge in Shrewsbury. Not surprising as both were by David Rowell & Co. of London who seemed to have erected these suspension bridges all over the country and as far afield as Chile.

Near here in 1787 John Wilkinson, described by Telford as '*the king of iron-masters*', launched the first iron boat ever made, *The Trial*. In fact, a barge, the idea did not catch on for many years. 'How can metal float?' people scoffed but Wilkinson was buried in an iron coffin in Broseley churchyard, obviously a man with faith in his own products. Brian Waters also describes one of the attempts to improve the Severn for '*fifteen years before the launching of the Trial, the tow-path was made between Bewdley and Meadow wharf, Coalbrookdale. A number of the landowners along the Severn paid a hundred guineas into a trust fund to make the path and keep it in repair, and tolls were exacted for horses, but not on vessels bow-hauled by men*': a curious incentive to use sweating and straining human beasts of burden rather than expensive horses perhaps. The thought of dragging barges upstream made us feel an exhausted sympathy for the bargemen.

From our lowly position on the river, though, we could see little of Apley Hall beyond the unkempt trees and scrub along the bank but much of its park seemed to be under the plough. At one point the earthen bank gave way to a stone wall of massive rock-faced blocks, once a quay, possibly for unloading stone for the house's recasting in the Regency period and for Victorian changes, as well as for house-party pleasure craft. There were mooring rings but it was all pretty overgrown. Brian Waters noted that '*this castellated mansion was once*

*considered as a residence for Queen Adelaide, after the death of William IV,*
*until it was decided that the fogs from the river would be injurious to the*
*Queen's health'.*

Opposite, a sandbank projected far across the river and another stretch of 'rapids fun' followed. The river bore steadily south-east before being forced south onto a new course by a heavily wooded escarpment rejoining the river just beyond the estate gates which we could see from the river. This escarpment is named Winscote Hills, its sandstone bluff rearing above us, and at its feet the water turned once again into rapids, the river narrowed by sandbanks. The boat grounded again and Richard was out of the boat, apart from one leg, with great alacrity: perhaps not unjustifiably fearing it would capsize if I tried such a trick. A lot of shoving and rocking and grinding of aluminium and we were afloat. The escarpment receded from the riverbank once past the Winscote Hills.

Nearing Bridgnorth we could see the sandstone once again closing on the riverbank. The modest and meandering River Worfe had cut

through the hills here, before merging with the mighty Severn. Ahead a massive crag ended abruptly, its sheer grey and reddish Bunter Sandstone cliff face masked at its base by trees and the main A442 road. We could also see other bare rock faces before we neared it partly screened by the wooded escarpment, Pendlestone Rock on the map. As we neared them a red sandstone two-storey building appeared in its lee with buttresses, stone mullioned windows and turrets. The OS map showed it as Fort Pendlestone but on old maps it was a yarn then a carpet factory named Pendlestone Mills built on the site of a medieval watermill. It is now apartments, industry long departed, and dates from the 1840s when this debased Tudor style was popular.

Then we were past and heading for the major crags ahead, High Rock, towering we guessed 200 sheer feet above the river. Most impressive and the river's surface was now less wind-ruffled, the bankside trees and scrub reflected sharp-etched in the water, the clouds higher and their reflections a less crisp grey-blue. As the river bore west of south the ripples and wind disturbance reappeared and we were back to a Severn we knew better. On the right bank numerous fishing platforms peeped from between the trees, and then Bridgnorth High Town came into view on its ridge.

Soon we were passing the outliers of Bridgnorth: a row of rather austere and lumpish modern blocks of flats with steeply pitched roofs: a missed opportunity to enhance the riverside. Then the wonderful, picturesquely situated tower and copper dome of Telford's St Mary Magdalene church, up on the ridge, came into view as we rounded a gentle bend. Hoping to land for a late lunch (it was now after half past two) the only possibility seemed the rowing club's steps on the left bank. We dismissed these, as there were too many people about, and pressed on to the heart of Bridgnorth and its river bridge.

The bridge has a history back into the Middle Ages: it even had a chapel on it until the 16th century, and there were wharves and warehouses upstream and downstream. The old bridge had eight arches, one rebuilt in 1773, and according to some sources Telford virtually rebuilt it as a six-arched one in 1795, presumably after the Great Flood, possibly doing more in 1823. Whatever the truth he was working on his church in High Town in the 1790s and was of course the county's Surveyor of Bridges. Unfortunately for the bridge, in 1960 a widened roadway deck replaced the balustrades to resolve a traffic bottleneck. Ruined in our view, like Montford Bridge. The two eastern arches almost blocked by gravel banks and spits, we rowed through the arch immediately next to them, this being the nearest Richard could get to the centre of a six-arch bridge.

Alongside the wharves in the 19th century there had been warehouses, iron and brass foundries, timber yards, breweries and malthouses and even a carpet factory. The Mill Street foundry on the east bank made castings for Richard Trevithick. Brian Waters, something of a champion of Trevithick, tells us that '*These* [castings] *he built into 'Catch-me-who-can', which, almost twenty years before Stephenson's Rocket, performed a circular run on rails near the present-day site of Euston Station, where it carried passengers at a shilling a head'.* Thus, although only going in circles, it was the world's first steam-hauled passenger railway. A precursor of the Circle Line, I suggested. By the 1940s Brian Waters noted the town had *'little manufacture and small exportable wealth'.*

We spotted nowhere to land so pressed on, swapping roles and I took the oars alongside The Bylet, an islet occupied by the town's 19th-century bowling greens. It must have been fairly exclusive as until 2004 it was only accessible across the 'barge gutter' by boat. Then Young Territorial Army volunteers built a bridge as a training exercise: no doubt welcomed by landlubberly locals. Looking back at its buildings along the ridge, Bridgnorth seemed decidedly French with the sublime tower of Telford's church a counterpoint to the Gothic one of St Leonard's Church. Had the castle survived the picture would have been complete. Rowing, I had the best view of the town receding as we rounded the first bend and, as the river passed beneath the 1995 concrete bypass bridge in choppy waters, we were fully past Bridgnorth.

# 11

# Quatford, Collieries and Back to Upper Arley

We rowed on and soon a river cliff reached the riverbank, as usual heavily treed and forcing the river and us south-eastwards. The more open left bank had numerous fishing stations, several occupied by anglers, and we exchanged greetings or waves, depending on their desire to talk. The water was smooth as we headed south-east, the wind no longer disturbing its surface. The wooded escarpment receded from the right bank, making room for the hamlet of Knowlesands.

There was rough water ahead, alongside a narrow islet. Richard got me to ship oars and chose a course as best he could but we banged heavily and loudly into a just-beneath-the-surface rock and scraped and ground our way across it, the violence of the collision turned us beam-on to the current. Ahead, two swans moved off from the bank and dipping their necks towards each other set off downstream, occasionally looking back to see how we were doing. A stretch of smoother water was followed by more rough water, Richard steering us into the 'V' of strong side currents racing over the rocks to merge in the middle of the river. Once through this stretch there was calmer but fast-flowing water and rounding the next bend more turbulence for Richard to steer through. All good fun and in one calmer stretch we watched a flock of gregarious long-tailed tits swirling between the bank and the overhanging willows.

Shortly, the first houses of Quatford village appeared, the water calmer as we approached. The river appeared to vanish into the ridge ahead, the water dark beneath a large overhanging willow jutting far out from the bank. Behind the riverside trees we glimpsed Quatford village and then we were round a sharp bend and heading south, the river forced to do so by the crags of Camp Hill, which ends in red sandstone cliffs, their feet in the water.

On the crest of Camp Hill, high above the river, are the earthworks of a motte-and-bailey castle built for Roger de Montgomery, Earl of Shrewsbury, in the late 11th century when Quatford was briefly a market town before his son Robert moved everything to Bridgnorth. Brian Waters relates that Adelissa who was to become Roger's second wife *'was nearly shipwrecked on the* [English] *channel crossing when on her way to marry Roger, and vowed to build a church on the spot where they should meet. This occurred at desolate Quatford, where Roger was hunting in the forest'*. She and Roger married and built the parish church, in theory on the site of this meeting. Its mid-1080s chancel

and various other bits survive
from their time at least attesting
an element of the story.

Looking at Camp Hill's
towering river cliff, it and its
heavily eroded strata of red
and pink Bunter sandstone,
turbulent water at its foot, the
epithet 'craggy' fitted the bill. Once beyond the crags, though, the hills
headed inland away from the river. We passed a replica of a Severn
'trow' moored by a riverside cottage and, on the site of Quatford ferry,
a cable-hauled one whose wire had near decapitated an Edwardian
honeymooning couple rowing downstream, the river in spate and
both drowning.

Beyond, the riverside meadows are filled by mobile homes for
a quarter of a mile or so. Another stretch of rapids and we passed
a settlement named on the map Lower Forge, a clue to the site of
Eardington Iron Works that had operated from the 1770s until 1889.
As Brian Waters puts it, they *are overgrown like the ruins of a deserted
civilization, and are of interest to the archaeologist of industry, for the upper
and lower forges are connected by an underground canal, fed by the Marl
Brook*. The forges made *wrought iron of the finest quality with charcoal,
brought by the burners from Wyre Forest and as far away as Wales*.

After more rapids we spotted a cast-iron bridge nestling amid
trees, scrub and the wreckage of tree trunks washed ashore by past
storms and floodwater. This bridge crosses the More Brook and
was first built as part of the 1770s barge towpath but must be a
replacement for it looks about 1820 in date. Was it cast by nearby
Eardington Iron Works? We had passed before I could see if there was

a date on its gently rusting russet ironwork. To the right or west, the Severn Valley Railway was now occasionally in sight from the river.

One more stretch of rapids before the river turned south and ahead of us Richard pointed to a bridge. Something of an anticlimax when I turned to look and certainly not by Telford or Gwynn: the Hampton Loade Water Treatment Bridge, also more attractively known as 'Chelmarsh Bridge'. Dating from 1963, of its type it is interesting with massive fabricated steel tubes forming quadrant arches with the deck supported on stays, all painted blue. These tubes seem grotesquely oversized until you realise they double as water pipes taking water extracted from the river to a reservoir half a mile inland and then pumping it back to water treatment works on the east bank: a multitasking bridge structure. Richard said it reminded him a bit of Isambard Kingdom Brunel's great 1859 Royal Albert Bridge at Saltash.

About a quarter of a mile south of Hampton we bounced down white-capped 'rapids' at a bend, the land now rising on both sides. There were glimpses and longer views of the Severn Valley Railway, sometimes with steam climbing into the calm air from copper-capped Great Western locomotive chimneys. The left bank then became more open and there were numerous walkers along the footpaths on both sides of the river, some seriously kitted out, others strolling with their families and dogs in the sunshine. Shouted greetings filled the air, a rowing boat exciting comment as we were virtually the only players afloat that afternoon.

After about a mile, past a small tree-clad island, we saw a concrete footbridge and assumed it had been built recently to replace a ferry but not so. It was indeed almost new, opening in 2006, having replaced a defective 1930s concrete bridge from the era of King Coal. It seemed somehow incongruous as we rowed amid such tranquil rural scenery that industry had once impinged on it, the old bridge echoing to the stout boots of miners on their way to and from Highley to extract coal from the mine in Alveley.

Coal deposits between the railway and the old village of Highley up on the ridge had been worked until 1939, Highley growing into a large mining village, many of the coal-hewing miners probably thinking about their evening rehearsing with the colliery brass band, just as in any Yorkshire mining village. A new shaft in Alveley, on the east side of the river, replaced the Highley one so the predecessor of the current footbridge was built to link the railway with the colliery via a rope-worked tramway to the sidings on the Highley bank. It replaced a ferryboat and according to Brian Waters *'miners crossed for the night shift would crowd eighteen at a time into the narrow boat'*. This pit also closed in the 1960s, its site now occupied by an industrial estate. The plant and railway sidings are no more, partially replaced by a new Severn Valley Railway station named Country Park Halt, and once again the area is wholly rural.

We rowed beneath Colliery Footbridge as it is now named, and rounding the next bend in the river, passed Highley Station which must have had a more industrial look than its current peaceful heritage-railway appearance. Highley Colliery was situated about 400 yards west of the river, behind the station and the popular Ship Inn. In its place is a golf course and a coal pit 'monument' set up by the people of Highley using a salvaged wheel from the cage winding gear that took the men underground, and now a peaceful Severn Valley Country Park picnic site. Gone now are Brian Roger's *field's lengths of barges … waiting at Highley, loading for coal, timber and stone*.

Here we changed over and I took the oars for the last miles to Upper Arley. We passed the mouth of the Borle Brook which meets the Severn under an elegant early-19th-century single-span cast-iron bridge manufactured in 1828 by the Coalbrookdale Company. The river wound south, both banks now in Worcestershire, and round the next bend Richard said the river ahead seemed largely blocked by a peninsula of mud and gravel running out from the right bank. As we neared, he found a route through by the left bank and we rushed over what was in effect a low weir, the boat scraping across rocks before we were into calmer waters for the row to Upper Arley around a left-hand bend.

Below Arley the river is lively with 'rapids' and gave us a fun bouncy ride, then we were nearly opposite Worrall's Grove. Out in midstream we drew level and I attempted to turn the boat and started heaving on the oars aiming slightly upstream thinking I could counter the strong current and cross to the bank but however fast I rowed we were pushed downstream instead. 'You'll exhaust yourself if you carry on at this rate and we're going nowhere. Row hard into the bank or at least as close to those willows as you can and I'll grab one.'

There was no way I could row upstream so I turned to shore and drove into willow branches which whipped at our heads and shoulders as Richard grabbed them to haul us out of the current. Much relieved, me somewhat shamefaced, we landed and hauled the boat ashore, after a twenty-mile row and no landings apart from at 'Firefighters Rapids' and certainly no lunch or drinks stop. The whole fiasco had been observed by a JCB digger driver working on bank clearance who stopped to lean on his steering wheel the more to enjoy the action, perhaps also amused that his efforts had turned the riverbank into loose knee-deep mud.

We struggled through and faced the daunting prospect of getting the boat through the narrow gate in the stone wall, up narrow steps and into Amanda's garden. Just at that moment a family walked past and the young dad peeled off to help us. Very kind, and between the three of us we got the boat onto the lawn above. Thanking our helper, we got the boat up the rest of the grass and into Worrall's Grove cart shed cum garage and, like Stanley and Livingstone, we shook hands and, unlike those two doughty explorers I suspect, grinned at each other. We knocked on the farmhouse door but sadly there were no rooms free.

Our voyage was over and our euphoria at having completed rowing the Severn from Wales to Upper Arley easily survived the 'housekeeping' task of getting my car back from the start at Crew Green. A further brief excursion across the Welsh border Richard endured affably enough, though pointing out he felt that the Welsh 'whinge' less than the Scots. As there were no rooms free at Brook House Farm in Crew Green we ended up spending the night at The Swan Inn at Knowlesands, a village we had rowed past earlier in the day.

Over supper we agreed that the Severn voyages had not remotely dimmed our enthusiasm for rowing or for the qualities of our boat, our eagerness to recreate the Hornblower escape down the river Loire remained absolutely undiminished. As the wine flowed, I suggested again to Richard that at a future date I would like to row more of the Severn actually within Wales. Perhaps we could walk from the source to wherever it became navigable to ensure full Hafren/Severn coverage. No idea how realistic that would be but I rather fear the general glee at completing the first phase of our project was going to my head. Richard seemed unenthusiastic and non-committal, I have to report, and suggested that if we rowed any more of the Severn it should be downstream and in England.

Back down to earth, he also reminded me that the river Loire project was our primary aim and we should shelve such wine-heightened nonsense. Hornblower and the Loire were briefly back in the room as well and an agreed desire to row again as soon as feasible. The last rites followed breakfast the next morning as we returned to Worrall's Farm for the last time to load the boat onto my car roof, and set off for our respective homes.

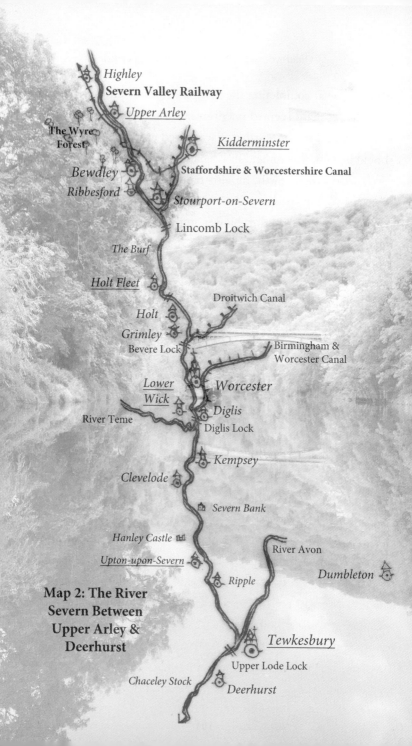

*Highley*
**Severn Valley Railway**
*Upper Arley*

**The Wyre Forest**

*Kidderminster*

*Bewdley*
*Ribbesford*

**Staffordshire & Worcestershire Canal**

*Stourport-on-Severn*

Lincomb Lock

*The Burf*

*Holt Fleet*

Droitwich Canal

*Holt*
*Grimley*
Bevere Lock

Birmingham & Worcester Canal

*Lower Wick*

*Worcester*

River Teme

*Diglis*
Diglis Lock

*Kempsey*

*Clevelode*

Severn Bank

Hanley Castle

Upton-upon-Severn

River Avon

*Dumbleton*

*Ripple*

**Map 2: The River Severn Between Upper Arley & Deerhurst**

*Tewkesbury*

Upper Lode Lock

*Chaceley Stock*
*Deerhurst*

# 12

# Back to the Severn: Bridgnorth and on to Bewdley

Within a week or so of having driven home from Upper Arley, we were planning following Hornblower down the river Loire, but for various reasons, again of no interest to the reader, it was back to the Severn to continue from where we had left off. I felt we should stay somewhere other than Worrall's Grove for the sake of variety and ended up booking a room at The Unicorn Inn in Hampton which we had rowed past during the earlier voyage.

Setting off from our respective homes, we arrived in mid-afternoon within ten minutes of each other and checked in to The Unicorn Inn, asking if we could leave our cars for a few days as we had no idea how far we would get downriver. No problem at all and no suggestion of a parking fee, so we repaired to the bar, Richard for a pint and me for a Peroni.

It being early evening, we decided to drive to Bridgnorth to look at the town we had perforce swept past on our earlier jaunt. We would have supper there as well and I was keen to look at Telford's church that dominates the riverside town. Arriving at Bridgnorth we parked at the Jacobethan-style Severn Valley Railway station. Built in 1862 and closed or 'Beechinged' in the 1960s, the Severn Valley Railway restored and reopened it in 1970. We walked to the riverbank in Low Town to have another look at the somewhat disappointing six-arched bridge and assess the river's water levels and flow.

We turned our attention uphill to High Town on its ridge where we would find the castle ruins, two churches and the old town hall. Linking it and the riverbank in Low Town is the remarkable Bridgnorth Cliff Railway opened in 1892, ascending steeply the 111 feet to High Town and unusually inland rather than at a seaside resort like Scarborough. Bridgnorth received the current rather odd streamlined cars in the 1950s, looking like transplanted jaunty motor coach bodies of that era. They are painted in blue and cream and proudly sign-written 'Bridgnorth Castle Hill Railway Co Ltd'. Tickets bought, the car moved off on an ascent stiff enough to justify its claim to be England's steepest, nowadays an admittedly much-diminished field.

From Castle Walk beside the cliff railway terminus the views across the river as the dusk settled were splendid and expansive with to the far left the wooded sandstone hump and river cliffs of High Rock whose looming shadow we had rowed beneath. At the end of Castle Walk we turned into St Mary Magdalene's churchyard, the church replacing the ruined castle's chapel. Here in the 1790s Telford worked in a strict and severe Classical style, using an attractive grey-to-buff sandstone quarried from Eardington, a couple of miles south of the town and more durable than other local red sandstones. In a bang-up-to-date, almost French style, Telford was careful to design the church so the pedimented and columned north entrance front with tall tower and copper-roofed cupola closed the vista along East Castle Street in some style.

Most impressive, while behind the church is the 'Leaning Tower of Bridgnorth': in fact, the remains of Henry II's castle keep built in the 1160s and a feature within Town Park which occupies the former castle bailey. The remains lean spectacularly as a result of incompetent demolition by Parliamentary gunpowder in 1646, in fact leaning more steeply than Pisa's famous tourist-infested campanile. Within the park is a substantial former drinking fountain of 1881, its columned granite plinth surmounted by a bronze statue of Sabrina, the spirit of the Severn, as usual shown proudly bare-breasted.

North through the town, past the frankly unattractive multicoloured-brick Italianate mid-1850s New Market Hall, the High Street opens out and is dominated by the Town Hall, a rebuild of 1652 after Civil War destruction with an arcaded stone ground floor and an upper storey in black and white timber-framing. To its east, in a grassy churchyard, sits St Leonard's, the town's other parish church. Its encircling lane surrounded by fine houses seemed to resemble a (very) small-scale cathedral close. Only its medieval tower survived the Civil War.

Back in the High Street at half past six our minds turned to supper. In Bridgnorth, according to a pamphlet we picked up at the cable railway, there are twenty-two pubs so we would be spoilt for choice. In West Castle Street we paused by one with a board outside describing it as a '*Husband Creche*' and asking '*Is he getting under your feet? Leave him here while you shop*'. This pub, festooned with colourful flowers in hanging baskets, troughs, window boxes and pots is The Old Castle, its 18th-century brickwork barely visible through a dense floral screen.

Numbered two in the pub trail leaflet, we entered and Richard ordered a pint of Wye Valley beer brewed on the Herefordshire banks of a rival river. After unbelievably vast supper portions, we waddled back to the car, me dreaming of more wine after I had finished driving. It was now virtually dark with the sun's afterglow feebly illuminating the fading blue dome of the sky. Back at The Unicorn Inn we had more drinks, the white wines of distinctly varying quality.

*****

Waking during the night on several occasions I could hear rain lashing the windows and roof. I willed it to ease off but when we got up it was raining more thoroughly. After we had partaken of an eventually delivered 'full English' breakfast accompanied by good coffee we could prolong our departure no longer, so suitably waterproofed we took our backpacks and our departure. I say 'waterproofed' but I had omitted to pack my overtrousers so was destined for a good soak in the trouser zone.

We drove towards the riverbank and by a parking area found a steep, muddy gully down which to slide and manhandle the boat into the river: it was no more than that and far from ideal. I wandered off a little upstream as Richard prepared the boat and looked at the remains of the cable ferry that ran between Hampton and Hampton Loade, its wide punt lying amid foliage and nettles. Out of action for some while it did not look old and is in fact a 2004 replica built by the Ironbridge Gorge Museum.

The car and trailer back at The Unicorn Inn's car park, our boat loaded and oared, we slid and scrambled the boat down the rain-slicked gully, climbed aboard and launched into the river once again. We were of course rowing a stretch of river we had rowed earlier in the year and I'm not sure Richard was over-enamoured of this but he said nothing as the rain dripped off our jackets, the world around us damp and grey.

Once past Worrall's Grove we were entering fresh rowing territory and had reached the parts of the river rather alarmingly described by Linsdall Richardson as rapids. He wrote that below Upper Arley the river flows through a gorge cut into the Coal Measures where the *sandstone beds, with interbedded shales cross the channel of the river and their outcrops have given rise to what some locals call 'rapids', and others 'fords'*. He considered that *probably the former designation is the more suitable*. Just downstream from Worrall's Grove the 'rapids' cross a shallow ridge, the water deepest by the opposite bank. It remained lively and fast flowing, shallows marked here and there by disturbed water and wavelets. The rain was somewhat wind-driven so which were shallows and which wind-raised wavelets was unclear but I felt there was little risk of grounding, at least until more convincing 'rapids' at Folly Point where the river turns sharply south.

Rounding a bend, one of the finest bridges on the river came into view through the murk and my rain-spattered glasses. This is the Victoria Bridge which carries the preserved Severn Valley Railway across the river and is best seen from a boat so you can admire the elegant cast-iron structure, a single-span of four parallel arches, each formed of nine sections bolted together, and a forest of smaller ironwork struts and braces. Dating from 1859-1862 it was designed by Sir John Fowler for the Severn Valley Railway Company, a line that ran from near Droitwich to Shrewsbury. Its detail and structural grace take it fully into the realm of architecture. We had rowed beneath Fowler's somewhat compromised and slightly later twin, the Albert Edward Bridge upstream of Ironbridge.

Both Fowler's Severn bridges carry cast inscriptions, that on the Victoria Bridge is at the crown of the arch and prominent for all to see: '*Victoria Bridge*,'*1861*' and below in smaller letters '*John Fowler, Engineer.*' More mundane information is in less prominent secondary locations: to the left '*Messrs. Brassey & Co., Contractor*' and on the right '*Cast and Erected by the Coalbrookdale Company*'. For a number of years along with Albert Edward Bridge its main span of 200 feet was the longest cast-iron single span in the world, and Fowler went on to design, with Benjamin Baker, one of the most famous bridges in the world: the extraordinary Forth Railway Bridge in Scotland (in 2014 I stood at the apex of its northern cantilever, some 350 feet above the Firth of Forth). The protean Fowler also designed complete railways from terminus to terminus, important stations and the world's first underground railway, the Metropolitan, which opened in 1863.

Richard took photos, brushed the rain off his glasses and I rowed on for a while. Then we let the boat follow the current although every so often a few firm strokes were needed to keep us away from the bank. Nothing to do with my incompetence, I should add, for it happened as much when Richard was steersman.

Looking back, this stretch of a mere three and a half miles could be described as the 'river of bridges', as well as good fun sweeping across shallows and finding deeper water as we wound towards Bewdley. Beyond Victoria Bridge, tree-clad river cliffs on the right bank rose some 300 feet into Seckley Wood. To our left riverside meadows were between us and the railway line, beyond which the land rose steeply. Since 1966, Trimpley Reservoir has occupied this lower ground and is used to clean and store water extracted from the river to feed into the Elan Valley Aqueduct which crosses the river a little downstream of Folly Point, running from that flooded Welsh valley to Birmingham. The city's water demands had increased greatly since the Elan valley was first dammed: hence the need for adding up to 30 million gallons from the Severn when required.

We could see nothing of Trimpley Reservoir, however, from the river as I steered us past and approached a narrow tree-clad island in midstream. About 150 yards ahead was white-crested rough water and a sharp bend at the ominously named Folly Point. We 'rode the rapids' and it was fun but hardly at a hair-raising-white-water-rafting level of excitement or indeed 'folly'.

Immediately round Folly Point the river headed south towards our second bridge of the day. This 1904 aqueduct carries the Elan Valley water across the River Severn towards Birmingham in huge pipes. As might be expected the great and dynamic leader of that city's Council, Joseph Chamberlain, was at the forefront of the scheme but you can guess what the inhabitants of these delightful and remote valleys of the Elan and the Claerwen in the Cambrian Mountains thought of all this. Compulsory purchase saw them off but needless to say only landowners were compensated, not the tenant farmers and their labourers for whom these valleys had been home and livelihood for generations.

The bridge itself is in a way not dissimilar to Victoria Bridge as the central span crosses the river in a single arch but in steel, rather than cast iron. As we rowed beneath we looked upwards into a mass of metalwork, this time of lattice form and the whole thing lighter and airier than Victoria Bridge. Richard, ever alert to technical matters, explained this relative delicacy as being due to the difference between a dynamic load (a moving train) and a passive load (water flowing evenly through a pipe).

The river was now running roughly south and the heavy rain was vigorously wind-assisted into my face. I looked into what I believe nautical types call the bilges and there was a fair bit of water slopping about and more to the point our packs were sitting in it. The river continued quite zippy and the hills and ridges retreated somewhat from the banks but a dense growth of willows, alders and other trees effectively screened views from the river for much of the time. Old photographs tend to show much clearer banks but nowadays bankside trees often have their boughs overhanging or in the water accumulating river-driven flotsam, branches and other detritus, but they are good places for ducks, coots and moorhens to shelter out of the current and for kingfishers and other birds to perch and peruse the water for passing fish and food.

It was this stretch of the Severn that so incensed Brian Waters in *Severn Stream* of 1949: '*Before one comes to Bewdley the riparian scenery is marred by warrens of wooden bungalows. Tawdry in their lack of uniformity, these dwellings, like cheap and gaudy clothes, first look blatant and then almost shabby. They have not the excuse or dignity of being homes, they are summer houses, and some, indeed, are derelict motor-buses; but they remain fixed on their location at all times of the year. They are the greatest misfortune that has yet befallen the river Severn.*' Waters carries on in this vein for a while but eventually, possibly realising some of the folk derided might one day read his books, admits that no-one can blame '*the townsman for desiring to return to the countryside that his ancestors left in the course of the last two hundred years.*' Doubtless feeling better for all this Waters headed right to Dowles stream, to digress on a more agreeable topic than humanity: the wood ants of the Wyre Forest.

Above Bewdley the river is still in its natural and unimproved state, hence the 'rapids', so we made the most of a last stretch of broken water and obstructions, while also noting the replacements for Brian Waters' post-war shacks along the left bank. After a mile two tall stone towers set in the river emerged slowly from the rain-swept gloom, like pylons guarding entry to a netherworld. They seemed most mysterious until we realised they were the strikingly tall 1860s brick-and-stone-dressed piers of Dowles railway bridge minus its track deck. I suppose our rain-misted glasses contributed to what should not have been remotely mysterious. Rising an impressive eighty-five feet from the river, they have a monumental presence as splendidly enigmatic memorials to a vanished railway.

We headed towards Bewdley with large caravan parks on either side. What would the fastidious antennae of Brian Waters have made of them? Reaching the historic part of Bewdley and its quayside north of a fine river bridge, Richard spotted stone steps, the lower slick with green weed and slime, and jumping onto the steps, painter-rope in hand, we arrived in Bewdley.

# 13

# Bewdley, Ribbesford and on to Stourport

Climbing the steps, everything left in the boat as usual, we reached the quayside, Severn Side North. A sign on a house, Quay Cottage, informed us that it was once called 'Coles Quay', an archaic spelling of coal, for this wharf was where it had been landed when Bewdley had been a thriving river port.

Now on dry land, having rowed about nine miles and despite the weather it had been good fun. The 'dry' land however was pretty wet in truth and a coffee seemed a warming idea.

Bewdley's name is a corruption of the French *beau lieu* or beautiful place. Brian Waters wrote that the town's origins '*were anything but respectable*', claiming it was a no man's land, not in any particular county, and a bed of thieves, pirates and outlaws. A ferry was replaced in the 1440s by a bridge, but it and the town were burned down in 1459 by Lancastrian forces. Perhaps that was why in 1471 the town sent its archers to support the Yorkist king Edward IV at Tewkesbury: smouldering resentment. A grateful Edward IV granted '*these illiterates their first charter*' in 1472 which included '*the privilege of travelling toll-free on the Severn*' in perpetuity, a right fully exploited over succeeding centuries.

The current river bridge is the most beautiful and elegant stone one along the whole of the Severn. A large claim I know but from the river we had seen its graceful, beautifully modulated rusticated arches and the elegant balustrades above the equally graceful curved road deck. Amazingly the medieval bridge survived all the floods and storms the Severn could throw at it until it finally collapsed in the catastrophic floods of 1795. There is an 18th-century print of the old bridge, clearly in decay, with buildings along it, one the town prison. Fortunately, the town was able to turn to neighbouring Shropshire's Surveyor of Public Works, no less than Thomas Telford. Paradoxically, the summer of 1798 when it was constructed was very dry and this helped a speedy rebuild, rising according to a contemporary observer as *'if by enchantment'*.

With his eye for townscape Telford rebuilt the bridge a little further north so you could cross it and look uphill along Load Street, the former market place, which rises bustling and picturesque towards the church. The old bridge abutments survived some yards further south but were buried beneath a later bandstand, now gone, its location commemorated by a circular area of paving.

We turned into Load Street with its 'vista-closers', to use an ugly but serviceable word. The first is a six-window, wide Georgian building that narrows the road from about seventy to forty feet and then beyond that and a bit further uphill the flat east end of St Anne's Church with a striking Venetian window, also Georgian and surrounded by roads, the east one the remarkably heavily trafficked B4190. The late 17th-century tower beyond is the climax and a survivor from the earlier church

Entering the church, partly to look at its interior but also to get out of the rain for a few minutes, it is plastered and white-painted, the austere Georgian nave with massive Roman Doric columns.

The earlier church was timber-framed and merely a chapel of ease to Ribbesford. By the 1740s it did not fit with the now prosperous town's Georgian pretensions and this much grander church was completed in 1748. Much of this we learned from an enthusiastic and well-informed volunteer who spotting that we were interested gave us a tour. He also persuaded us to have tea and a slice of cake in the informal café within the church.

*****

Back in the boat shortly after midday, a number of passers-by peered over the quayside railings to watch and Richard waved as I rowed off. Almost immediately, we passed beneath Telford's bridge and then alongside the grander Georgian fronts of Severn Side South: a contrast to the cottage-scale houses to the north, presumably merchants rather than wharfingers and boatmen. Across the river were the splendid 17th-century timber-framed and brick houses of Beales Corner in Wribbenhall.

After a bit of lively water and beyond the 1980s bypass bridge, the river was forced west by Blackstone Rock, a striking bare crag emerging from tree-clad surroundings, feet firmly in the river. This is an outcrop according to Linsdall Richardson of Bunter sandstone crossing the riverbed. I couldn't help thinking of Billy Bunter, Greyfriars School's Fat Owl of the Remove, rather than its translation from the German *Buntsandstein* meaning colourful sandstone: its red hues are certainly that. The rocky riverbed caused no problem to our boat but in olden days three feet of water was needed beneath the keel to avoid a laden barge or 'trow' running aground. When the river was low the boats queued awaiting a flush of water, a 'fresh', to carry them to Stourport. Sometimes, the boats would be partially unloaded and waggons would take cargo to Ribbesford and deeper water for reloading to continue onwards to Stourport.

Blackstone Rock has old caves hollowed out that were once inhabited, so it is no surprise that it attracted tales of hermits. One was 18th century, presumably a local eccentric, and there are tales of boatmen throwing him coins and gifts to seek his prayers for a safe voyage. Another story is more fanciful, involving a much older medieval knight marrying a younger woman who fell in love with one of his pages. On Bewdley Bridge, so the story goes, he ran his disguised wife through with his sword instead of the page. Appalled, he lived in the cave as a hermit and later the page, not recognising him as the cuckolded knight, sought absolution for his adultery. They fought and plunged off the summit of Blackstone Rock into the river below never to be seen again.

We were soon looking for a place to land on the opposite bank, now about a mile south of Bewdley, so we could visit Ribbesford Church which I knew had an unusual 15th-century timber nave arcade. Richard spotted a fishing platform and I rowed vigorously to it, Richard leaping ashore, painter in hand. Remarkably and completely fortuitously, when we scrambled up the bank through the scrub and nettles we emerged at the road opposite the lime-avenued drive to the church and Ribbesford House. We squelched along this, or at least I did in my mud-filled neoprene boat shoes, their thin soles jarringly transmitting every speck of gravel.

The name Ribbesford indicates that there was a ford here but Linsdall Richardson notes that *'the name … suggests the proximity of a ford, but the writer has not succeeded in locating it or in obtaining any information about it'.* Reaching the church, just past various red sandstone-built Ribbesford Estate farm buildings now converted to houses, we entered its churchyard, surprisingly large for what is now a hamlet. However, as the 'mother' church of Bewdley, many burials were of townsfolk and inside are many wall tablets to Bewdley's carriage folk. We entered via the white-painted timber north porch proudly dated 1633. It shelters a good Norman doorway, the tympanum between the arch and the lintel carrying a rather good if crudely carved hunting scene showing a Sagittarius (often understood to represent Christ in medieval sculpture) aiming his bow at a monstrous beast and accompanied by his dog.

The church had been half-demolished by a lightning strike during a fierce storm in 1877 and the great art critic John Ruskin loftily opined that it should be left as a '*dear old ruin grow[ing] grey by Severn's side in peace*'. No doubt poetically put, but the parish was having none of that and spent over £4000 restoring the building, including rebuilding the chancel and adding a fine stained-glass window in memory of Hannah Macdonald, designed by Burne-Jones. He had married one of Hannah's daughters, Georgiana, so there's the connection. A good medieval stained-glass window includes a 15th-century St George nonchalantly thrusting his lance into the dragon's throat. There are Norman carved fragments and much of the north aisle wall is Norman, the rest is mostly 15th century, including the timber nave arcade with its octagonal piers. The standout features for us, though, were small and easily overlooked: timber tracery panels, also from the 15th century and part of the former chancel screen incorporated into a Victorian pulpit. Salvaged from the 1877 wreckage, the medieval carpenter had undoubtedly had a field day inhabiting his tracery with vigorous vignettes. These include a sow eating a giant acorn while five piglets suckle, a pig playing the bagpipes, various faces with their tongues sticking out, a couple of whom are Green Men, and a fox preaching in a friar's clothes to an audience of foolish birds, a medieval insult from the regular clergy who hated friars.

Leaving the church, we could see little of Ribbesford Hall requisitioned like so many country houses during World War II and used to train Free French officer cadets. Not open to the public, we squelched back to the boat and cast off, me rowing and aiming to get to Stourport-on-Severn for lunch.

We rowed steadily downstream, initially with Ribbesford Woods, its oak and Corsican pine-clad hills climbing steeply away from the right bank of the river. In contrast the left bank was much flatter and less rugged so almost inevitably partly occupied by mobile homes and holiday caravan parks, some with pontoons, one per plot and almost all with a river cruiser neatly tied up. Beyond these the river curved and then straightened so we could peer through the rain and gloom towards Stourport's river bridge. We were now entering Canal & River Trust permit waters.

With jaunty blue and tan paintwork, the bridge was a welcome splash of colour in the murk. Mind you, there was no bridge (and no Stourport-on-Severn either for that matter) until the late 18th century. The main road from Wales to London crossed the river at a ford by Redstone nearly a mile south of the bridge near another of the striking red sandstone outcrops towering over a rocky, shallow riverbed. Richardson writes that it *'was an important crossing especially in the 14th century. When the river was sufficiently low, wagons used the ford: when it was high, traffic had to be adjusted to the capacity of the ferry.'* Apparently, it was serviced by hermits, a type of person apparently not in short supply along this river.

Redstone Ford briefly blinked in the glare of history when the body of Prince Arthur, a teenager and the first husband of Catherine of Aragon, was carried across it to Worcester for burial. He had died at Ludlow Castle in early April 1502 apparently of *'a malign vapour'*. Had he lived beyond fifteen years of age and had Henry VIII, his younger brother, not married the grieving widow, one wonders whether the Reformation would have reached England: one of English history's great 'what ifs'.

*****

Stourport was built at the mouth of the Stour, a river reaching the Severn, according to Brian Waters through the wilderness of Hartlebury Common, *'a sandy, barren unprofitable heath, with only a few lonely scattered cottages, exhibiting a picture of desolation and poverty'*. That was soon to change with the arrival of the Staffordshire and Worcestershire Canal built by the celebrated engineer James Brindley. He had intended to reach the river at Bewdley, but the town was hostile, so the canal route continued along the valley to the tiny hamlet of Stourmouth. The canal basins were dug by 1771 and had large entrances so the Severn trows could enter and exchange cargo with canal narrowboats.

Later in the year Richard gave me a framed print of the route of the proposed canal, which had been published in the splendidly named *The London Magazine or Gentleman's Monthly Intelligencer* in 1753. This had belonged to his father, Tom Robinson, who was the author of the definitive study, *The Longcase Clock*, about what you or I would call 'grandfather clocks'. The print is entitled '*A MAP of the New Intended CANAL to join the Rivers Severn and Trent*'; there is no trace of Stourport at that date. Nor was the canal named: it was years before its enabling Act of Parliament.

A new river bridge was built upstream of the canal mouth at the expense of the canal company and had a long, arched causeway leading to the three arches actually crossing the river. Opening in 1775, Richardson says that twenty years later during floods two arches over the river collapsed to be replaced by '*a single iron arch with a 150-foot span and a 50-foot clearance above the surface of the water.*' In old prints it appeared to have been similar to the famous Iron Bridge, but in 1868 another Scottish engineer, Edward Wilson, replaced it with the present elegant metal bridge.

The town grew rapidly and as Brian Waters noted the basin is '*still the most picturesque feature of the Severnside town that grew around its rim.*' Tactfully, put and further mistreatment of the town during the 20th century was all too apparent both from our vantage point on the river and within the basin we rowed into, hoping to tie up. The 1805-built Engine (or Crown) Basin's surroundings are now a car park and a permanent funfair, the Riverside Amusement Park and Arcade, its sign proudly if dispiritingly declaring it open all the year round. It looked a bit risky so we rowed back onto the river passing two other canal basins accessible only via locks. We tied up at the public pontoon just beyond and, more to the point, in a less public location.

Climbing the steps from the pontoon we headed towards the town, passing The Angel pub. Beyond it we reached a long and rather grand three-storey Georgian building, framed by pines and beech trees. The former Tontine Inn had over a hundred beds when built with high hopes in 1771 and its now grassy terraces were once formal gardens. The hotel trade died and the pub survived a 1977 demolition attempt by the brewery: a crass but typical Stourport approach to its built heritage. Some years ago, walking the Staffordshire and Worcestershire Canal, I sat in warm sunshine at outside tables, The Tontine packed; so still a pub in 1993. Locals told us it had closed in about 2000 and was now apartments.

Retracing our steps to The Angel Inn, a neat three-storey Georgian red-brick building, we encountered some elderly smokers in a smoking shelter who between puffs on their cigarettes offered humorous comments on us emerging from the river in pouring rain. Alas, we were too late for food so lunch was a pint and a packet of crisps but to be truthful we weren't hungry. The place was convivial and we talked with the locals, the landlady and her daughter but we felt, rather like Stourport itself, the pub had seen better days.

# 14

# Rowing to Holt Fleet in the Rain

Dried off (a bit) and our drinks finished we reboarded the boat, the rain easing for a while and Richard taking over the oars. There would be no further 'rapids' for we were now fully on the Severn Navigation. Why the river needed a 'navigation' is succinctly put by Richardson who observed that in '*its natural condition the Severn was a difficult river to navigate*'. Along the stretch above Worcester which he termed the Upper Reach it was '*crossed by numerous outcrops of hard beds ('rock-bars') interstratified with softer, and was locally encumbered by gravel-shoals. At low water the river in this upper reach was little better than a series of deepish pools separated every mile or so by rock-bars over which the water seldom exceeded eighteen inches*'. In most years there were only two months in which barges could get upstream or down.

Brindley found the river presented serious problems for his canal barges. These included primitive weirs of wooden stakes and fast by-lets formed beside small artificial islets through which the trows and boats had to 'flash', an often hazardous process. On the Thames upstream of Oxford, Horatio Hornblower had to contend with 'staunches', rough wooden dams with a gap for the boats, in low water guarded by lock paddles at one end: flash locks. In winter the river was higher and faster and the lock paddles were left open and, as on the Severn, all boats had to hurtle through.

On the Severn several efforts to improve the river foundered through local opposition to any perceived threat to *'free' navigation, fear of flooding, harm to fishing, particularly the eels and because the watermen were against it'*. So even early and relatively minor improvements in the 1780s were reversed when watermen took their complaints to Worcester Assizes. Nothing much happened between the 1830s when a Severn Navigation Company was formed and the 1850s, bill after bill failing in Parliament. For readers who would like to follow these twists and turns Richardson provides the detail. Eventually, the river trade, of course, benefitted greatly with the shoals and rock bars excavated away and weirs bypassed by vast locks that raised the water level between Gloucester and Stourport so vessels could use the river without let or hindrance.

Rounding the first bend a caravan park seemed to stretch for half a mile, then another on the left bank, before we reached the sandstone of Redstone Rock, its strata dipping gently towards the river, the cliff edge above lined with pine trees. Boats of a bewildering variety were moored along the left bank as we passed the entry to Stourport Marina in which we glimpsed launches and cruisers neatly lined up alongside their pontoons.

Beyond was a line of red warning buoys marking Lincomb Weir. Signs directed us to their left for the run-in to Lincomb Lock which had opened in 1844. We tied up and debated what to do. Should we lift the boat out and portage it below the lock? There was a very large river-cruise boat, the MV *Edward Elgar*, already in the lock. We watched as the lock gates opened and she edged out of the lock, grinding along the side walls and, eventually liberated, surged forth towards Stourport.

The lock-keeper spotted us and beckoned us to row into the now-open lock. Feeling mighty insignificant and complete frauds Richard rowed us in and the lock-keeper told us to put our painter loosely around one of the stout wire ropes that were set in vertical recesses in the stonework. Shutting the upper lock gates behind us he opened the lower gates' sluices. As we slowly descended, he told us that the *Edward Elgar* had been built for cruising the Severn but the boatbuilders had assumed all the locks between Gloucester and Stourport were identical in width. Nobody had noticed that Lincomb Lock was some six inches narrower than the one measured and as a result the *Edward Elgar* has to batter its way in and out of his lock. He warned us of the cills at each end, presumably being ironic as our boat took up only a bare ten per cent of a one-hundred-foot lock. I shouted our permit number, greeted with a dismissive wave, and we were on our way again to rejoin the main river. Our first lock had been navigated and thankfully we were not beneath the notice of lock-keepers.

We were by now soaking and my non-waterproof trousers were sopping as rainwater coursed from my jacket to augment the water slopping around the bilges. I had noted on the map two signs for pubs further downstream, the first at the curiously named The Burf and the second nearer Holt Fleet. I said I would rather press on a bit further to Holt as there was plenty of gloomy daylight left, while any lurking hunger pangs had long passed. The sign at The Hampstall Inn at The Burf said boats were welcome but did not offer bed and breakfast. Old photographs often showed the long-defunct Hampstall Ferry, a near-flat-bottomed punt, an oarsman in the stern. Later back home I looked up what 'The Burf' might mean and apparently it is a corruption of the name of a nearby wood 'le Barrave' or 'Bearffe', not that that advanced me very far.

We rowed on, the rain again setting in hard, to our right heavily wooded sandstone hills gradually closed with the river to form distinctive but low red cliffs before receding again. This was Shrawley Wood and round the next reach a long line of motor launches and cruisers were moored along the left bank, presumably related to the mobile home park behind. To the right loomed a large, cream-rendered building of two sprawling storeys. This was The Lenchford Inn and the site of yet another small punt ferry, also long-defunct. Richardson writing in 1964 stated that '*the ferry ... is in use, but not for the public: it is worked by the landlord of the Lenchford Hotel for the convenience of his customers.*'

The Lenchford Inn had a 19th-century hip-roofed three-bay element at the right, complete with sash windows, but the rest was a flat-roofed motel-style building. But it had a mooring pontoon and the signs indicated that it had accommodation. This was a relief as we were not sure whether the Holt Lock half a mile downstream would still be open with a lock-keeper in attendance. We tied up, picked our soaking backpacks from amid the water slopping in the bows, left the oars shipped, and squelched through the rain to the reception desk where we dripped onto the carpet and asked if the inn had any rooms free. In whatever circumstances you enter a B & B, pub or hotel, there is a ledger to consult, the receptionist assuming a worried frown and saying that he or she is not sure but they will have a look as some kind of special favour. Invariably, the following morning very few breakfast tables are ever occupied.

After what seemed an age she emerged, wearing an expression of triumph and relief, as though solving Fermat's Last Theorem, and announced that they did indeed have a twin room free. We asked about supper and a table was booked, remarkably one having been found to be free for 7.30pm. The puddle on the reception carpet steadily increased during this lengthy performance before she finally handed over the room key and we trekked off to the flat-roofed block fronting the river, our room's French doors opening on to a dripping balcony unlikely to be of use on this particular visit.

Relieved to have found a bed for the night and stripping off our saturated clothes, we examined our packs for water penetration. While we had waterproof 'stuff bags' these were too full to guarantee no seepage. Sure enough the upper levels of clothes were decidedly wet. By the time we had finished laying clothes out to dry the room resembled a laundry and the windows were steamed up. Warmed up by showers, we found just sufficient dry clothes and went down to a restaurant with remarkably few of its tables occupied.

We mused on where the other guests were eating, the mobile home site immediately south of the inn a potential dining 'catchment area'. The room had tables along the outer edges and a raised, white-painted balustraded central area, accessed via steps edged in health-and-safety-era black-and-yellow-banded tape. Timbers had been applied to the walls in a half-hearted way to simulate 'Olde Worlde' timber-framing, odd in a decidedly post-1660 building. We ordered drinks and dinner and looked back at our day and eighteen miles of rowing: two major towns, Bewdley decidedly more attractive than Stourport-on-Severn, and a fine village church at Ribbesford. While the weather had been poor, there was something oddly satisfying about achieving what you hoped for despite unceasing rain. Would the rain fill the boat and sink the unsinkable? I don't think we thought this likely but it seemed vaguely amusing at the time.

\*\*\*\*\*

Opening the curtains in the morning we saw that although the sky was pretty grey at least no rain was actually falling: so good news. Richard nipped out to check the boat while I navigated the labyrinthine corridors and arbitrary staircases of the inn's modern blocks to reach last night's restaurant, now doubling as the breakfast room. Returning, Richard confirmed that the boat was still afloat but with more water shipped. We agreed emptying it out would be a sound idea on two counts: the boat would glide through the water more easily and our packs would enjoy a break from near-floating in the bows. During a good breakfast we looked at the OS map and into our trusty Pevsner's hefty *Worcestershire* volume to see what interest lay along the river between the inn and Worcester where we would probably stay the night. It seemed that Holt village and Grimley fitted the bill, the latter probably for lunch.

Back at the boat, the three oars resembled the Isle of Man's three-legged badge and not nearly as neat as we had left them. Apart from the mud-rich water half-filling it, all was well. It proved easy to lift the boat onto the landing-stage pontoon and pour the river back where it belonged. I untied the painter and pushed us off from the pontoon while Richard took the oars, in fact he rowed until we left Bevere Lock after lunch. Before any reader thinks me idle, Richard positively wished to row and who am I to stand in a determined man's way?

Beyond the mobile homes the river started to turn and the right bank rose steeply for about eighty heavily wooded feet. A direction sign guided us to Holt Lock, avoiding the weir stretching across the river to the right of an 'island' between it and the lock. The 'island' was created in 1844 by cutting the lock and its approaches through a meander, the weir built across the river's more circuitous course.

A large motor launch coming upstream was in the lock and, when it had passed us, we rowed in and I looped the painter through the vertical cable in the middle of the lock's towering side wall just as we had done in Lincomb Lock: we were getting dab hands at looking as though we knew what we were doing. We had another shouted conversation with the lock-keeper and gave him our licence number although he didn't seem particularly interested. Eventually he decided he'd better write it down and with a wave disappeared back to his control cabin. The river now about six feet lower, Richard rowed out towards Holt Fleet Bridge.

Heaven knows what Thomas Telford would now make of his bridge. Waters informed us that '*Holt ford and ferry were replaced by Holt Bridge, a fine iron structure of single span, designed by Telford, which was opened in 1828 and widened in 1928*'. It was a typically elegant Telford iron-arched bridge designed late in his very long career but had to be 'reinforced' in its centenary year and cocooned in concrete with a widened roadway. I dare say the engineer Hammond was responding to structural problems in its 150-foot iron span but you have to peer carefully to discern the original core amid the battleship-grey paint. The mellow red sandstone of the unaltered abutments and approach causeways contrast markedly.

Immediately through the bridge the extraordinary Holt Fleet Inn reared above the right bank. Spotting a landing stage, no doubt for the inn's passing boating trade, if any, I steered to it and we tied up a mere mile downstream from the Lenchford Inn. At half past nine The Holt Fleet Inn was not open. It had all the hallmarks of 'roadhouse' and Richard said it looked like an oversized liquorice allsort and I could see what he meant.

Built in 1937 it had replaced a more modest, stuccoed 18th-century inn which in the age of the Victorian and Edwardian Midlands day trippers added tea rooms of prodigious length. A popular destination for cheap rail and steamer tickets from Wolverhampton and the Black

Country, people boarded boats at Stourport, the ticket including alcohol-assisted or Total Abstinence lunches or teas at the Holt Fleet Hotel. A victim of its own success, the charming lower-key buildings were demolished to make way for the current grander ones. It now combines oodles of black and white timber-framing to the upper floor and gables with stone bands amid the brickwork of the ground floor and the striking chimney stacks. I suggested to Richard that the whole ensemble looked like both streaky bacon and liquorice allsorts. We could see it was 'of its time' and showed how the Arts and Crafts style had got somewhat overheated by the 1930s. Landed, we knocked at the hotel's front door to ask if we could leave the boat while we walked south to visit Holt church. Eventually, a side door opened as a delivery van arrived, a man in kitchen overalls emerging. Presumably, the van's arrival was expected but it gave us a chance to ask our question. No problem, and he returned to his real interest: unloading the van.

A public footpath left the pub grounds through a gap in a tall conifer hedge to climb through woodland via an escarpment (a modest 'cliff' about seventy-five feet high). After all the rain the previous day the going was wet and muddy, my neoprene rowing shoes slithering mightily until we reached firmer ground on the plateau. We joined a track made difficult by prodigious puddle-lakes that spanned from side to side and well into the fields. Reaching Holt's historic core, it felt remote from the river. The village 'centre', such as it is, mainly consists of parish church, manor house, Holt Castle, and a substantial 19th-century red-brick model farmyard whose buildings have been converted to houses, the complex unsurprisingly named Holt Castle Barns.

I am always a sucker for a robust round-arched Norman parish church and Holt's churchyard is entered through a Norman-arched stone lychgate: a bad sign, though, as such things don't exist from

the Norman era. Annoyingly, we had left Pevsner in the boat which meant that we had to work out the church from our own observations but I remembered that the Norman church was 'obscured' by vigorous Neo-Norman work of the 1850s. For us, 19th-century Norman revival architecture seems on the whole pretty unsuccessful, a style that had a brief burst of popularity until swamped quite rightly in my view by the full-blooded Gothic Revival style. We had to disentangle the impact of the 1850s Neo-Norman 'restoration' and 'augmentation' from the original mid-12th-century building: always good fun. The then Rector's wife, Mary Sale, a self-taught sculptress, had in the 1850s carved the Neo-Norman stone pulpit, the lectern (now replaced) and some of the arches: clearly a talented lady. However, the *Building News* at the time delivered a witheringly patronising and much-quoted put-down: '*we refuse to criticise them as they are the work of a lady and it is pleasing to find [them] taking an interest in these matters.*'

The Rev and Mrs Sale were also responsible for the mosaic above the chancel arch, visiting Ravenna to view the 5th-century mosaics in the Mausoleum of Galla Placidia and even bringing back an Italian mosaicist to undertake a copy in Holt. Not surprisingly, the

parishioners felt this a trifle too Catholic for their tastes. The Sales' gravestones can be seen in the churchyard, albeit relocated with all the other ones to line the churchyard walls. I always think this removal of gravestones, while convenient, a great loss to a churchyard's numinous character.

There is also some good late-medieval stained glass within and the genuine 12th-century parts are well worthy of Pevsner's view that this is one of the most impressive Norman parish churches in Worcestershire. It also features in Simon Jenkins' *England's Thousand Best Churches* so we were not breaking new ground in our admiration. The whole church, whether Norman, later medieval or Victorian,

melds together as it uses the same local pinkish-red sandstone, now mellowed delightfully. While the lychgate is an 1850s confection in the same sandstone it does re-use a complete Norman arch.

Leaving through the lychgate we looked east across the lane towards Holt Castle, also in the same mellow pinkish-red sandstone, its drive framed by two fine and spreading cedars of Lebanon. The frontage is dominated by a crenellated four-square, four-storey tower, the oldest part of the building, seen to good effect across freshly mown and striped lawns. The range beyond is also battlemented, an 18th-century embellishment but no less attractive. The tower was built for John Beauchamp who was knighted by Richard II in 1385 and ennobled as Baron of Kidderminster in 1387. Falling out of favour, he was beheaded in 1388 for high treason by the Merciless Parliament. We assumed the fortified house would date to between his meteoric rise and his equally meteoric fall.

To the right, the wall to the kitchen garden has much interesting evidence of the earlier medieval stone building for its first length before changing to 18th-century brick. There appeared to be a stretch of battlemented walkway and then a gateway. We wondered whether this related to the 14th-century castle or the 15th-century rebuild. Did it have a fortified courtyard or bailey between the tower and the lane? Richard always poses awkward architectural questions to which I normally have some kind of answer, often plucked from thin air.

We headed north along the farm track, retracing our steps and, with a repeated slither in the mud for me, back downhill to the river.

# 15

# With Swans and Sculls
# to Worcester

Back at The Holt Fleet Inn, it was still firmly shut so we resumed our leisurely way downriver, mainly using the steering oar to let the current move us, interspersed by short bursts of rowing. The escarpment on which Holt stood receded from near the river and we came abreast of what had earlier looked on the map a promising, if non-footpath, access to Holt, but there was nowhere to land, so The Holt Fleet Inn landing stage had been the only practicable way of getting out of the river.

Rounding the first bend a row of (mostly) stylish Scandinavian-style timber-clad houses lined the river, each having its own mooring and a terrace overlooking the water. Past these we started looking for a landing place in order to visit Grimley. Although the bank became open and lower on the right and cattle grazed the pasture (and presumably drank from the river) there seemed nowhere to land easily. Eventually, I spotted a portable metal field fence that extended its feet into the river's margins.

I steered towards it so Richard could grab the fence and tie up. Although we had rowed a mere three miles since leaving The Holt Fleet Inn it was very much lunchtime. Looking at the map we were about a quarter of a mile south-east of the village. The 'beach' was churned, deep mud, no doubt cattle-trampled and soggy from the recent rains but we could shuffle along the fence and, unmuddied, reach the damp pasture beyond.

The Severn Way follows this bank, but after a few yards we left it and bore half-left gently uphill towards the village. The public footpath was a bit indistinct and we ended up on the wrong side of a tree-girt pond. The farmer who was doing something agricultural in the field did not seem to mind and waved us towards him and pointed us through a gate back onto the footpath that led us into Grimley. Turning right we headed past the brick barns of Church Farm, now converted to houses, and then the village school, partly built in 1856 but with modern additions. Its humbler 1834 predecessor had been by the churchyard gate in a red-brick cottage.

Red sandstone piers flanked the iron gates into the churchyard, the path beyond an avenue of tall conifers. Awaiting us was another piece of Neo-Norman in the form of a porch with a round-headed archway and at its left side a staircase leading from the porch to the nave gallery with an arcade whose columns diminished in height as the stairs rose. This seemed a faithful copy of the Norman stairway at Canterbury Cathedral priory. Inside the staircase steps were worn by a century and a half's countless feet. The 1845 architect was from Worcester, Harvey Eginton, one of whose pupils was William Butterfield who went on to greater things.

The porch protects a more modest Norman 12th-century south doorway into the church where the chief glory is a fine 15th-century stained-glass Annunciation: our second of the day. The chancel was rebuilt by Ewan Christian in the 1860s, known among architectural historians as a 'rogue' architect but here keeping himself in check.

Having attended to our spiritual needs, we headed to the Wagon Wheel, a thatched pub just past the church, to deal with our now quite sharp hunger. Here a genial Indian host in a formal dinner suit greeted us and showed us to a table. The pub was full of regulars, all greeted as old friends: their age profile close to ours, mostly around seventy. None the worse for that of course, although one elderly regular arrived with an oxygen cylinder carried by his son, a mere fifty-year-old stripling. We could see why there was repeat business for the portions were vast and the menu traditional. We had given up attempts to empty our plates when the waiter, a dapper chap in a double-breasted suit and pencil thin (obviously he did not eat here) and looking a bit like an actor in a 1950s British film, collected them. We eventually left the pub, full to the gunwales, and descended a lane towards the river and then along the riverbank amid inquisitive cows.

Back on the boat and just before the river bore west, a landing stage/pontoon screened the entrance to a lock where the Droitwich Canal reaches the River Severn. It opened in 1771 as a barge canal capable of handling Severn trows and almost needless to say it was by the great James Brindley. Mainly intended for salt transport, then coal, it followed the meandering valley of the River Salwarne, but fell out of use in the 1930s. Through prodigious effort it has now been restored to working order (for leisure of course).

We reached Bevere Island and beyond it our third lock. Richardson reports that the island is a natural one but according to its then owner it lost 'a *lot of land every winter, especially at the north end where the river divides, and is covered by high floods'*. It also features in history as '*a refuge of the inhabitants of Worcester in 1041 when Hardicanute sent a force to destroy the city because its inhabitants had refused to pay the danegeld and had killed one of his tax collectors'*. In fact, the *Anglo-Saxon Chronicle* records that two of the king's 'housecarls' were murdered and the townsfolk outrageously '*slew them within the town, inside the minster*' (cathedral church). Fleeing to Bevere Island they escaped the Danish King of England's 'harrying', a near-standard response in those wilder days to defiance of this type, involving razing an offending town to the ground and slaughtering its inhabitants. The town was indeed destroyed by Hardicanute but he abandoned his siege of the island. As we rowed past towards the lock the island looked pretty peaceful, mostly grass with a fringe of the usual riverside trees.

Bevere Lock and its weir, according to Richardson, *'are built upon a bed of gravel, a real shoal, that required sheet-piling to secure the foundations.'* Before we heeded the signs and bore to the right of the island we glimpsed a rather good and substantial iron footbridge from the riverbank onto the island, dating from 1844 and part of the lock works. The island came to an end before we had reached the lock and

a row of bright red buoys kept us on the straight and narrow for without them the careless boater might have had a distinctly rocky ride over a weir.

The lock was shut against us and, for the first and last time, the insignificant size of our boat told against us. Tied up to a steel companion ladder upstream alongside high sheet-piling, we were invisible to the lock-keeper in his cabin. Hollering 'ahoy' and similar no doubt irritating nautical calls had no effect. There was no boat in the lock as far as we could see so there was nothing for it but to clamber up the metal ladder and walk to the lock-keeper's cabin. This I did and he looked up in surprise for he had not seen us approach, no doubt more used to larger craft. He was most apologetic and I returned to the boat while he opened the lock gates. Further shouted chat, our licence number given, the usual good wishes and we were through.

Below Bevere Lock we soon passed the Camp House Inn where there had been another now long-defunct ferry. Linsdall Richardson was told that it was a *'punt ferry, for no rope could be put across because of the steamers'*. Richard suggested it would be a good idea to book a hotel or B & B in Worcester so I used my phone while he rowed on. A twin room in The Crown in Broad Street sounded good so I booked it but as we found out later all was not as it seemed: but more of that anon.

Soon afterwards we swapped over, Richard taking the steering oar and correcting my erratic line with hand gestures and a faintly exasperated expression each time, the river gently winding. After about a mile we passed a somewhat saggy metal footbridge carrying the footpath across a marina entrance and then houses on the left bank above us: the northern outskirts of Worcester. There were large numbers of elegant swans; then we were amid oar-driven rivals, both to us and the swans.

Everywhere we looked there were eights, fours, pairs and even a few single sculls speeding along the river in both directions, nearly all from the rowing clubs of the University of Worcester and the King's School Worcester. We pottered along, close to the right bank, as fit young people were urged on by their coxes, or by coaches following in small motorboats while yet other coaches cycled along the riverbank. We had seen very few boats thus far in our passage downriver and their speed and the complexity of keeping oars in synch with each other was impressive. Unlike us who rowed with the oar ends not quite meeting, they rowed with each oar pulled to their stomachs, one above the other. It looked tricky; particularly as Richard somewhat unkindly pointed out I can't even get the stroke equal between my two oars let alone face the stiffer challenge of coordinating with six other oarsmen or women.

Soon we were gliding past a park with an avenue of trees just inboard of the riverbank. The thundering of hooves told us this was a Worcester race day, so the town would be teeming. We could not see the galloping horses but could a stark white modern grandstand. This had replaced the Grandstand Hotel, and next came a modern rebuild of the Worcester Rowing Club's boathouse.

We were keeping a weather eye out for moorings but did not feel a rowing club would welcome us among its racing shells. We eased below the first of three bridges that span the Severn at Worcester, this one a fine modern pedestrian one, Sabrina Bridge. Only completed in 1992, it is a cable-stayed type with an A-frame only on the right riverbank so appeared asymmetrical for its 200-foot span from our vantage point on the river. Not dissimilar in fact to the two we had rowed beneath in Shrewsbury.

To people of my age, of course, 'Sabrina' was the name of a full-breasted, wasp-waisted TV and film star of the 1950s and needless to say the butt of innumerable coarse jokes. There was even a railway wagon, the Prestwin Silo wagon, that had two circular silos and these were universally known to 1960s railwaymen as 'Sabrinas'. However, the bridge is obviously not named after the film star and we had already seen a proudly bare-breasted statue of Sabrina in Bridgnorth.

'Sabrina', the Latin for the River Severn, may be a corruption or a Latinisation of 'Hafren' by which it is known in Wales. There is a fantastical tale in Geoffrey of Monmouth's notoriously unreliable and fanciful 12th-century *History of the Kings of Britain* about how Sabrina became the goddess of the river. It all started with the fiction that Brutus fled the Siege of Troy to end up in Cornwall where he became

King. Sabrina was a daughter by his son Locrinus and Estreldis, his lover. Sabrina was cast into the river, along with the offending mistress, by the king's outraged and deserted wife Gwendolen. A kind of Boadicea cum Amazon figure, Gwendolen had led the Cornish army that defeated and killed Locrinus in battle near where the River Stour enters the Severn: a convenient spot to throw in the mistress and her offspring. She decreed that henceforth the river be known as Habren. While there is no evidence for a King Locrinus, Geoffrey was not one to let facts spoil a good yarn. Anyway, that's apparently how Britain's longest river got its name.

History is a very different beast these days and Geoffrey of Monmouth's attempt to give British history roots in the classical world of Troy now cuts no mustard. In some ways this mythological stuff is more interesting than cold facts and all along the Severn are statues of Sabrina, usually naked to the waist to show off her assets, although usually considerably less than her namesake film star.

Beyond Sabrina Bridge were two old-stagers in the river crossing stakes: a railway bridge and beyond it a road bridge. We also got our first sighting of the cathedral and its pinnacled central tower from north of the railway bridge, albeit somewhat in blue-grey silhouette on this cloudy, gloomy day. The railway bridge of 1860 has a curving sixty-eight-arched viaduct before it meets the lattice-girder spans over the river which replaced original more attractive cast-iron ones in 1904.

The cathedral was looming larger but also in the foreground was the very tall, elegant spire and tower to another church. This turned out to be all that remains of St Andrew's Church, the rest having been demolished in 1949. It is 155 feet high and bizarrely the spire is topped by a Corinthian capital rather than a more normal medieval finial, dating I imagine from its 18th-century restoration or complete rebuild. In white limestone in a region dominated by red sandstones it stands out: a fine and dominating landmark known locally as the Glover's Needle, its parish being where most of the city's glove makers once lived. The road bridge beyond was designed by John Gwynn and replaced a medieval one a little upstream which in turn had replaced a ford. The ever-informative Linsdall Richardson tells us in '*early*

*days there was a good ford on hard Keuper Marl linking Tybridge and Newport Streets, the use of which was replaced by a bridge that may have dated from pre-Norman times as it is on record that it was repaired in 1088.*'

John Gwynn's bridge was a somewhat conventional Georgian design lacking the flair and elegance of Telford's bridges. We had rowed through his other two, the English Bridge at Shrewsbury and the one at Atcham. Described by James Boswell who of all men should recognise one as '*a fine, lively, rattling fellow*', Gwynn died at Worcester in 1786. The bridge, completed in 1780, has five arches across the river and a narrow towpath arch on each bank. It underwent considerable change over the years before a total rebuild in the 1930s, reverting to Gwynn's original design, albeit three times as wide, a similar fate to that of his English Bridge.

As we drifted on, we saw several old warehouses converted to flats, but our focus was now on finding a safe place to tie up for the night. We passed the cathedral, its west front's great traceried west window towering above the river, and beyond it the sublime central crossing tower. The riverside promenade was full of people walking, school pupils on their way home and the atmosphere very relaxed. Behind the promenade with trees along its landward walls, the ground rose up with fine buildings at the west end of College Green, then some buildings of the King's School, finishing on the river front with its startlingly modern boathouse of 2012. This resembles a boat with sharp bows projecting almost to the river above the tiers of steps down and up which the rowers carried their boats. It is a clever building by Associated Architects with boat stores and workshops below while the boat-prowed upper floor appears to float effortlessly above. Immediately beyond is the Georgian Diglis Hotel, the now somewhat faded name painted in large letters on the boundary wall at the back of the promenade.

Beyond a long terrace of Edwardian houses, their ground-floor bay windows and chimney stacks marching into the distance, was a modern complex of flats loosely modelled on old warehouses and that had replaced sawmills and woodyards. They overlook canal basins filled with narrowboats and were built for the Birmingham and Worcester Canal that opened in 1815 to carry coal and salt, although in decline by the 1860s.

Richard had spotted pontoons ahead and we rowed past the canal's junction with the river, the entrance lock behind a pedestrian bridge across the canal. The lock's northern 'bastion' projects beyond the canal entrance and is surmounted by a signpost giving distances and the number of locks en route: Stourport, Gloucester and Tewksbury for the Severn (only one lock to Tewkesbury), the fourth arm pointing along the canal towards Birmingham thirty miles away with a somewhat daunting fifty-eight locks to climb the 400 feet to that city. The pontoon almost immediately beyond the canal entrance obviously relates to canal traffic but Richard rowed us to its far end where we would be less visible to passers-by while we left the boat overnight, although to be on the safe side we took the oars with us.

The eights and other sculls obviously used Diglis Lock as their turning point before heading back to the city. Thus, when I fell into the river there were numerous witnesses on the river and on the riverside path above us. I did not mean to fall in and it happened like this: Richard had climbed onto the pontoon and I had passed him the oars we had removed from their rowlocks. This is not quite as easy as it sounds as they are locked in position and have to be rotated fully to allow them to be lifted out: achieved without embarrassment. Next I passed up the packs which he hefted onto the pontoon. The effort of this pushed the stern away from the pontoon, although the painter secured it at the bow.

My mistake was reaching across the watery gap to grasp the pontoon in order, I hoped, to pull the stern back to the pontoon. The boat tipped and I had a simple momentary choice of which way to go: either continue tipping the lightweight boat over with me in it or continue falling into the river, leaving the boat afloat. I took the latter course and the water welcomed me. I was hanging on to the pontoon and sank up to my armpits, praying inwardly that the waterproof document pouch was doing its job.

It is amazingly difficult to haul yourself out of water fully clothed so I turned sideways and got one leg onto the pontoon. This achieved, Richard grabbed my lifejacket to give him purchase and I pushed as hard as I could and, between us, we got me floundering onto the pontoon. Hmm. I had grazed my arm badly and bashed my leg too, presumably because the pontoon's matting had very uneven edges, resulting in plenty of blood on my forearms and a scraped left shin. I stood up, water streaming off onto the pontoon deck, my head and shoulders fairly dry. Several eights and fours, all rowed by girls, watched this mortifying and amateurish procedure with amusement.

Checking the waterproof pouch around my waist, I opened it with some trepidation. The wallet was damp in places but the phone was fine, which was more than could be said for my pride.

I did not much fancy squelching and dripping around Worcester so I removed my boat shoes, trousers and underpants. Semi-naked, I faced away from the inquisitive scullers and replaced trousers and pants. It was also farewell to the neoprene boat shoes and with relief I put on my sandals. My upper garments were of course soaked and I could not dry myself properly so there were patches of damp appearing in strategic areas of my pale grey trousers, giving an impression of some form of incontinence. I trusted that by the time we had walked into town this would all have dried (sadly, not so).

# 16

# A Glamping Night
# and Worcester

Climbing off the pontoon we set off for our hotel with our packs on our backs and carrying the oars. We worked our way along the promenade, eliciting a few strange looks, then beyond the cathedral, turned into town to head for the Crown Hotel, looking forward to a shower and then eating somewhere in the city. Richard went into the hotel reception while I stayed outside with the packs and the oars, enduring humourists pointing out that I appeared to have lost my boat. Richard emerged: 'You booked for next week, not tonight and as it's the races every hotel and B & B will be full to the gunwales.' I thought the nautical reference a bit of a cheap shot. 'Fortunately, I was able to sort it without cost.'

'That's great. Let's try the Premier Inn over the bridge. If not we'll have to get on Booking.com again. If out of town or miles away we'll have to get a taxi.' I still felt a chump but Richard was gracious and we hefted our packs and oars and set off westward to the river. Richard disappeared into the very modern and stylish hotel, the Worcestershire County Cricket Club just to its south. This is a ground that regularly floods but has one of the best outlooks of all cricket grounds with the cathedral towering above riverbank trees. Richard emerged: 'No luck. Time to get on the website again.'

Not trusting me, eventually he found a place not far away and booked. He told me it was a yurt in a place called Worcester

Glamping, 'glamping' apparently being an inelegant fusion of glamour and camping. Well, any port in a storm and it was only a mile and a half away in Lower Wick. We called a taxi and the driver didn't turn a hair at the three oars which had to poke out of the left-hand front window. At Lower Wick the taxi driver turned down a lane that became a muddy farm track at the end of which were a couple of buildings. Depositing us he executed a tricky multi-point turn and left, we having booked him to pick us up in the morning at half past eight from outside the nearby Manor Tavern carvery.

There was a chap doing some form of maintenance by the building beyond which we could see a number of yurt tents, not a form of accommodation with which I was familiar. He looked up in surprise as we approached with our packs and of course the three oars. Richard told him we had booked via the website which threw him somewhat as the site was not really open. Richard's brows darkened and the proprietor (for it was he) said he would open one of the yurts and check it was aired and equipped. Richard's brows cleared. This did not seem very businesslike but I suppose yurt camping is pretty 'alternative'. We said we would leave our packs (and oars) by the shower hut and head off to the carvery for a meal, as it was now about 7.30pm. He showed us which yurt and would leave the key in its door. He was clearly keen to get away, having finished whatever task had fortuitously brought him to the site: otherwise we really would have been high and dry (except for me of course).

We set off back up the muddy track, past Bennetts Ice Cream plant in modern barns behind the Manor Tavern. I was not particularly hungry after the spectacularly large plateful we had almost finished at the Wagon Wheel in Grimley and the place looked disappointingly like a Beefeater if you know what I mean.

However, this 'Crown Carvery' was excellent and a fellow diner told us their breakfasts were 'brilliant'.

I had noticed that the buildings incorporated a courtyard of farm buildings and barns with pyramidal-roofed louvred vents to their roof ridges: the word 'manor' should have given me a clue. The conversion was well done, I thought, as I explored inside to see how much was adaptation and how much new build. A further range behind has the remains of a medieval chapel dedicated to St Cuthbert which closed as a chapel in 1371, its subsequent 'half-life' in agricultural use a long one indeed.

Richard did full justice to the menu. I didn't but there was excellent wine and coffee. Back at the yurt, the toilet and shower building had a common room with coffee and tea-making facilities but these were indeed scanty: a couple of tea bags and a coffee jar with no coffee and certainly no milk. On the plus side we had the rest of Richard's bottle of Malmsey so we repaired to our yurt.

Yurts are clever circular structures utilising lightweight trelliswork to support vertical walls and slender 'rafters' meeting at the apex support a canvas roof. The floor was conventional floorboards and the furnishings traditional beds and so on. An unlit log burner occupied part of the space and we used its extensive fireguard to finish drying our clothes from the previous days soaking and from my impromptu dip in the Severn. Awoken early on Thursday morning by the sounds of a *'lowing herd winding slowly o'er the lea'* or rather cows noisily assembling nearby for morning milking, I opened the incongruously house-like yurt door and peered out to an intensely blue cloudless sky.

Richard emerged and we set off to the shower block and after much flicking of switches and guesswork, rather to our surprise, got some tepid water for our showers. Alongside the yurt field was what

I thought was a stream amid the trees but turned out to be manorial fish ponds first mentioned in 1299. Quite by chance we had hit on a site rich in history and we later found out that part of the 1651 Battle of Worcester took place at Manor Farm, the Royalists defending the nearby Powick Bridge across the River Teme. To the south this river winds east to join the River Severn: 850 yards away as the crow flies but twice that as it meanders about, perhaps reluctant to merge with its big sister.

We packed our rucksacks, locked the yurt and headed for the Manor Tavern for a very good breakfast. Last night's taxi arrived and deposited us at the end of Broad Street in Worcester, again the problem of the oars being brushed aside by our amiable driver.

*****

I had not been into the centre of Worcester for twenty or so years and I had mixed memories: the cathedral cut off from the historic core of the town by a large fume-filled roundabout overlooked by the appalling

1960s Lychgate Centre. This had ridden roughshod over the historic street layout and exposed the cathedral to the horrors of modern flat-roofed mediocrity. Rebuild or die seemed the motto in those days as city fathers excitedly adopted desperately ill-conceived attempts to ape East Croydon. If you turn your back on the shopping centre, the full glory of the cathedral and College Yard cannot be bettered. In this green space are three towering plane trees with wonderfully gnarled trunks, all leaning away from each other in their search for light and screening fine terraces of Georgian houses. Across the Yard, we entered the cathedral's north porch, our packs and oars left in a secure location after a quick word with a verger.

Worcester had been a key player in late Anglo-Saxon reforms under two canonised bishops, Oswald and Wulfstan. The cathedral was built and rebuilt several times after its foundation in 680AD, the present one started by St Wulfstan in 1084: a rare Anglo-Saxon bishop who kept his see after the Norman Conquest, dying rich in honour and esteem in 1095. My first visit focused on the surviving crypt and transepts of Wulfstan's building, the late 12th-century Transitional nave west bays being too 'modern'. This time I was determined to appreciate the whole of the church and its medieval Gothic grandeur. Mind you, the crypt is still just as magical with austere cushion capitals to its four rows of columns carrying the vaults to the choir floor above.

In the choir we again met Prince Arthur, Henry VII's eldest son. Henry had commissioned an ornate chantry chapel in his memory where a priest would say masses and pray for the prince's soul in perpetuity. Within the chantry a statue of Henry VII eternally grieves for his fifteen-year-old son. It had, though, little future for Arthur's younger brother Henry VIII began suppressing chantries, a task completed by Arthur's nephew Edward VI.

Back in the main body of the choir the other notable monument is that to King John, topped by a superb Purbeck marble effigy of the highest quality, dating from about 1232 and the earliest surviving royal effigy in England. He had sought burial at Beaulieu Abbey in Hampshire but apparently on his deathbed opted for Worcester Cathedral: he must have enjoyed his 1206 visit. Next we did our usual trawl of choir stall misericords, those tip-up seats that allowed the clergy to take the weight off their feet while appearing to stand respectfully through long services. These misericords provided splendid opportunities for medieval carvers to show off their skills. The best here dating from 1379 cover all bases from sacred to profane. The latter include a joust, a sow and piglets, a huntsman and a woman writing. The most curious illustrates an old riddle of the Clever Woman riding a goat naked, carrying a rabbit in a net.

A splendid cathedral and we had one more treat in store: the cathedral café occupying the Norman 'slype' or passageway between the south transept and the chapter house with groin vaults and wall arcades to each side. We bought coffee and a cake and sat down to admire the architecture. After this we needed to move on, and, gathering our oars and packs, we made a suitable donation to the maintenance fund and emerged into the sunshine.

Beyond the great west front of the cathedral we reached College Green, formerly the medieval priory's Great Court: now with fine houses on its east and south sides and the medieval monastic refectory range to its north. We descended off the higher ground through the 1378 Water Gate, the lower part in severely eroded red sandstone. Back on the riverside walk we passed again the boat-shaped King's School boathouse and the Diglis Hotel. Across the footbridge over the canal with its distinctive finger guidepost, we descended to the pontoon where our boat waited.

Richard busied himself with getting everything shipshape and we packed away rain gear, put the lifebelts on over short-sleeved shirts and donned our hats, Richard's a floppy blue sun hat and mine a natty but misshapen panama that had  suffered in yesterday's rain. We cast off to head towards Diglis Lock, a mere 450 yards away, the accompanying weir roaring away to our right. There are two locks, one narrower than the other but, surprisingly, the lock-keeper waved us into the larger one.

Linsdall Richardson informed us that for Diglis Lock, completed in 1844, '*two locks were needed because of the additional traffic accruing from the junction of the Worcester and Birmingham Canal with the Severn immediately above.*' The impact of the navigation works is striking for he says that '*Before Diglis weir was built in 1844 and penned up the water it is quite likely that it* [the river] *was generally fordable down to Diglis during times of low water*': a nightmare for the river and canal trade.

This time the lock-keeper asked for our licence number, another shouted conversation, and we were on our way, almost immediately passing beneath the rather beautiful and graceful Diglis Bridge, a cycle and footbridge that opened in 2010 and a near-twin to Sabrina Bridge. The river wound southwards as I rowed, relaxing in the warm sunshine. We passed the somewhat low-key confluence with the River Teme, last night's neighbour at Worcester Glamping. Under the more workmanlike southern bypass bridge we were finally away from Worcester's suburbs.

The left bank had long runs of moorings, the first for the Severn Motor Yacht Club, a splendidly old-fashioned name, then countryside again, the river on both sides with its customary fringe of trees. Approaching Kempsey where we hoped to land for lunch, a long row of moorings hove into view fronting the mobile homes of Seaborne Leisure, many miles from the sea and merging with Kempsey village to its east.

Drifting gently past we looked for a landing place beyond and spotted some fishing platforms. I rowed to one and Richard leapt ashore with the painter, securing us to a substantial tree. Scrambling up a steep bank through thick grass and bushes, we found ourselves on a path that turned out to be the Severn Way itself. The unprepossessing field in front of us was once thought to be the site of a palace of the Bishops of Worcester but current thinking however places the site amid the less attractive mobile homes and caravans of Seaborne Leisure. We turned inland past a fisherman's car park and followed a lane towards the battlemented and pinnacled tower of the parish church.

Although much rebuilt in the 19th century (a common refrain, of course) there is sufficient Norman evidence to show it was then an aisle-less cruciform 'minster church' whose priests tended the needs of surrounding villages. The church is set in a large churchyard fenced by metal estate railings, the grass lush and green, I recalled a fine monument from an earlier visit but no more than that. We entered through the north porch, a Victorian one by Ewan Christian whose handiwork we had seen in the rebuilt chancel at Grimley. Inside, an attractive lady with a clerical-grey shirt, dog collar and a shock of honey-blond hair welcomed us. She was the Rev Philippa Sargent, Kempsey's curate. After twenty-two years in the Royal Navy's Engineering branch she left to train as a priest. Looking her up when I got home, she had served in both Afghanistan and Iraq. She told us she had trained for the priesthood at Ripon College, which I assumed was in Yorkshire. In fact, it was at Garsington on hills with long views towards Oxford and a mere ten miles from my Buckinghamshire home.

Eventually, she said she had to go so we turned to the superb Jacobean monument to Sir Edmund Wylde, a local big shot (he died as Sheriff of Worcestershire). His effigy, now recoloured as if in life, lies in an arched and columned Classical structure. The inscription notes he was only thirty-two when he was '*visited with a most painfull and grievous sickness whereof he died being then in the strength of his age & of great hope*'.

Kempsey had been rather dismissively described by our old friend Brian Waters as '*a favoured village. In the days of its decline it houses an idle population of retired tradesmen and gentry of modest means.*' A bit down on the retired, but then he always seemed keener on working river folk and craftsmen. It was now lunchtime and the curate had suggested the Talbot pub on the main road. Leaving the churchyard through the lychgate we headed along Squire's Walk and over an attractive single-arch brick footbridge crossing Hatfield Brook. Reaching Main Road, the Talbot was a short way down, late-Georgian stucco with curved bay windows flanking a central doorcase. Doubtless built to take advantage of coach traffic between Worcester and Tewkesbury, we had a beer and a sandwich sitting in warm sunshine. Retracing our steps to the river we rowed on.

# 17

# Down to Upton-upon-Severn

With Richard at the oars and/or me steering, we soon passed the site of Pixham Ferry, its location marked by a small car park screened by tall poplars. Replacing a ford lost when the 19th-century navigation works raised water levels, our trusty Linsdall Richardson pointed out that it was popular but *'the introduction and subsequent multiplication of motor-vehicles had much to do with the decline in usage – particularly by pedestrians who once sought short-cuts over usually exposed and frequently soggy fields. The Pixham ferry was for many years a big horse ferry, which often took the Hunt, with horses, hounds and cycles, across to Kempsey Ham. This big ferry went out of operation some time before the last war, but a rowing-boat ferry was used until 1947, the year of the big flood when the boat was completely ruined and never replaced.'*

The river passed Clevelode, also the site of a ferry, then ran straight for about a mile, a caravan park on the right bank, before heading south-east at Rhydd where there was another ford, *rhydd* meaning 'ford' in Welsh. Cliffey Wood climbed from the riverbank onto higher ground, forcing the river to change direction before straightening again. Ahead we saw a white castle on a well-wooded ridge ending at the riverbank.

As we got nearer it was obvious that we were not looking at a medieval castle, despite the battlements. Three storeys of Gothic-arched windows towered above the flanking bays, a further range largely obscured by trees. A Romantic confection forming a superb 'vista closer' to this long reach, we identified it from the map as 'Severn Bank'. It appeared early 19th-century Gothick (that is, academically unsound Gothic Revival) and its gleaming cream stucco showed it had recently been refurbished. Built as a fishing lodge for the Earls of Coventry of nearby Croome Park a little further inland; presumably his lordship had to descend some sixty feet to the riverbank with his fishing rod over his shoulder or more likely carried by his gamekeeper. The highlight of the river between Kempsey and Upton, it was completely unknown to us. Set on a ridge, we would never have guessed it was a fishing lodge so far above anything less than a biblical flood.

Brian Waters in *Severn Stream* does not mention Severn Bank: only telling the story of a pistol discharged in the parish church of St Denys, Severn Stoke: '*John Somers, father of the future Lord Chancellor, shot at the parson in the pulpit, fortunately without effect. This happened in Cromwell's time when feelings ran high*'. This anecdote is not one of Brian Waters' more fanciful flights. The vicar was a Mr Wybrough and a Jacobite ballad, quoted in Noake's 1868 *Guide to Worcestershire*, commemorates this incident:

> *His Satanic zeal at Stoke it was such*
> *That he shot at the parson; you'll think it too much*
> *But he loved the Old Cause as his son loves the Dutch.*

A clergyman's life was apparently exciting in the 17th century, particularly if you offended the local gentry.

Discussing the fishing lodge occupied us pleasantly enough as the river curved south-west, flat fields above the tree-lined bank to our left. Hanley Castle was away on our right, a lane coming to the riverbank, but Pevsner reported there was little to see, the castle built as a hunting lodge for King John disappearing by the 16th century. By the 17th century William Habington, a local poet, stated sententiously there was only a *'lytell rubbyshe and a seely* [silly] *barne to teach us that the glory of the World vanishethe to nothinge'*.

The river bore south-east past a four-square Georgian brick house on the right bank: Pool House, once a farmhouse, and beyond it Pool House Caravan Park. Upton-upon-Severn's old church tower came fully in view, a curious structure resembling through half-closed eyes an 18th-century lighthouse.

Just upstream of Upton's road bridge we spotted public pontoons with two or three canal narrowboats moored. Beyond the last boat Richard, painter in hand, scrambled onto the pontoon. Tying the boat fore and aft to avoid it swinging to smite the nearest narrowboat, we hefted our backpacks and talked to the narrowboaters. One couple lived on their narrowboat full time and moved up and down canals and rivers at a leisurely pace.

*****

From the pontoon we had noticed that the current bridge does not lead directly into the town centre, so in bridge terms Upton is the complete opposite of Bewdley where Telford relocated the bridge to centre on the town's principal street, Load Street. At Upton the bridge had formerly reached the town at the north end of the High Street and was moved west in the age of the motor car to avoid the town centre. This bypassing had the beneficial (and probably unlooked-for) effect of creating a quieter town river frontage so all was perhaps not lost.

This latest bridge had, as usual along the Severn, numerous predecessors, the first one mentioned in a late 15th-century document replacing a ferry first recorded in 1307. This much-patched and

rebuilt stone replacement had its hopelessly compromised structure washed away in 1852 to be replaced by a bridge of iron. The current 1940-built bridge itself is elegant if stolid and being rebuilt west of the original location diverted traffic along Church Street with its fine timber-framed and brick houses. It is no longer the narrow lane of old photographs.

More surprising to a new visitor, the tower we saw as we rowed towards the town is all that's left of the Georgian parish church. It is now named the Pepper Pot Heritage Centre, 'pepper pot' a reference to the octagonal top to the tower. The rest of the flood-prone, ruined and roofless church was demolished in 1937.

A more recent change along the riverbank has been the building of an undoubtedly very necessary flood defence wall, although rather a solid barrier it has to be admitted. Upton, like Tewkesbury, has always been very prone to flooding: on an earlier trip to the area I couldn't even get into the town because of deep floodwater. Completed in 2012, these defences have proved their worth in subsequent floods.

We had asked the narrowboaters if they could suggest a B & B or hotel and one of them named the White Lion Hotel as a possibility, an old coaching inn in the High Street. 'You can't miss it because it's got a stone lion on the porch.' From Church Street we turned right at the High Street, a wider street, still flanked by a mix of black and white timber-framed buildings and brick ones, some of them rendered.

Before reaching the White Lion, we spotted The Map Shop, its shop window and the first-floor oriel window above painted a jaunty green. Both of us love maps and often buy from them online: their next-day service is unbeatable. So, we popped in and Richard asked about difficulty getting large-scale Greek maps. Happy to meet customers, they explained that the Greek financial crisis was the cause. We resisted the temptation to add more maps to our packs and said our farewells. Always good to put faces to names, if you see what I mean.

Beyond we could hardly miss the White Lion with its large Doric porch, surmounted by a statue of a white lion, its flowing mane picked out in gold and its raised left paw on a golden globe, all glistening in late afternoon sunshine. The façade of about 1800 is the grandest in the street, flanked by fluted pilasters rising to a moulded cornice. A room was available with twin beds, although not within the frontage block but in a 'courtyard' room in the more utilitarian single-storey range at the rear adjoining the beer garden (or rather nowadays smoking zone and several men were busy there doing just that amid desultory conversation).

We left our packs in the room and before setting out to explore the town, we looked at various pieces of historical information framed on the hotel walls. There was also evidence of an earlier building behind the grand stucco façade and we were informed that the building dated back to 1510 and there was certainly 16th-century timber-framing. Of the historical information the visits of Alec Guinness and other actors in a gilded picture frame were rapidly passed over in favour of the one next to it about the Civil War. Prince Rupert, Charles I's dashing, if reckless, nephew, stayed the night here in 1645 and apparently he and his officers got roaring drunk.

The other piece of information related to *Tom Jones*, the Henry Fielding novel published in 1749. Its full title is *The History of Tom Jones, a Foundling* published in six volumes, so a meaty read. I remember the 1963 film with Albert Finney as Tom and Susannah York as Sophia, his beloved, directed by Tony Richardson with a script by no less a luminary than 'Angry Young Man' John Osborne. One of the most memorable scenes was set in 'the inn at Upton', although the White Lion was not actually used for the film. Tom and Mrs Waters, played deliciously by Joyce Redman, memorably eat an enormous meal in a thoroughly suggestive way (this was after all the seduction of young innocent Tom). Amazing what can be done chewing a chicken leg, an oyster and an apple. Earlier there had been brawling with the innkeeper and his wife: not a good advert for the inn '*which, in their eyes, presented the fairest appearance in the street*'.

While not specifically named in the novel, the White Lion is the only one Fielding himself had stayed in so it is pretty conclusive that he had it in mind. Having seen the film I read the book and greatly enjoyed Fielding's confiding and somewhat arch style. As a result I eagerly devoured his and other 18th-century novels by Smollett and Sterne, many of them picaresque and all witty, finishing with Sterne's *Tristram Shandy*, a novel quite unlike any other before or since. I never got on with Samuel Richardson, though: too wordy, prosy and humourlessly didactic.

We left the hotel and halfway along New Street, which may have been 'new' in the 17th century, we looked in the window of Upton-upon-Severn Wines. Clearly, a small town with a lot going for it: not only probably the best map shop in England but also what looked a most impressive wine shop. Our Malmsey supply had been exhausted during our sojourn at Worcester Glamping so we went in to see whether there were any dessert wines and selected a couple of half bottles of Sauternes. At the till the co-founder of this family business asked us whether we were staying in the town, if so she thought we might be interested in an Italian wine tasting dinner that evening. A few tickets were available so we left the shop with our Sauternes and our evening sorted.

The wine tasting dinner (five courses of Italian food) was in The Boathouse on Riverside so we walked past it to look. It is a tapas and wine bar and looked promising so we 'changed for dinner', the change mainly consisting of putting on long trousers and shoes but the same shirts above.

There was a riverside balcony above the entrance so we sat there contentedly looking at the River Severn bathed in evening sunshine with a glass of wine. There were about twenty or so guests when we were called in as the least smart of the company but after initial awkwardness and a slight feeling of gatecrashing people who all knew each other we soon integrated. Talking about the river defences warmed a few of them up. It transpired that some lived beyond the eastern floodgates in Dunn's Lane so had not escaped the post-2012 floods. The wine flowed and courses came and went; we did our best to nod wisely as the wines were introduced, the party discussing them in great detail. We left with a feeling of general well-being and probably too much wine and good food on board, the evening an unexpected adventure on our picaresque Severn voyage.

Next morning we looked at the maps and Pevsner over another good breakfast. We thought we could get to Tewkesbury by lunchtime and perusing Pevsner we saw that Ripple, the medieval mother church of Upton, had two full pages so we decided to try to land there.

# 18

# Rippling to Ripple
# and Tewkesbury

Back at the boat all was well and we cast off, Richard rowing under the bridge, then passing the town's river defences that had been so warmly discussed the previous evening. We rowed on past a waterworks and then Ryall Quarry wharves where large barges were loading aggregates via a conveyor belt emerging from a tunnel cut through the bank's bund. These were the first industrial-scale vessels we had seen on the river and we passed several more powering up and downriver. There was also a perceptible change in the nature of the river: it was losing its upper-river charms, the scenery flatter on both sides and the banks higher, tree-clad and largely restricting our view of the world beyond. South of the quarry wharves, we passed beneath a cable spanning the river from a concrete tower on the left bank, apparently a monitoring station, the cable having some role in this. Where it reached the right bank, we could see the tree-clad embankment of a former railway line, the Tewkesbury and Malvern Railway. Its bridge, dismantled in the early 1960s, apparently had a sliding central span to let tall ships through. Soon after was Saxons Lode where according to Richardson there was a ford until the 1840s navigation improvements, adding that *'the river swings westward and then south–south-eastward, the nose of the alluvial ground within the bends being Sandy Point'*. Beyond this Point we started to look to land at Ripple. Two private pontoons for houses on the bank were not promising but beyond two fishing platforms beckoned and Richard rowed for the second one.

Atop the riverbank was a public footpath and we turned along it towards a house, then right to curve inland past a fishing lake to a car park. Several fishermen were setting up their tackle and told us in broad West Midlands accents this was a Birmingham Anglers Association's water, Uckinghall Pool. The hamlet of that name is separated from Ripple by the deep cutting of the old Tewkesbury and Malvern Railway.

From the car park a lane wound to the village, emerging at a small triangular green by a sign naming the lane '*Ferry Lane*', a ferry ignored by Richardson, perhaps looking forward to bigger fish nearer Tewkesbury. This little green is at the heart of Uckinghall hamlet and has the base and lower part of the shaft of a medieval village cross. The parish is unusually well endowed with medieval crosses for in Ripple village itself is one with its tall stone shaft intact and another less complete in the churchyard.

Heading towards Ripple village, the road crossed the trackbed of the old railway in its well-treed cutting with the village station, closed in 1961, converted into a house, its platform largely intact, far below. In the heart of the village is a charming small triangular green with its medieval cross, the (now disused) village stocks and the churchyard beyond.

St Mary's, a large cruciform church with a central crossing tower, has a churchyard dominated by row upon row of gravestones still in their proper locations. It is another church, like Kempsey, that was probably a minster church for surrounding villages and had two priests noted in Domesday Book. The transepts and lower part of the central tower are late Norman, but the tower upper parts are 18th century topped by an incongruous balustrade, replacing after a surprisingly long interval a spire destroyed by lightning back in 1583. The 18th-century work is a poor climax to a fine church, and one richly endowed by the medieval bishops of Worcester. This is another church with a superb set of 15th-century misericords in the chancel: under the tilt-up 'seats' lively scenes represent the twelve farming Labours of the Months, and the sun and the moon. Richard thought it worth taking a few photos and reached for his camera: not there.

'I borrowed Vicky's waterproof camera.' The furrowed-brow look was again very much in evidence.

'When did you last have it?' I asked.

'Not sure.' After a pause he continued. 'Now I come to think about it I seem to remember I took it to The Boathouse last night thinking I might take a few sunset shots.' A vision of many years of twiddling my thumbs while he set up sunset shots flashed before me. Richard was talking: 'I remember hanging it over the back of my chair. I don't remember taking it back to the hotel. Do you think it could still be there?'

'We passed a pub on our way through the village. If it's open, we could find The Boathouse's number and ring. If it's there, ring for a taxi.'

'No point in us both going to Upton so can you stay in Ripple and mooch back to the boat? But the pub didn't look open,' Richard added and I agreed but it seemed a reasonable starting point for a camera rescue mission. He was very much right: The Railway Inn was closed for refurbishment and in any case did not open normally until midday, but we knocked anyway. After a certain amount of discussion and a surprising reluctance to put down paintbrushes, we got a phone number for a taxi and also the number of The Boathouse.

Back outside Richard phoned and to his evident relief they had the camera. A taxi was booked and emerged from the Tewkesbury direction to collect him and he headed back to Upton. I suppose this made us equal in the cock-up stakes after my Worcester dip. Still, I restrained myself from smart comments and set off to retrace my steps, reaching the fishermen's car park just as Richard returned, looking a tad tense despite having his wife's camera back. After the taxi had roared off, he said he had been charged a rather hefty £30 fare but, shelving his normal combative self, had not argued and coughed up without protest. His brow cleared and we chatted to the same Brummie fishermen before heading back to the boat.

I rowed on, heading generally south-east, passing under the M50 motorway bridge, the river crossed in a single span. Immediately beyond was another wharf for loading sand from pits on the left bank, the still-active workings continuing beneath the motorway. Three quarters of a mile south of the bridge Richard looked up from the map and told me our left bank was now a Gloucestershire one: we had rowed the Worcestershire Severn and had only a few miles to row before both banks were in Gloucestershire. Hardly a crossing of the Amazonian rainforest it has to be admitted but a good feeling. I put Pevsner's *Worcestershire* volume away and placed *Gloucestershire 2* in the waterproof case, Tewkesbury Abbey being keenly anticipated and one of my favourite larger churches. I have also seen it with the flooded Severn lapping close: clearly the monks chose their site well but the town has never been so lucky.

We were steadily approaching Mythe Bridge, a fitting name as it is an Anglo-Saxon word meaning a place where two rivers meet, in this case the Severn and the Avon merging at Tewkesbury. We were looking forward to rowing beneath another of the great Thomas Telford's bridges, this one finished in 1826, and a late one, he being sixty-nine years of age when it opened. Telford considered Mythe

Bridge one of his most elegant and Linsdall Richardson allows himself a rare exclamation mark and even an underlining: '*It is an iron bridge of single arch with a span of 176 feet: it was cast in Shrewsbury and brought to Tewkesbury <u>by river</u> before the river had been canalised!*'

Tewkesbury was nearer now and as the town is not on the banks of the River Severn Richard pointed out we would have to turn into the River Avon and row against the current to moor in the town. Bearing in mind the strong current in the Severn I steeled myself for some vigorous rowing. At Richard's signal I turned the boat eastwards and upped my stroke rate, although the flow seemed less strong than on its mighty sister river. After about 300 yards Richard said the river widened and he could see pontoons where we could tie up and land. This was Quay Pit overlooked by the massive Borough Flour Mills. He steered me to the pontoons and I shipped oars, climbed out painter in hand, and pulled the boat to the rear of the pontoon where willow scrub would hide it from prying eyes.

The pontoons served the narrowboats waiting to enter the canalised section of the river, Mill Avon, via a lock into what on historic maps is 'Old Avon'. This canalised 'cut' is thought to be 12th century and powered the Abbey's watermills. Signs informed us that there was no mooring or fishing allowed so we climbed the steps from the pontoon and walked as nonchalantly as possible through what appeared to be the lock keeper's garden, then along the canal path towards the old flour mills. Behind us we could see King John's Bridge across the Mill Avon, rebuilt in the 1960s. We gathered that it got this name only in the 19th century having previously been Long Bridge, Wide Bridge and even in medieval times 'the bridge towards Mythe'. King John's Bridge sounds more romantic, and justified by his allocation some of the market tolls to bridge repairs.

The first major Tewkesbury buildings we looked at after leaving the boat were the towering Borough Flour Mills. Replacing earlier watermills, they are high, five to seven storeys, the northern block named and dated '*Borough Flour Mills Erected MDCCCLXV*' while the southern higher and larger block is dated '*1889*'. Mainly red brick, other coloured brick was used to create ornamental patterns in a style cumbersomely known as 'constructional polychromy' and popular with leading Victorian architects such as Butterfield. Steam powered from the start they used the river to transport raw materials and finished products, the last grain barges mooring here in 1998 and the last flour milled as recently as 2006. Their original use gone, they forlornly await conversion into flats. We crossed the Mill Avon on an elegant arched iron bridge with plaques on the railings, '*This Bridge was erected in the year 1822*', and next to a rather more utilitarian one that formerly carried railway tracks into the mill.

From the mills we followed a lane, Back of Avon, alongside the Mill Avon and now a riverside walk. Once there had been warehouses along the banks: all now gone and replaced by riverside car parking. Disappointingly few of the long narrow burgage plots that ran towards the river from High Street survive. The lane curved away from Mill Avon and in Talbot Lane we at last saw our first black and white timber-framed buildings, so we knew we were closing on the High Street.

Turning right into High Street we passed the 1920 war memorial cross on the site of a medieval market one, then a fine mix of buildings in timber-framing, brick and stucco. The rich vista is closed by the end gable of a long timber-framed range, Abbey Cottages. I remember them as a conservation cause célèbre of the late 1960s, eventually saved by the National Trust. The monks of Tewkesbury Abbey built this terrace of over twenty single-bay houses in the late 15th century specifically for renting. I can't think of any longer single terrace of medieval houses anywhere else in England. They are two-storeyed, the upper floor jettied or projecting beyond the lower, and they delightfully follow the curve of the road as it skirts the abbey churchyard.

Ahead of us were the three gables of The Bell Hotel, another fine black and white timber-framed building, the first floor and gables all jettied. This seemed a good place for lunch as it overlooks the churchyard of the abbey. It dates from 1697, rising from the charred ashes of its medieval predecessor, the former monastic guesthouse. Another literary connection here, as with the White Lion in Upton. The Bell features in that now largely unread but thoroughly improving novel *John Halifax, Gentleman* by Mrs Dinah Craik, published in 1856 and set mainly in a thinly disguised Tewkesbury. Inside amid the timber-framing a convivial group of late middle-aged friends lunched.

After lunch we left The Bell to revisit the magnificent Norman abbey church founded by Robert FitzHamon in about 1087 and complete by 1123. The west front is dominated by a soaring full-height Norman arch with six orders of shafts (there were originally seven) framing a 17th-century great west window in a convincingly medieval Perpendicular Gothic style. Inside as ever we were staggered at the scale of the nave with its eight bays of towering drum

columns receding towards the crossing arches, rather more Burgundian than what might be termed 'mainstream' Anglo-Norman and also used at nearby Gloucester Cathedral and Pershore Abbey. Strikingly

similar in fact to the great 11th-century Abbey of St Philibert at Tournus in Burgundy, a building that I finally visited in 2010 with my wife Jill. Deerhurst later would be another first for me but I avoid modish terms like 'bucket list'.

The great nave piers rise austerely for about thirty feet and then sprout an astonishingly delicate forest of Decorated (14th-century) lierne vault ribs: it is probably a cliché to say it is like walking into a stone-built medieval forest but clichés are clichés for a reason. Beyond, within the east end, the Norman drum piers were shortened and a

Decorated Gothic upper storey added with a further soaring spread of vault ribs. The crossing tower received a similar vault so the effect is breathtakingly beautiful with an ethereal net of 'branches' floating and intersecting above the robust Norman work from end to end of the old church.

Back inside, the lighting scheme is one of the best I've seen in any church. Warm lights point upwards into complex mouldings of arches, aisle vaults and within chapels and transepts. To complete the lighting scheme, three fine chantry chapels set within the arches of the choir have each been sensitively lit within, each a small room with unglazed traceried 'windows' and complex stone vaults. The Trinity chantry chapel has fan vaulting and a delicate late-14th-century painting of the Trinity and kneeling donors on its east wall. Above the arcades with their chantry chapels and elaborately canopied medieval tombs, the seven tall windows of the chancel fortunately retain most of their high quality mid-14th-century stained glass. Our interest in misericords was also met for Scott's 19th-century choir stalls incorporated the original 14th-century ones, mainly birds and various beasts, real and mythological.

The abbey was dissolved by Henry VIII but the townsfolk bought the church for the then princely sum of £453: they must have cherished it and its role in the life of the town for they also bought eight of its bells. Their purchases undoubtedly saved one of the finest medieval churches in England from destruction although the monastic buildings went, leaving only traces of the cloisters' Perpendicular Gothic blind arcades veneering the lower nave and south transept outer walls.

Outside again, the fields to the south have been kept free from modern development, so the church is seen largely as it has been since the monastic buildings had been cleared between it and Swilgate stream. Brian Waters reports that '*there is a tradition, now hardly remembered, that stone from Caen (Normandy) was brought by sea, up the Severn and into the Swilgate for the building of the Norman abbey*'.

It was now three o'clock in the afternoon, and Deerhurst beckoned. As with Worcester's great cathedral we could have spent much more time in the abbey and the town but headed back down Church Street and then High Street, pausing to buy a take-away coffee. I spotted

Welsh cakes in the food display, a delicious scone rich with currents and spices and generously rolled in sugar. I wanted to introduce Richard to something Welsh that he might actually like. I bought us a couple each and we headed for the boat back over the elegant 1822 bridge. The Welsh cakes found favour so that was progress and, wiping the sugar off our hands, we boarded the boat.

# 19

# Journey's End and the Tidal Severn Abandoned

Casting off from the Tewkesbury pontoon, Richard took the oars with the easier task of going with the Avon's flow to rejoin the Severn. Heading westwards, we approached the Upper Lode Lock, the last before Gloucester. Linsdall Richardson informed us that lock and weir took five years to build due to funding and geological problems, finally opening in 1858. Nowadays, the weir is protected by linked bright orange floats and as ever a large sign directs the heedless towards the lock rather than the weir.

While the waters lowered, the lock-keeper rather forcibly took the view that tangling with Gloucester in a small rowing boat was not a good idea. I must say we had been looking at the map to see what was of interest downstream between Deerhurst and Gloucester. There did not seem much and Linsdall Richardson hinted that the river becomes duller: '*the shallow valley of the Severn broadens southward from Lower Lode to Ashleworth and the river has a broad level tract of alluvium on its west side, the meadows on which are subject to frequent flooding.*'

The river is now tidal and the famous Severn Bore reaches here, discussed by Brian Waters in his earlier book *Severn Tide*, which follows the river from Tewkesbury to the Bristol Channel in his discursive style seeking out craftsmen, fishermen and the like. He reported that the '*Bore still has enough power to gush with splendid force into the 'Old Severn'. This still backwater was once known as the Upper Lode, and was the main stream of the Severn, until the river was diverted to run over Tewkesbury weir, when the lock was built. The highest Bores knock against the lock gates, which open up before them, and all four gates are on occasion thrown open by the force of the tide which continues to flow upstream. The weir itself can be submerged when there is a considerable amount of water flowing over it'.*

Pondering the lock-keeper's advice, we decided to continue to Deerhurst and then take stock. The river had widened appreciably, the banks seeming higher, perhaps not surprising to defend fields from the Severn Bore. We passed where the Mill Avon merges with the river from the left, opposite Lower Lode. Here amid campsites and caravans sits the Lower Lode Inn, and the site of a ferry used by the monks of Tewkesbury and revived by the inn during the summer months.

Rowing on for a mile and a half, we saw Deerhurst Priory's tall, slender tower to our left and, spotting a fishing platform on a muddy 'beach', we rowed to it, tied up and climbed the bank to the Severn Way footpath, turning south amid vivid green meadows to a remarkable, entirely hollow, ancient but otherwise thriving oak tree, the cavity a giant surprised mouth to landward. It marks the junction with a track heading across the

fields to Deerhurst. Through a gate the track bore left and beyond a few fine trees was Odda's Chapel, one of the two fascinating Anglo-Saxon buildings that survive. The chapel in rubble stone is attached to a fine half-timbered farmhouse, Abbot's Court. We entered the chapel through a tall, narrow Anglo-Saxon doorway. Inside a high nave and a chancel arch leads into the chancel that had been incorporated into the farmhouse. On its east wall is a replica of the dedication stone, the original since 1675 in what became Oxford's Ashmolean Museum. This dates its dedication exactly and affirms the building's high status. Translated it reads:

> '+ *Duke Odda ordered this Royal Hall to be built and dedicated to the honour of the Holy Trinity for the soul of his brother Ælfric who was taken up from this place. Bishop Ealdred (of Worcester) it was who dedicated the same on 12th April in the 14th year of the reign of Edward, King of the English.*

This was Edward the Confessor and the year 1056 while Ælfric had died or been 'taken up' in 1053. Odda himself also died in 1056 and was buried at Pershore Abbey. The chapel was only 'discovered' in 1885 when repairs exposed an old window and a slow restoration followed, only completed in 1965. The nave had a long second life as a kitchen: sensible as it was more fireproof than the attached timber-built house. The chapel (but not the house) is open to the public. Waters haughtily remarks: '*Though a visit to Deerhurst is an experience for the antiquarian, to the historian it serves as a reminder of the poverty of Saxon civilization*'. Other comments are equally disdainful but we thought this group of ancient buildings of quite outstanding interest. I have dwelt on Odda's Chapel partly because it is so unusual: an

Anglo-Saxon nobleman's private chapel. Much is also known of the Earl (Duke in the Latin of the inscription) adding more interest to Brian Waters' dull stone boxes.

We moved on to the old priory church of Deerhurst and, it has to be admitted, it presents a somewhat unlovable appearance. I think it is down to the row of 14th-century aisle windows with their flat heads and the plain west tower, rectangular in plan and seventy feet high. Closer examination shows much Anglo-Saxon stonework and evidence of later cloisters while at right angles a long stone house incorporates some of the priory's medieval buildings. The original foundation date of the abbey, later priory, is unclear but it is first referred to in a land grant of 804AD while extensive later Anglo-Saxon work added to and enlarged it. The tower looks odd because it started life as a rectangular porch with an upper floor with an external timber gallery on three sides that was progressively raised to produce a five-storeyed structure. Above the west door and the third storey doorway/window are curious stone beast's heads projecting from the wall like the figureheads of a Viking longboat or Classical *prokrossoi*.

Inside it is tall in proportion to its width and with a remarkable amount surviving of the Anglo-Saxon abbey church, its nave and the east end of the aisles which were actually two-storey side chapels or 'porticus',

now without the floors to the upper storey. The west porch and much of the tower above it remain while to the east foundations and a bit of apse walling can be seen. The present east wall of the church has the blocked great arch into the lost chancel and on either side are the openings into the former side chapels/porticus.

Turning and looking west, the nave's far wall shows evidence of a first-floor nave gallery accessed by a now blocked doorway. Above this, opening into the nave from within the second floor of the tower/porch, is a two-light triangular-headed opening with stumpy fluted pier and jambs, presumably for the Earl's family to watch services in privacy. A complex Anglo-Saxon abbey church and very much more interesting to us than to Brian Waters firmly in a then mainstream of scorn for Anglo-Saxon architecture.

The font is also a remarkable Anglo-Saxon survival, being dated to the 9th century. Like many old fonts, it had been used elsewhere, in this case as a washtub until found in a garden near the river by a Miss Strickland of nearby Abberley Court in 1870. She then asked

the vicar of Longdon in Worcestershire for what she believed was the original base and both were reunited (if her theory was right, of course).

Back at the riverbank there was a pub, The Yew Tree Inn, on the opposite bank a little downstream and beyond it what looked like a sailing club, marked as Chaceley Stock on the map, the club on the site of a former Victorian brickworks. I rowed the quarter mile or so to the pub's moorings. The pub not yet open, we sat at one of its outside tables.

'Let's face it, it's nearly six o'clock. We're not enjoying rowing here, there's not much to see in the stretch between here and Gloucester, the scenery sounds dull and Gloucester sounds a bit scary for us in our tiny boat amid the giants. The lock-keeper also said we would have trouble getting into the docks. Do you think we should leave the boat here and get back to Hampton to pick up the cars tomorrow?'

'Well, the pub's closed but the sailing club has a slipway,' Richard replied. 'If there's anyone around we can ask if we can leave the boat there overnight. I'm sure it'd be safe. What do you think?'

'I think we should get back to Hampton tonight. We could get a taxi to Tewkesbury station. The Severn Valley Railway goes from Kidderminster to Hampton but will be closed by the time we get there.'

'No problem. How about staying the night in Kidderminster and catching a train to Hampton in the morning? I assume we can get there this evening,' Richard concluded.

Climbing the low fence between the pub garden and the Avon Sailing Club, we could see no-one. By chance a chap drove into the site and we asked if we could leave the boat. 'Sure, no problem at all,' he said. 'I suggest you put it near the entrance gates, but you won't be able to get your car and trailer in as the gate has a key code.' He puzzled for a moment. 'I know, I think you look trustworthy, I'll give you the code.' He wrote it on a piece of paper. With the camaraderie of boaters, he waved away offers of payment. Having moved the boat into the yacht club and, the pub now open, we had a beer before the taxi arrived.

There was another view of Mythe Bridge as the taxi crossed it to head into Tewkesbury, crossed the M5 to Ashchurch and its station beyond a modern industrial estate. The station name has a splendidly old-fashioned ring as 'Ashchurch for Tewkesbury': a reminder of a long-lost branch line into the town. Tickets bought from a machine, we had a mere quarter of an hour wait for the train. During an amazingly smooth and speedy journey we changed trains at Worcester Shrub Hill and at Droitwich, reaching Kidderminster station around 9.00pm. Richard had booked a B & B online and we got a taxi there. A balti restaurant was still open in the town centre so we walked to it, crossing the Staffordshire and Worcestershire Canal, first encountered as it entered the River Severn at Stourport. It seemed many days ago but was in fact a mere four.

# 20

# Homage to Paddy Leigh Fermor at Dumbleton

Another fine day greeted us: a perfect blue sky sprinkled with small, fluffy alto-cirrus clouds. Over breakfast (another excellent, freshly cooked one) I asked our host, David, about the model steam locomotives on the mantelpiece and shelves, hoping to talk about trains. No interest: a previous owner had left them there but he did have copies of the current timetable for the Severn Valley Railway (SVR) and the first train to Hampton Loade left at 9.45am.

Our breakfast could thus be fairly leisurely and with time to walk to the station rather than take a taxi. Packed and replete we set off into

the town again, our packs on our backs. We worked our way through the town to the stations. The mainline one to the east of the SVR's was damningly described by Pevsner as a miserable replacement for an 1863 half-timbered Great Western one. The SVR station next to it looks authentically Great Western of a late-19th-century type, even having J E Danks French Second Empire-Style pavilions similar to ones at Slough. We assumed it must be the terminus of the 1878 loop from the old Severn Valley Railway but not a bit of it: entirely modern and opened in 1984 on the site of the old goods yard. It is apparently a replica of Danks' Ross-on-Wye station demolished in 1975. It was a while before I realised it was indeed a replica.

Buying a coffee, we walked along the platform beside our train before boarding, the coaches the SVR's set of wonderful LNER Gresley teak coaches dating from the 1920s and 1930s, all beautifully restored. As a boy it was all London and North Eastern Region of British Railways for me, though fated to live in Great Western and then Southern Electric territory for much of my childhood.

The train was full of families out for the day and, after it had crossed the canal and rumbled through the Bewdley Tunnel, it puffed past the West Midland Safari Park where everyone played spot the 'wild' animals. Beyond Bewdley Station the line skirted between Eymore Wood and the Trimley Reservoirs to emerge into bright sunlight and onto the memorable Victoria Bridge across the river. We spotted Worrall's Grove on the opposite bank and a little reluctantly we left the train at Hampton Loade Station.

Our euphoria at having completed rowing the Severn from Wales to south of Tewkesbury easily survived the 'housekeeping' task of collecting the cars from the Unicorn as we set off back to the Avon Sailing Club, the trailer bouncing around behind Richard's car. After an uneventful drive, the gate's passcode was not needed as people were there getting their yachts ready for the river. Again, we tried to press money on the club members but they wouldn't hear of it, so we sneaked off and put a fiver in the clubhouse letterbox.

The boat loaded upside down on the trailer and secured by the webbing straps, we discussed what to do next over a pint at the adjacent Yew Tree Inn (again). Richard was already thinking about modifications to the boat to make it 'match fit' for the Loire while I contemplated a return to Greece for more superb walking in Paddy Leigh Fermor home territory before Hornblower and the river Loire.

The two Severn voyages, totalling about 115 miles, had failed to weaken our enthusiasm for rowing or for recreating the Hornblower escape down the river Loire which we had merely deferred until next year, 2017. Reluctant to end our trip and tamely head home, I was idly scanning the road map, thinking that crossing the M5 east of Tewkesbury and heading towards Stow-on-the-Wold would be the best route. As my eyes moved eastwards, I spotted Dumbleton.

'Richard, why don't we go to Dumbleton: it's only a few miles east of the M5 and we could do what I've been meaning to do for ages ...'

'Visit Paddy and Joan's graves in Dumbleton churchyard,' Richard finished my sentence for me.

Paddy Fermor had died as recently as 2011 while Joan his wife had died eight years before that in their Kalamitsi villa. We felt it a fitting end to our May voyage that had first seen the light of day as an idea in their beloved Mani and indeed Paddy and Joan's names appear in the Introduction: a satisfying topping and tailing to our trip.

We set off heading east, back past 'Ashchurch for Tewkesbury' station, pressing on along the Evesham Road and via country lanes to Dumbleton. Parking near the church we entered the churchyard

through its smaller east gate and there by the path was a row of three gravestones side by side: Paddy, Joan and her brother, Henry, Viscount Monsell who had died in 1993. Beyond the church is Dumbleton Hall where Joan grew up, a hotel since 1959.

Joan's gravestone adds that she was Paddy's wife, and sister to the 2nd Viscount Monsell. Both her and Paddy's gravestones have a relief carving of a sprig of olive, Joan's with Kalamata olives. Below his name is a Greek quotation (of course) which can be translated '*he was that best of things, Hellenic*', a quotation from the Greek poet Constantine Cavafy. Perhaps modesty (or space) prevented the previous line being used: '*he was just, wise, courageous*'. On the back of the stone, compass points symbolise his travels. It was profoundly moving to see these three gravestones side by side in a quiet country churchyard, rooks cawing from the nearby trees. Seemed a good place to rest forever.

Time to go: standing in front of Paddy and Joan's graves we had a keen sense that the trip had come full circle. We had started thinking about it in the Mani in 2015, had visited Paddy and Joan Leigh Fermor's villa the following year and here we were, having made the pilgrimage to where they lie side by side. Reluctant to let our voyage end, we stood grinning like idiots, then we parted company amazed at how enjoyable the whole thing had been, even rowing in the rain, and how relaxing rowing down a river like the Severn had been. Firm in our minds and whatever happened to delay us, we would be back, the oars creaking in the rowlocks as soon as practicable and as commitments allowed, the French sun warm overhead and the shades of Hornblower with us in the boat.

# PART II

# THE RIVER LOIRE

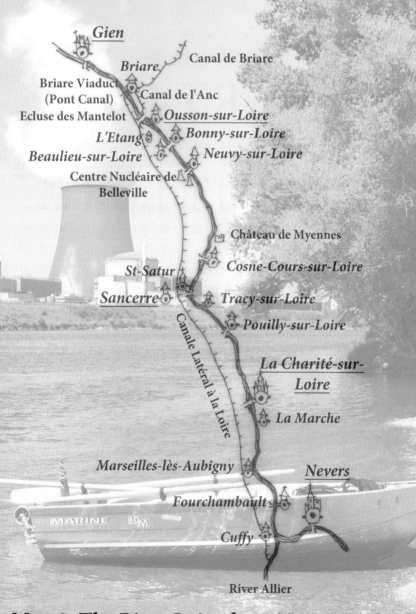

**Map 3: The River Loire from Nevers to Gien**

# 21

## To the Loire at Nevers, June 2017

In the Introduction Richard and I were hauling our boat, by then evocatively named *Flying Colours 70*, to the waters of the river Loire at Nevers to start our recreation of Captain Horatio Hornblower RN's 1811 escape down that mighty French river to the sea. Part I of the book took us in a different direction with the Loire postponed and our then unnamed boat voyaging down the River Severn from Wales to Deerhurst. In June 2017 the Loire was back 'on stream'.

We would follow in Hornblower's footsteps as far as possible downriver in the time available. While this would not be the first recreation of Hornblower's Loire voyage, we were undertaking it in a rowing boat as had our hero, rather than in a kayak, canoe or a boat with any form of power other than muscular. As far as we knew no-one had ever recreated the escape in a rowing boat. Even the fictional Hornblower in his more hazardous version of *Three Men in a Boat* made occasional use of sail.

Obviously, kayakers paddle the whole river, but in no way reproducing Hornblower's escape. We had not been sure it had been done in a powered boat either but, in early 2018, I corresponded with Ludwig Heuse of the C S Forester Society who had travelled down the Loire in a boat he had himself built, for most of the trip powered by an outboard motor. He did it in two stages, firstly from Nevers to

Beaugency beyond Orléans and then subsequently from Beaugency all the way to Nantes. Indeed, he sent me a photograph of him in his boat *Geneviève* rushing the many-arched bridge at Beaugency through turbulent water, one hand on the outboard motor casing, one on its tiller, Ludwig wearing a panama hat and pretty nonchalant in the rough water although it looked a pretty heavy boat for portages. We also knew from C S Forester's memoir, *The Voyage of the Annie Marble,* that he and his wife Kathleen had voyaged along the Loire, having joined it from the Canal d'Orléans in the summer of 1928, all the way to Nantes. There is a photograph in the book of the *Annie Marble* passing beneath Beaugency bridge, the waters smooth and deep, unlike when Ludwig rocketed through.

Nevers is a long way from Orléans but Forester presumably revisited the area and took a boat trip downstream in 1938 before the book was completed. The description of the first day on the river from 'Graçay' to Briare is an accurate representation of its character that could only have come from travelling by boat, apart from anomalies and errors that only added to the fun of our voyage (such as completely ignoring La Charité-sur-Loire). We also suspected that Forester got no further along the river than Briare or Gien as there is a surprisingly cursory coverage of the rest of Hornblower's voyage. As on the Severn we would be virtually the only rowing boat.

Richard and his wife, Vicky, had previously prospected the Loire above Nevers to work out where Hornblower had stolen the rowing boat on that snowy night of 19th December 1810 (the precise date, at least according to C Northcote Parkinson in his *The Life and Times of Horatio Hornblower*). In *Flying Colours*, the escape is said to have taken place four miles above Nevers. They found the likely spot but impossible for a launch, so we settled on Nevers with its convenient campsite next to the river.

In C S Forester's book, Hornblower's stolen rowing boat was dashed to pieces in rapids downstream of Nevers' bridge before the Loire met the Allier. He, Brown and Bush survived and overwintered with a sympathetic French count at his Château de Graçay, supposedly situated somewhere between the town and the Allier. It should be said that there are no near-river candidates for this château, let alone for the weir that destroyed the stolen boat.

A little more information came in Forester's further novel, *Lord Hornblower*, where in 1815 our hero revisited the Comte de Graçay and his sister Marie, who had been Hornblower's lover during their boat-building winter at the château. Hornblower headed south from Briare by coach with the Loire on his right and he and Brown looking across the river remarked on the confluence with the river Allier. After a few miles they reached the château which thus placed it on the Nevers bank of the Loire.

Richard and I would row, we hoped, in calmer waters and confident we would not be dashed to pieces somewhere between the town and the Allier. Our voyage would be in mid-June, some three months later in the year than Hornblower who, according to Northcote-Parkinson, commenced the voyage on 17th April 1811. Disappointingly, Northcote Parkinson devoted just over five lines to the voyage, evidently more interested in Hornblower's naval battles and voyages.

*****

As a footnote, after the Severn voyage, we registered the boat with the Small Ships Register in Cardiff, and having batted various names back and forth chose *Flying Colours 70.* This seemed quite neat, as the '70' was our ages in 2017 and 'Flying Colours' of course the title of the novel.

The previous day we and our boat had had a somewhat fraught journey from England. The problem had been getting past Paris, the Périphérique heavy with road works and diversions that seemed to take the whole of its traffic through hot, narrow-roaded and densely populated suburbs. We were eventually spat out somewhere north of Fontainebleau but after that all was plain sailing to Nevers, although we arrived amid ominous thunder and lightning.

The view north from the campsite, once we had taken possession of our cabin with its verandah (no roughing it in tents for us), was spectacular. St Cyr Cathedral's tall south-west tower and its flying-buttressed chevet dominates the city, clusters of grey slate-roofed stone houses climbing towards it from the river. To its right the towers and pinnacles of the old palace of the Dukes of Nevers peer above the trees, but then the architectural quality falls off sharply with 1960s intrusively dominant white-painted concrete buildings, including, somewhat ironically, the whopping eight storeys of the Maison de la Culture.

Unlike Hornblower whose boat had rushed the bridge at night, we were free to cross it and seek a well-earned supper. The old bridge had been rebuilt with fewer and wider arches so potentially less tricky rowing. Not so: peering over the parapets, it was clear that the boat could not get through the bridge and survive: sheet-piling on both sides all the way across and a fearsome array of rocks beyond, no doubt for sound riverine reasons but with water at lowish levels hazardous to say the least. Our chosen guide, Souchard's *La Loire Vue du Fleuve*, indicated the bridge's three arches nearest the town could be navigable but not so that evening.

The thunder and lightning pyrotechnics had moved on and the sun emerged as we left the bridge. The town did not impress the author of John Murray's 1844 *Hand-book for Travellers in France*, describing it as *'unprepossessing, dirty, but ancient'*: not a fitting modern description. Meandering through the narrow lanes and streets there were many old houses, even some 16th-century timber-framed and stone ones.

I had visited the cathedral with my wife Jill in 2010 on a grey and rainy day but this evening its mellow golden stonework glowed in warm evening sunshine. It seems a slightly disjointed building with the 170-foot Tour Bohier, completed in the 16th century, tucked into the angle of nave and transept: a splendid beacon for shipping. Most of the building is good 13th-century Gothic but it suffered considerable damage in 1944 when allied bombers aiming at nearby ironworks and railway yards bombed the choir by mistake. Superb modern stained-glass windows replaced shattered Victorian ones, using rich medieval colours to splash the interior stonework with vibrant patterns.

For us with our lifelong passion for Romanesque architecture the glory of the cathedral is the west end which has a fine, airy transept and great west apse raised above a crypt. They survive from a church dedicated in 1058 and I assume were retained out of respect for the shrines of St Cyr and his mother St Julitta in the crypt, everything

else being swept away in the 13th century. The apse has a magnificent Byzantine-influenced Christ in Majesty painted in its half-dome, surviving French Revolutionary desecration by being whitewashed.

There were large number of visitors, many in the crypt whose 11th-century stone vaults support the floor of the apse. Down here amid the white stonework and the limewashed walls is a staggeringly good and moving Christ's Entombment scene, 15th century and possibly from Flanders. All in stone, seven figures prepare Christ's body, including Nicodemus, Joseph of Arimathea and of course the Virgin Mary.

Outside we paid particular attention to the great 11th-century west end before moving on to the nearby Duke's palace, now an annexe to the Mairie. Referred to by Hornblower by its 18th-century name, the Gonzaga Palace, from the ducal family who owned it until 1810, its south front architecture is pure 'Châteaux of the Loire' style. Consequently, it is regarded as the most easterly of these great buildings, many of which we hoped to visit. It replaced a castle, the duke wanting more 16th-century comfort and fashion, but he retained a couple of 15th-century round towers at the rear. The best feature is one of those splendid stair towers where the windows climb with the spiral stairs: unsymmetrical notes struck in otherwise rigorously controlled designs. From the south front we looked across the palace's former parterres and terrace, towards the Loire and our campsite.

The other church I had hoped to visit was also Romanesque: St Etienne, well to the north-east of the palace. We headed there, part of the route along the Rue Saint-Martin, a gently curving road flanked by the fine stone houses of prosperous 18th-century citizens and with a spectacularly fruity 1630s Baroque church at its heart, the Chapel of St Mary, a remnant of the Monastery of the Visitation (of the Virgin Mary).

When we reached St Etienne it was unsurprisingly closed. Built between about 1080 and 1097 it is contemporary with many fine Norman churches in England. The Count of Nevers, as he then was, had granted it for the good of his soul to the mighty Cluny Abbey in Burgundy. In a mellow golden stone, it follows the 'Benedictine' plan perfected at Cluny: the east arm has a semicircular aisle or ambulatory passing behind the high altar as a continuation of the choir aisles so the monks could worship without disturbance from pilgrims. It is on one of the great medieval pilgrimage routes to Santiago de Compostela in Spain, so the city would have seen thousands upon thousands of pilgrims pass through its gates.

The church looked pretty heavily restored, and if the two west towers and the central tower look a bit underpowered it is because upper storeys and spires were demolished during the French Revolution. Now hungry, we sought out a restaurant. One seemed promising: named La Cour Saint Etienne. Shown into the garden at the rear, the west front of the church towered above us, bathed in late evening. What a location for supper! After chicken and goat's cheese salads, our hostess was delighted to report that she had made an English apple crumble. We couldn't resist. Before daylight finally faded we headed to the western part of the old city where medieval city walls and two gatehouses survive. We passed through the city's great west gate, the Porte des Croux, which dates from 1393 but was heavily restored after 1944 bomb damage and pristine, unlike when described in Murray's guide as '*black with age and dirt*'. The other archway nearby is a Roman-style triumphal arch erected after the Battle of Fontenoy in 1746: a briefer entry in Murray as it was a French victory over British, Dutch and Hanoverian troops. We continued south towards the river along the self-explanatory Promenade des Remparts, a path in a linear park with the 14th-century city walls alongside. Back across the river we sat on our verandah with a bottle of wine to chew over the day.

# 22

# No Château de Graçay
# and on to the Iron Town
# of Fourchambault

The next day, as described in the Introduction, we rowed away from Nevers, some three months later in the year than Hornblower's apple orchards in full blossom. We thought it more likely that C S Forester voyaged downriver in June when water levels are lower and running aground more frequent than in April. Forester's nettle-infested islands would be an all too accurate observation for June, as we discovered with islets and riverbanks heavily and virulently nettled to snare the unwary.

However, there was one unsettling issue at the back of our minds: Hornblower had rowed from the Château de Graçay to an islet beyond Briare in one day (actually Gien in Forester's mind) where they camped. This would have given Hornblower an epic first day's rowing of sixty-five or even seventy miles. A suspicion crossed our minds that to do such a distance in a day would have required engine power: an impossible day's work with Hornblower's frequent groundings and portages consuming time and straining their every sinew manhandling a much heavier boat.

I have to admit such thoughts were not in the forefront of my mind as we rowed off into a wide and wind-ruffled river, the easterly

sun running across the caps of the ripples, the cloud ahead thinning with patches of blue sky emerging. Through the railway bridge we turned the boat to look back at Nevers and its two bridges, safe beyond the bankside gathering of French officialdom. According to a plaque the 1850 railway bridge's ironwork came from the foundries of Fourchambault, the first town we would reach after Nevers. Still in use, the bridge is elegant with latticework metal spandrels to the arches, all carried on robust stone piers.

Just past the bridge and moored off the north bank we saw our first Loire sailing barge. Black-painted and with a shallow draught, a near flat bottom and a single tall mast, these boats were for centuries the workhorses of the Loire trade. They varied in size, of course, either the larger *gabare* or the smaller *toue*, and were sometimes linked together as 'trains', all barges having a large, single white or reddish sail. There are plenty of these boats as well as the smaller ten-metre-long punt, the *fûtreau*, also with a sail and mast, moored or tied up along the riverbanks, presumably a fraction of 1811 numbers. Forester assumed there was very limited river traffic then, stating that lateral canals carried most of the trade, an essential element in his claim that the river was quiet and suitable for Hornblower's purposes. Unfortunately for Forester, the Canal Latéral à la Loire, parallel to the river all the way to Briare, opened only in 1838: a quarter of a century after Hornblower's voyage. We suspected that there would of necessity have been heavy commercial traffic on the Loire above Briare due to the Royal Navy's highly effective blockade strangling both coastal and long-distance shipping. Nowadays, traffic actually is minimal and the river as quiet for us as purportedly for Hornblower.

The river headed south-west, theoretically wider than the Severn of our previous voyage but effectively narrowed and diverted and sandbanked by islets, banks and deep beaches. Richard guided me through with care, hoping to avoid grounding or other mishaps. Hornblower had found selecting a navigable channel no easy task in *Flying Colours* and it was no surprise that we grounded alongside one of these sandbank islands, still with the tower of St Cyr Cathedral in sight. I had previously checked Souchard's Loire guide and there were only two islands marked on its map between Nevers and the confluence with the Allier. Clearly, the islands marked were schematic tokens, the river continually shifting its gravel and silt to make new islands and wash away the old.

We looked along the right bank for the Château de Graçay or a building that could have served for its riverside location if not its architecture. Nothing doing, as we really already knew, and nor were there any weirs like the one that had wrecked Hornblower that winter night. All was tranquil, the clouds thinner and higher, the peace disturbed only by barking of a succession of dogs sent wild by the sound of our creaking rowlocks.

It was also noticeable that there were no insects out on the river: something of a relief, perhaps a result of the numerous wheeling sand martins hunting insects on the riverbanks and islets. The main river was the preserve of terns, many flying alongside us, beaks full of small fish. We also saw the first of many heron, this one standing tall and dignified on a narrow sandy islet, terns at the other end of the spit as though deferring to a more powerful hunter.

Round a long bend the river turned westwards and we eventually lost sight of the cathedral. We did not ground again and, nearing the Allier, waved to a fisherman on the riverbank. His lively Dobermann was, to his evident irritation, running excitedly in and out of the water disturbing the very fish he was trying to catch. The north bank was heavily overgrown with willow and alder scrub where there was no riverside woodland (and no sign of châteaux). Richard pointed beyond me and I glanced behind to see what looked like a sandbank across the whole river. He thought it was the Allier, Hornblower noting a great increase in water where the rivers met. I was looking forward to resting on my oars while Richard steered a faster, fuller river but I was a bit sceptical due to the number, size and meandering nature of the huge sandbanks and beaches ahead. Much silt and shingle had been deposited where the two river flows met, forming a very substantial sandbank island, so picking our way past the Allier confluence was challenging as we began to turn our boat northwards.

Oddly, the Loire looked narrower as we rounded the bend at the Allier confluence. To our left the stone houses and cottages of Cuffy village, wisely set well back from the riverbank beyond a long scrubby meadow, peered nervously towards the river from behind great flood embankments. A quick glance at the map in our Souchard guide showed a wider channel and a narrower, curving one to its west skirting a substantial island occupying the centre of the river, the island even named on our IGN 1:100000 map as the Iles de Marzy. In reality it turned out to be exactly the other way around, the combined rivers following the narrower and curving westerly channel. We supposed that the more powerful current of the Loire had stifled the Allier, absorbing and shoving its contribution west, the wider channel now a mass of water-deprived sandy silt.

However, trusting in C S Forester's description I shipped oars hoping that the boat would cruise merrily along in the narrower western channel, guided solely by the steering oar. Well, it was pretty disappointing for we made little progress and it seemed evident that, despite a profusion of islands, sandbanks and ridges narrowing the main stream, the Allier's waters made little difference. On the other hand, it was almost an hour before we next ran aground so perhaps there was some increase in water volume. We may have been a long musket shot from land, not that it mattered in 2017, but everything was as Forester described it with an extensive no man's land of sand and willow flanking the riverbanks. Hornblower dwelt on the difficulty of steering a course with the gravel shelving and rearing into ridges under the boat without warning and upon which it would get stuck fast: again, more likely in summer than spring.

Overhead, buzzards wheeled effortlessly, while heron flapped along the banks, businesslike but not nearly as elegant. Many of the islets had lines of snowy white egrets and crows contemplating the river. Opposite the village of Courcelles the boat grounded again for we chose the wrong line through the tangle of sandy islets and deceptive channels. As Richard climbed out to free it into deeper water a kayak swept by in the correct and deeper channel, we exchanged slightly red-faced greetings. Round the next gentle bend, we saw Fourchambault

Bridge, a steel one of 1950 painted a jaunty sky blue. It replaced a fine six-span suspension bridge of 1836 dynamited in World War II by the retreating French army, hoping to form a defensive line along the Loire. For five years there had been no bridge, merely the ruined suspension bridge's stone piers sitting forlornly in the river, until the present more utilitarian trussed girder one was built, carried by these old piers.

Through the bridge's second span that appeared to have a better water flow we crossed towards sandbanks and shingle spits to beach near the third arch. Jumping out we used our anchor to hold the boat on the sand, still some 200 yards from the willow-lined riverbank. Halfway across the gravelly mud and sand we climbed a bare ridge or levée. Admittedly, it only rose about a metre and a half above scrub, weed and grass-tangled beaches but ran from the bridge diagonally through the sand and shingle for about 300 yards to end with its feet in the river. We rather assumed this might have been something to do with the 1830s Canal Latéral à la Loire which had a spur joining the river via a lock not far downstream. Or perhaps it was a breakwater protecting the town's quays after vast ironworks had been established in the early 1820s.

The riverbank to our north was named Quai de Loire and the ironworks had run alongside and behind it. In the 19th century the quays would have been alive with barges unloading coal and iron ore for the furnaces, with the finished products lowered into empty barges: a very different picture from today's tranquillity. Reaching the river embankment, we scrambled up to where a riverside walk amid trees stretched away in both directions. Sitting briefly on a bench before setting off into town, me wearing my wafer-thin-soled neoprene boat shoes, visions of leafy squares and outside tables at cafés rose alluringly to our minds' eye.

*****

Fourchambault rarely gets more than a few words in guidebooks and is certainly not one of the gems among towns along the Loire. It was little more than a village by a watermill until industry arrived, some of which remains, including a Renault lorry factory. Didn't sound a winner but the tree-shaded riverbank promenade seemed promising. Reaching the road bridge, we turned towards the town, on our left young people doing various vigorous and earnest forms of exercise in the Stade Municipal. Through the town's suburbs, a mix of late 18th and 19th-century houses lining the road, modern suburbs to the south, we turned left into its main street, the Rue Gambetta, a sign indicating that the Hôtel de Ville was somewhere on this long road and in the distance was a church spire. The centre was pretty dispiriting: a meagre 19th-century Neo-Romanesque church and the Hôtel de Ville set in a soulless miniature 'square': merely car-parking spaces indented from the road frontage. All shops seemed closed and the couple of open bars looked uninviting.

Time for a rethink: near the church was a mini supermarket. We ended up buying an unappealing-looking emulsion-like pâté de Sancerre, a town we wished to visit further downstream, packet croissants, hard tomatoes and cans of lager. Clutching our goodies and avoiding eye contact with various idling groups of youths, we headed back to the riverbank. I took the opportunity to remove my boat shoes and give my feet a chance to recover from their pavement pounding. We were disconcerted to see that the lager was not a light Dutch version of a Peroni but a power-packing 8.6 per cent 'heavy-brew': an instant headache for me and by the time we landed at La Charité-sur-Loire my head was thumping.

Richard told me as we munched discontentedly that the ironworks had been founded by a Jean Louis Boigues using ironworkers recruited

from Britain, smelting with coke rather than charcoal. Most of this expertise came from Wales via Merthyr Tydfil's Cyfarthfa ironworks, their process known in France as the 'English method', doubtless to Welsh annoyance. Sadly, there seemed no direct connection with Coalbrookdale on the Severn, although William, a brother of that great Shropshire ironmaster, John Wilkinson, contributed to setting up the Le Creusôt works. So, who knows, he might also have advised Boigues. Murray's 1844 guide notes there were *'extensive iron furnaces and forges, perhaps the largest in France, where the iron conservatories of the Jardin des plantes (Paris) … the framework for the roof of Chartres Cathedral … were cast'* and *'they employ between two and three thousand men'*. Nowadays, the town is unlikely to attract more than the most accidental tourist.

It occurred to us that Fourchambault had gone the way of much of the once-industrial Severn gorge, where the riverbanks are nowadays serene and unruffled by the polluting bustle of industry with forests of foundry chimneys belching fumes and sulphurous pollution.

# 23

# La Charité-sur-Loire, la Fille Ainée de Cluny

Clearing our lunch remnants into a nearby waste bin and recrossing the sand and shingle ridges to the boat, we cast off at two in the afternoon, Richard at the oars. Passing the lock gates to the Canal Latéral's spur branch, the riverside road was carried high across the lock on an elegant stone bridge. We suspected this spur was little used, for below the lock gates it was virtually blocked by a river-deposited sandbank. On the opposite or Fourchambault bank was a rather elegant brick factory chimney, visible from the river in a presumably deliberate gap in the riverside trees. It may be all that remains of the vast Boigues ironworks.

The next stretch of river had a striking number of heron, terns and egrets, mostly contentedly squatting on sandbanks and islets in the afternoon heat. After forty-five minutes we ran aground again; a sandbank having reared up towards the river surface. This time I got out of the boat, for as navigator I had to rectify what Richard rather unkindly termed an 'error of judgement'. Clambering inelegantly back in, we were off downriver. It widened as we rowed on and a bright green dragonfly sat on Richard's shoulder for some time while a dipper flew busily alongside the riverbank, occasionally disappearing beneath the surface to root out tasty morsels amid the stones. Clouds built up and rain came but spluttered to an end after a mere ten minutes, but it remained overcast, hot and humid as we rounded a bend to pass Marseilles-lès-Aubigny, a riverside village that became a river port when the Canal Latéral arrived in the 1820s. The canal could not be seen from our lowly river position but there were numerous Loire-style traditional sailing barges moored along the village's riverfront.

Ahead as the river bore north we could see the dramatic effects of the river in winter spate with wrecked barges hanging precariously from the steep banks and massive washed-away trees littering the shoreline. We swapped roles and I took the oars as far as La Charité-sur-Loire, our intended stop for  the night. Soon afterwards we saw children swimming from a sandy beach, their mothers gossiping under parasols. This set us thinking and a dip in the river seemed alluring, although our swimming shorts were inaccessible in the bottom of our packs. Richard pursued the swimming idea with enthusiasm. 'Not to worry: there's nobody about and we'll land on an island for a swim.' I knew what that meant for Richard has a somewhat disconcerting propensity for 'skinny-dipping' wherever he sees an attractive stretch of water or indeed seashore. So north-west of Tronsanges we beached on an islet, stripped off and sunk into the refreshing water, accompanied by disapproving rumbles of thunder from the heavens. Pulling our clothes back on I rowed on, much cooler I must admit as the sun emerged at last.

We passed the village of La Marche, more important than La Charité before the latter's priory arrived in 1059. La Marche became a backwater, its castle largely demolished under pressure from the prior,

his power enhanced through possessing the right hand of St Savin and the metaphorical ear of popes and bishops: Adam, Count of La Marche, had no chance.

By now thoroughly convinced that Hornblower had not rowed sixty miles in his first day, round the next bend, La Charité-sur-Loire started to come into view, partially obscured by trees on the right bank, the bridge looking pretty odd, as though constructed of blue-green steel sheets. It turned out we were not seeing the bridge at all. Undergoing restoration, its stone structure was hidden beneath cheerful plastic sheeting. Looking to tie up we headed for the island opposite the town where a number of boats were moored and nosed between the boats, landing at half past six, well satisfied with twenty miles rowed.

\*\*\*\*\*

The rather beautiful town of La Charité-sur-Loire and its river bridge gets no mention at all in Forester's *Flying Colours*, the first downstream bridge mentioned by Hornblower was at Briare (actually Forester meant Gien). Accordingly, while our stopover town is not in the book, we were going to make the most of it. I had learned about the Romanesque priory at La Charité-sur-Loire as a postgraduate student at the Courtauld Institute of Art in the late 1960s and early 1970s and was looking forward to seeing the great medieval church in the flesh. It is situated on one of the four main pilgrimage routes to Santiago de Compostela, this particular one starting from Vézelay. Indeed, La Charité was one of the most important monastic churches in medieval Christendom, second only to its founder, Cluny.

Emerging from the boat on the island of Le Faubourg, its name nailing its medieval status as a suburb, our priority was to find a bed for the night. We followed a footpath between walls leading to the bank of the western arm of the Loire, thanks to a weir and a long dyke now very much a backwater. Archaeologists think this was the original course of the river until the 13th century, the island connected to the town by a causeway through marshes and sandbanks. Near the modern bridge across the old river course we found our bed for the night at Le Bon Laboureur. We got the last remaining room, saving us a trek into town to seek another hotel.

An omelette paysanne consumed, a beer drunk, my headache receded and we set off to walk over the bridge into town, noticing halfway up the ground floors of various buildings flood marks for very high floods in 1836, 1846 (the highest) and 1866. Quite astonishing, and we tried to visualise how traumatic and damaging three such floods in three decades would have been, the whole island under water. Because of the scaffolding and screens we could see little of either the bridge or the river until we got to the La Charité bank. I must say it looked a tricky dash through in the boat. Souchard's guide shows the third arch from the La Charité bank as a route through. Richard sucked his teeth a bit for the water was rushing through in a foam-topped torrent. No other arches would suffice with their rocky downstream hinterlands and very shallow choppy approaches beneath the bridge itself.

Old prints show the 17th-century bridge with a gatehouse halfway across, removed in 1738 when three arches were rebuilt. During World War II the bridge suffered partial destruction both at the hands of a retreating French army in 1940 and retreating Germans in 1944. The bridge across the old river, west of Le Faubourg, just to complete the story, had a succession of bridges, including one destroyed by floods in 1789, the current concrete one dating from the 1950s.

It was now nearly 9.00pm but the sun was still out, bathing the upper parts of many buildings in a warm, late-evening glow. We set out to see as much of the exterior of the abbey as possible before darkness closed in. I suppose I must have known that the church was somewhat truncated but it was still a shock to see how much of the nave has gone. The great west doorway led into an open courtyard with the remains of the nave arcades as its north wall, saved no doubt by finding a new life as front walls to houses. All did not look well, with timber raking shores and stone buttresses to two of the blocked nave arches, the highly enriched triforium arcade teetering above.

Looking back towards the river, the far west bay of the nave and the great north-west tower remain intact along with the west front's ground-floor elevation. All this reminded me of 18th-century lithographs of decaying great churches or mansions as warrens of housing, crowded with colourful locals. Was this a demolition following the French Revolution, we wondered. Well, not in La Charité's case: the destruction followed a disastrous fire that swept through the town in 1559 taking out most of the nave, the choir vaults, the priory buildings and over 200 houses in the town. It was not until 1695 that the four east bays of the nave were rebuilt, the six western ones left ruinous. In survival terms the priory fared better than its mother church, Cluny in Burgundy, where merely a south transept remains of the second most important church of Western Christendom after St Peter's Rome.

Only fragments of La Charité's monastic buildings survive in which over 200 monks served God and their prior. Murray gives a glimpse of the scale of the prior's secular power and influence for '*in the 16th century the pope found it necessary to interfere and regulate the number of knights who should form their* (the prior's) *escort*'. By half past nine the sun had sunk to the horizon, dusk overwhelmed us and we left our musings about the priory church to head back across the river to our hotel.

*****

Over excellent breakfast croissants and coffee in our hotel, seasoned with further chat from our somewhat flamboyant patron, Richard confessed that while I snored contentedly full of good wine he had lain awake worrying and planning the route through the bridge's only navigable but turbulently watered arch. This plan apparently involved rowing hard across the river, aiming upstream to avoid being dragged perilously towards the bridge by the current, turning at an appropriate moment into the narrow channel beneath the third arch. In this scenario I would row so our skilful skipper could direct operations.

That excitement would have to wait, as we wanted to visit the priory and the town on what was now a bright and sunny day. Our voluble patron was happy for us to leave our packs at the hotel and we set off. Many of the houses and shops in Le Faubourg seemed shuttered, closed or in need of repair, large satellite dishes attached to dormers being in some cases the only indication of occupation behind faded paintwork and general decay. The route beneath the bridge still looked tight and it extended a further narrow rock-girt twenty metres beyond the bridge, at the far end of which a fisherman stood nonchalantly on the rocks. Downstream, islets, shoals and white water coursed over numerous rocks.

All that could wait, and we continued up to the priory. Looking at its sadly diminished grandeur, it was difficult to imagine that it had briefly been the largest church in the whole of Western Christendom until Cluny itself was rebuilt on an even grander scale after 1088. La Charité remained second largest for some years and in 1107 it rebuilt its east arm copying the new Cluny Abbey. Perhaps wisely Prior Odo

drew back from out-scaling Cluny, then still under construction, but did secure Pope Pascal II, a former Cluniac monk, to consecrate the new work. Inside, the soaring elevations with their narrow bays create a magnificent sense of scale, the attached columns between the bays continuing as arches across the stone vaults emphasise this rhythm. The masons used a pale limestone but there are areas green with mould marring the upper parts of the south transept, doubtless caused by long-term roof leaks.

Not surprisingly in a building with a chequered history of destruction and fire there are numerous repairs as well as blocked openings and complete renewals, but as the Michelin guide puts it, 'malgré ses blessures': it is a building of great historic significance. There are other interesting features to see such as a blocked doorway in the south transept with a superb carved tympanum in the arch above the lintel, with a Christ in Majesty and numerous finely carved figures, all lively twisting shapes and swirling drapery. Outside there are enough Romanesque arches and blank arcades to satisfy even the most demanding. To the east under a protective modern roof are the recently excavated remains of the predecessor priory. Astonishingly, traces of original paint on the long-buried walls representing masonry blocks survive but, as usual in medieval churches, unrelated to the actual joints of the stone beneath the limewash. It was now nearly ten o'clock and we felt we needed to be back on the river and, as we crossed the bridge, Richard took another quick glance at its third arch, muttering and nodding to himself.

# 24

# The Wine Country of Sancerre

Bags retrieved, we headed to the boat to disentangle our ropes from adjoining ones and set off, Richard keen to implement his plan for running the bridge. At his Hornblower-style command I rowed like fury across the river but the going was easier than Richard had expected and surprisingly soon we were in position. I turned the boat towards the third arch from the town and after a few strokes was ordered to ship oars. We shot through, the boat buffeted from edge to edge in the swirling waters. We swept past the startled fisherman on his rock into somewhat calmer, rock-strewn water.

Clouds of deep blue damselflies were out on the water or landing on our boat and we were now rowing through the Réserve Naturelle

Val de Loire, designated in 1995. A leaflet picked up in La Charité informed us it ran from the town north as far as Tracy-sur-Loire, 12.5 miles downstream along both banks and extending for varying distances inland. The map marks beaches and various vegetation types. Photographs were as one would expect: a pair of contented-looking natterjack toads copulating (how very French), beaver damage to trees (they have recently been reintroduced) and nesting terns.

At one point at Mouron about a mile from La Charité a rather grim Victorian château loomed, remarkably in Scottish Baronial style. A towering cedar of Lebanon tree, immediately to its north, was probably planted in the 1840s when the château had been built. It and the trees reflected in the dark, glassy waters ahead, the mirror image frequently ruffled by intermittent breezes. Now a hospital for young people, we hoped it was a welcoming place despite rather forbidding grey walls, crow-step gables and battlemented turrets.

Ahead of us a school canoe camping party in kayaks pulled their kayaks up onto the beach and sprinted up and down, splashing around in the shallows. Looked great fun. We decided to land and beached on the opposite bank but our legs sank into glutinous mud, a surface crust of small stones masking its treachery. Clouds of flies sprang from the ooze, so we relaunched to cross the river and beach upstream of the children. They, their teachers and kayaks moved off downstream, laughing and splashing each other with their paddles: made us feel rather old, I must say.

It was certainly a much firmer island, this Ile du Lac. We were on the southernmost tip of the island and between us and dry land a narrow channel created the island. At this time of year there were areas where you could walk across to the 'mainland', your feet barely wet. Just beyond the tip of the island a single small willow had its

feet in the water acting as a natural cutwater. While Richard busied himself with the boat, I was struck by the number of butterflies both flying and basking, including red admirals and purple emperors, the latter an exciting find in England but less so in France. Relaunching with Richard at the oars I looked forward to leaning on the stern transom and daydreaming, the occasional course correction given to the labouring crew. We coasted past a long islet where there were hundreds of rooks lining the water's edge and darkening the trees, secure in the knowledge that they were in a nature reserve. In gazing at them I took my eye off the steering ball and grounded the boat, as Richard rather forcefully pointed out.

Approaching Pouilly-sur-Loire village we deliberately ran onto a shingly beach on the opposite or west bank. We could see the road bridge over the river and the broach spire of the parish church. It was very hot, well over thirty degrees, and a swim cooled us off. Back in the boat, I pushed off the shingle with the steering oar, the displeased crew pointing out somewhat acerbically that I would fray the oar blade. Weathering this, we headed under the road bridge and beached beside it, on the Pouilly bank.

*****

Out of the boat we looked at the bridge: a lattice-girder type carried on seven stone piers, similar to many others across the Loire and dating from 1902, it gave access into the heart of the Pouilly-Fumé vineyards around Pouilly (the clue was in the name but we only put two and two together after leaving the boat). Landing to see the tablet on the bridge marking the halfway point of the Loire, we found it easily enough on the Pouilly bank abutment wall. Cut into the stonework and picked out in red, it informed passers-by that it was 496 kilometres from the source and 496 kilometres to the mouth or embouchure, a total of 992 kilometres. A rough calculation showed we had rowed about twenty-six miles to reach this point. We took comfort from the fact that we were merely emulating Hornblower's route, but that still left a little over 300 miles to row.

Back afloat I took the oars but we had left the main channel to land at Pouilly so were soon out of the boat to haul it through a 'channel' across the sandbanks where water trickled, an inch deep in places. Back in the main river which had more sensibly passed beneath the westernmost span of the bridge, we ran aground again before landing for another swim. Richard steered us onto a substantial spit cum beach upstream of Tracy-sur-Loire and once again cool and refreshed we relaunched. This stretch of river meanders amid innumerable sandbanks, islets and spits: amazingly, only a single further grounding. We had intermittently seen the hill upon which Sancerre sits, surrounded by its vineyards, and had decided we would land at the next bridge and seek accommodation by the river or up in Sancerre. I knew the town from a previous stay with my wife as a fine historic hill town with long views over distant hills.

It was only a mile and a half and what could possibly go wrong? Four kayakers overtook us, engrossed in playing splashing games with their paddles, their laughter echoing across the water. I looked right and saw a very long freight train flickering amid the trees on a railway line running close to the riverbank, the train double-headed with powerful-looking locomotives and the wagons besmirched by as much graffiti and 'tags' as any New York subway train.

Beyond Tracy-sur-Loire, another village with a broach spire to its parish church, the still-shallow river bore north and widened, the riverbanks pockmarked by the dark tunnel entrances to the nests of sociable sand martins. The St-Thibault road bridge came into view, clearly modern with concrete shallow-arched spans and piers: very much post-Hornblower. Opened in 1966, it replaced another suspension bridge that had been destroyed in August 1944 by the French 2nd Parachute Regiment, the Free French SAS. They landed in ten gliders, each with a machine-gun-armed jeep and they and the local French Resistance blew up the bridge to impede the German retreat from southern France.

Our trusty Souchard kayak guide indicated we should land upstream of the bridge, just beyond a large island. All well and good but St-Thibault's beach above the bridge is now protected by a miniature Great Barrier Reef of rocks and shallow rock-strewn water. We could see turbulent white water and rocks protruding menacingly from the water. I steered for what looked to be a reasonable crossing of the barrier but hit rocks just below the surface with an almighty clanging and grinding: we stuck fast with an eighteen-inch drop the other side.

The metallic noises had drawn the attention of people on the riverbank, in particular a large family picnicking. We rocked the boat frantically and, amazingly, managed to get free, then I set Richard rowing against the current upstream and we repositioned for another crack at getting through to the beach. This time I chose a better route, although to be honest it did not look much different. We crashed over the rocky dam, dropped into the water beyond and shot onto the beach. The audience turned away disappointed but perked up when a couple of kayaks also tried to land here and similarly stuck fast on the rocky barrier. A shared embarrassment that also indicated that when their and our kayak guides were written it was an easy paddle (or row) to the beach.

We beached some thirty metres from the actual riverbank at about half past five, having rowed fourteen miles in the day. I sat near the boat while Richard walked to a hotel we had spotted near the bridge. He returned to say that the Hôtel de la Loire was full but the owner had been helpful, telephoning and booking a hotel up the hill in Sancerre, organising a taxi for us in an hour and a cold beer in the café opposite.

The boat was rather prominent on the beach so we hauled it across to the bank, ran it into waterside rushes and grasses and tied up. From the crest of the riverbank we could barely see the boat. At the café beers appeared from the fridge and they vanished very quickly. A second beer went the same way, as we eased into a contented torpor until the taxi arrived.

*****

Our taxi crossed the Canal Latéral and wove through the town of St-Satur and, looking out of its windows, we were surprised to see a towering but truncated Gothic church, basically the choir with huge clerestory window openings and the crossing east arch blocked with later stonework: no sign of crossing, transepts or nave. This was the substantial remnant of the former Augustinian Abbey of St-Satur, its lower fringe of choir ambulatory chapels also surviving.

It was an unlucky abbey, despite having obtained relics of St Satur, a third century Christian martyr from Carthage. The surviving choir is the substantial Gothic remnant of an ambitious rebuild that followed an earlier church's destruction by English armies led by the Black Prince. A rebuild started in 1367 but funds ran low, despite the miracles no doubt wrought by St Satur's relics. Only an ambitious choir had been completed before the English arrived again in 1420. This time they plundered and also shockingly threw over forty of the monks into the Loire to drown. Desultory repairs and rebuilding took place until in 1567 during the Wars of Religion the Protestants of Sancerre descended from their hill town and all but destroyed the hapless abbey. It revived and limped on until final suppression a few years before the French Revolution.

Beyond it we passed beneath an old 1890s railway viaduct that curves strikingly across the valley in which St-Satur sits. The taxi driver told us it is now for cars; the railway having long gone. The taxi climbed to Sancerre, and our hotel, Le Panoramique, looked north-west across vineyards and from our room they draped rolling hills and valley sides as far as the eye could see. Behind a very blue swimming pool on the terrace below a prominent sign read '*Clos La Demoiselle*' with a suitably demure statue of a maiden beside it. This blatant bit of advertising is by one of the main Sancerre wine producers, Alphonse Mellot, most of whose vines are south-west of the town and out of sight. Advertising his wines worked: dining later in the hotel, we ordered a bottle of La Demoiselle.

At about a quarter to seven we left the hotel to look at the town which has some quite steep, winding and picturesque narrow streets. In the centre is a sloping square with tables for the cafés that surround it. In this restaurant-centre of town, everything was quiet and we could only get a beer before moving on. From the rampart road a spectacular view opened out east and north-east across the Loire Valley, St-Satur Abbey dwarfed by two gigantic concrete grain silos on the banks of the Canal Latéral of a type Le Corbusier praised in the 1920s.

Sancerre had once had a mighty castle and town walls but in the 1570s during the Wars of Religion the town was besieged by the King's Catholic forces. The defenders were reduced to eating rats, leather and an ersatz bread composed of ingredients including ground slate, presumably to simulate flour, and chopped straw. Unsurprisingly, there were reports of cannibalism. We ended up eating in the solemn and reverent cathedral-hush of the hotel dining room attended by waiters of the dusty old school, but we did at least have the bottle of La Demoiselle and raised a glass to her image beyond the swimming pool.

# 25

# Portage and an Involuntary Dip at Ousson-sur-Loire

Breakfasting looking across the vineyards from our eyrie in the hotel dining room, the clarity of the early morning sunlight was striking and I felt I could make out every leaf as a pruning tractor moved slowly amid the vines. The sky was very blue with wispy cloud and criss-crossed by vapour trails. Following significant inroads into bowls of fresh figs and apricots, and after a final cup of coffee we packed. Downhill in the taxi booked by the hotel, under the great sweeping railway viaduct, through the town, again with glimpses of St-Satur Abbey, we were deposited in St-Thibault. The boat, however, was now much more visible from the riverbank as the recent rain had raised the river level sufficiently to float it out from the bankside reeds and bushes. It was now riding at the full stretch of the painter which, fortunately, Richard had secured to a scrubby tree trunk.

We scrambled down the bank and hauled the boat to shore, loaded our bags and cast off, hoping the fuller river would help us across the rock-scattered riverbed by the shore. Richard rowed us out, the keel scraping over a rocky obstacle course, reaching open water relatively unscathed. We swept through the bridge, the 18th and 19th-century houses of St-Thibault sun-bright and contented. Almost immediately we passed canal lock gates for a very short spur from the Canal Latéral. A campsite had several Loire sailing barges moored alongside, mainly *fûtreaux*, their masts attractively octagonal in section, splaying to square at the lower ends.

We hoped there would be more current and perhaps a day of lounging back, oars shipped and the occasional slight course adjustment from the steering oar. This worked for a couple of hundred yards or so, but the wind got up, blowing from the north-north-east along the river and the boat stopped dead, the current completely negated. With a sigh Richard took up the oars and we had to row all day with only very brief moments on the steering oar. Many trees were lying in the river and we had to steer around them. They either lurked below the surface or had a few branches poking above the surface to provide useful perches for terns, heron, cormorants, rooks or gulls. We assumed these trees were remnants of winter storms, though which winter would be difficult to say.

Behind us we could see Sancerre perched on its hill but surprisingly from this direction it peered from above heavily wooded slopes. Not so odd when we thought about it for the vineyards would of course be on its southern and western slopes, facing the sun. As we passed Les Vignes Sainte-Brigitte strange noises echoed from the village's grassy riverbank slopes. We thought they must be ducks but it dawned on me that they were frogs and making a deuce of a racket. After that numerous noisy frogs croaked at us along the riverbanks as we rowed past.

We rowed on and the next Loire bridge came into sight, a steel lattice-girder type with the usual stone piers supporting it. Built in the 1890s for a now-closed railway line, it is one of many Cyclorail lines you find all over France, using old tracks along which people pedal a rail car, side by side. I've cyclo-railed on a few myself: it's fun but on long, slow inclines it can be sinew and lung-bursting. What struck us about this bridge, though, was the prodigious amount of river-borne detritus trapped against the stone piers amid scrubby bushes and reeds around their plinths, much at least three metres above current water level: an insight into winter river levels.

Through this long bridge, ahead we saw the next town, also with a river bridge: Cosne-Cours-sur-Loire. Distracted by four heron immobile on a sandbank in the middle of the river, we hit a large rock that just broke the surface and ground our way across. The heron and egrets were put to flight by either the graunching of the boat or Richard's fruity oaths directed at the helmsman.

Back in control, it appears that Cosne-Cours-sur-Loire was yet another town severely damaged by World War II, its strategic river bridge having been destroyed, along with much of the town. Looking from the boat it is difficult now to picture a substantial medieval walled town with a castle, but it had revived in the 19th century with iron and steel foundries producing cutlery and files: Sheffield on the Loire but smaller.

A suspension bridge was first built in 1833 but photographs seem to be of a later one with curious stone cable towers with curved crests over which the cables crossed, an unlikely design for the 1830s: more like the 1890s. However, destroyed in 1940, it was not fully replaced until 1959 by the current one with its elegant concrete cable towers and utilising two of the old bridge's stone-built piers.

We did not land but swept through the bridge, the Cosne bank lined with pleached lime trees like neat lollipops, trim houses beyond the riverside road on its grassy embankment, a couple of Loire barges moored, sails furled. Richard rowed on, the river tending north-north-west and after a while we passed the 17th-century Château de Myennes at l'Île de Saulois, its two towers topped by slate-roofed cones.

At La Celle-sur-Loire we swapped seats and I took the oars, two cooling towers soon appearing. These belong to the Centre Nucléaire de Belleville, built in the 1980s and drawing its prodigious water needs from the river. Today only one cooling  tower had steam and to our surprise it was rising vertically, bearing in mind the strong headwinds at river level in which I struggled to make headway. At about 200 feet the steam clouds executed a ninety-degree angle to head near-horizontally towards us, sufficiently high to cast the vertical column of steam into its shade: quite a striking effect. Indeed, so powerful was the headwind that the boat was again blown upstream and I had to up my stroke rate considerably. Near la Baubutaine we beached to relieve ourselves of too many cups of breakfast coffee and I photographed a Peacock butterfly sunning itself on the muddy shingle.

Back in the boat, Richard took the oars and we passed Les Grands Ormes where the outfall of La Juddle, a curiously named stream, is controlled by three sluice gates. There seemed no sign of the elm trees of the village name, though. Looking at the map, La Juddle appeared to be canalised into an overflow or relief channel for the Canal Latéral a couple of kilometres inland. The cooling towers loomed larger and, although rowing against the wind reduced progress, the combined railway and road bridge crossing the river beyond was now in sight, the former a branch line supplying the power station inbound and for nuclear waste trains outbound.

Still upstream of the cooling towers, we saw signs on the right that seemed to direct us into a channel, with a picture of a kayak on

one and a right-pointing arrow on the other. We tried to follow the 'channel': a mistake. There appeared to be water but after getting out twice to push the grounded boat off the shingle we gave up and hauled it back to the river. Undergrowth had obscured the lower parts of the signs indicating we should continue on the main river for a kilometre more before landing. Muttering about regular pruning back, turquoise dragonflies skimmed alongside the boat. Soon a sign (unobscured) directed us into the right-hand channel and at two o'clock we landed at the foot of a portage ramp.

We lowered the wheels attached to the transom, one of Richard's good ideas, and easily pulled the boat up the concrete ramp, our packs still on board. Certainly saved carrying the boat. The portage ramp passed beneath the road and rail bridge which crosses the river virtually above the barrage, so for once we did not row beneath a bridge, but walked. Four lads larking around on bikes on the ramp back down to the river offered to help us back into the water. We could see that the barrage was impossible to kayak or row over, so this post-Hornblower portage was unavoidable.

*****

Thanking the boys who had helped us back afloat, we were perhaps a shade too nonchalant, for with me again at the oars we grounded noisily on a mass of jumbled rocks. Afloat again, Richard muttered that there seemed no easy way over or between so we headed away and towards the bank instead, rather than try and manhandle the boat over what looked an impassable barrier. A modest channel inshore got us past the rocks and as we edged alongside Neuvy-sur-Loire's riverbank we hungrily scanned the houses beyond the embankment road for any sign of a café or bar.

Nothing doing, so we landed on a sand-cum-shingle beach opposite Le Port, in effect a suburb of Neuvy, for a swim and 'lunch'. I say lunch but we had a scanty galley, and had to make do with a couple of bone-dry biscotti, unrelieved by meat, butter or anything else, and a few swigs of distinctly warm bottled water. The swim was more enjoyable.

At half past three we were back on the river, Richard now at the oars. The next bridge had been in sight from our swimming beach, and was yet another suspension bridge, this one at Bonny-sur-Loire. The town was mainly out of sight, some half a mile inland from the bridge, as was the town on the opposite or west bank, Beaulieu-sur-Loire, twice as far from the banks of the river it claims to be alongside. In fact, Beaulieu expanded when the Canal Latéral passed between it and the river. The suspension bridge, a modern steel one of three spans, was rebuilt about 1950 and, I need hardly add, replacing one destroyed in that fateful summer of 1940.

A little further on, opposite a hamlet named L'Etang, we exchanged roles, and rowed for the next few miles. The navigable water wandered about within its banks with numerous spits and islets and false-friend channels trying to entice Richard. However, he avoided running aground or venturing into the wrong channels and after about three miles a settlement appeared, the river's main channel running close into its north bank alongside the village. It had the usual introduction: houses beyond a steep, road-crowned riverbank and well-trimmed limes.

The village was marked on the map beside me as Ousson-sur-Loire. We did not particularly want to row on as far as Briare, the next riverside settlement. Richard spotted a slipway with the slate-clad spire of a church behind it. The slipway actually stopped short of the current water level and we could not run onto it. I climbed out of the boat into the water and soon regretted taking off my shoes after our swim.

The water by the slipway was slimy, weedy and rank, uncleaned by river flow. I lost my footing on treacherous stones from the collapsed lower section of the slipway. Soaked, I clambered back to the vertical, my legs and shorts thick with mud and stinking river detritus, much of it stirred up by our oars and made worse by my floundering. My next mistake was to try to wade out and wash the muck off but I fell in again and this time hit sharper rocks and collected a number of gashes in my legs, the deepest one on my right foot. Dripping blood and mucky water I stumbled ashore after a painful object lesson: never try to land barefoot where there are rocks.

Richard meanwhile had pulled the boat onto the ramp, scrambling up to tie the painter to one of the immaculately shaped lime trees. Trying to blank out the stinging pain in my legs, we walked to the top

of the ramp and contemplated the delightful parish church, set on the north side of its former graveyard, now grassed over and no longer in use. Benches, a picnic table, neat garden beds and a children's see-saw rather gave the redundancy away. A concrete pillar by the churchyard's riverside wall recorded the unnervingly high levels of various floods, the plaque nearest the top marking the levels of super floods of 1856 and 1844. These were some 2.85 metres above the road surface, the river itself many metres below this.

Nearby, we saw a notice that there was a *chambre d'hôte* by the church so we walked there, Richard dry and casual, me dripping water and blood. Fully booked, the charming lady who opened the door told us, but there was a good place to stay at the far end of the village. More expensive of course but we would find the cuisine excellent. To men who had merely had a couple of biscotti since breakfast this last was the clincher. She telephoned and booked us a room, pointing us northward towards the D2007 that passes the village from the Briare direction towards Bonny-sur-Loire. The historic part of this picturesque village lies beyond the parish church and we headed through the triangular Place de la Liberté, modest in scale with room for half a dozen heavily pruned trees and a stone-plinthed drinking fountain. We walked north along Grande Rue, modest 18th and 19th-century cottages, then modern suburban houses.

Dripping blood and no doubt stinking to high heaven, I felt every metre of the walk carrying my backpack, and was relieved when after about three quarters of a mile we reached the main road with its inns and farms. Rounding the corner onto the D2007 there was our night's rest: the Clos du Vigneron hotel and restaurant. Richard, smelling sweeter than me, was despatched to complete the formalities and book dinner. He emerged and said we had one of the rooms in a modern building at the rear. He said we had landed on our feet here, an image I did not particularly appreciate.

Showered and in clean dry clothes we headed off to dinner. It did not disappoint. In fact, it was superb, washed down with good white wine: foie gras, superb veal sweetbreads, cheese and sorbet: a gastronomic delight. Well satisfied with twenty miles rowed and, replete with good food, we tottered off to our room to sleep the sleep of the just.

# 26

# Briare's Aqueduct and Gien

My hand-washed clothes dried overnight and clear of river-mud fragrance, my gashes stinging less and no longer actively bleeding, well-rested and breakfasted, we set off back to the river with a jaunty step looking forward to a day's rowing below an intense blue and cloudless sky. This time I was wearing sandals to make sure that there would be no repeat of yesterday evening's unhappy landing. We reached the bank soon after nine in the morning and had another look around the churchyard, hoping the church might be unlocked: not so. We launched onto the river, Richard at the oars accompanied by the raucous croaking chorus of innumerable frogs in the reeds and grass along the riverbank.

Opposite the Ousson bank was a vigorous-looking weir, so we steered between it and the shallows; mud flats and sandy islands on our right pushing us towards the west bank. Shortly, we passed towering stone walls that framed a lock, for at this point the Canal Latéral à la Loire emerged into the river, the Ecluse de Mantelot. A towpath runs atop the embankment named the Dique de l'Escargot Most impressive but largely redundant after the canal was continued inland to the aqueduct at Briare in 1895-1896.

L'Escargot dike ended at the foot of the left pier to the suspension bridge's main river span at Châtillon-sur-Loire, the other five traversing a tree-covered island and back stream. There was a curious feature at the foot of the suspension bridge pier, rather like a stone

helter-skelter ramp which puzzled us. The suspension bridge, largely rebuilt in the late 1940s after destruction during World War II by the retreating French, had a chequered history, having been rebuilt several times between 1830 and the war. We could see patching of numerous shell and gunfire pockmarks on the stone piers and suspension towers.

The helter-skelter survived the latest rebuilding, and was simply a spiral ramp circling the bridge pier so unhitched draught horses and men could plod up to the bridge and cross the river to rejoin their barges at the downstream lock. At this point we realised why the dyke was named 'L'Escargot'. It had puzzled us but was blindingly obvious: nothing to do with the snail's pace of barge haulage but simply a picturesque description of the convolutions of the helter-skelter ramp.

This crossing of the Loire was highly unsatisfactory for boats and barges, as water levels in this notoriously shoally stretch caused all sorts of problems for bargees. Apparently, depending on river conditions, crossing the river from the helter-skelter to the lock on the east bank would take between two and four hours downstream and a fearsome three to six upstream. It was also hazardous with about ten boats being overturned or swept away annually. In 1881 a tugboat was installed, *Le Progrès*, with a steam winch: some improvement but the aqueduct at Briare entirely replaced all this and saved many tricky hours for boats, crews and their sturdy draught horses. Forester, however, in *Flying Colours* describes it as where barges were warped across the river, years before the Canal Latéral even existed.

Beyond the suspension bridge we passed the downstream lock, the Ecluse des Combles, from which barges and shipping emerge to be hauled upstream to the helter-skelter. The Canal Latéral à la Loire had been our constant if largely unseen companion since Nevers, running parallel to the left or south bank of the river and ending here until the 1890s. This lock led into the Rives de l'Anc, a short canal to Briare running parallel to the north bank of the river. Here it joined the Canal de Briare which headed north, one of France's oldest canals, completed in 1642 when Louis XIV, the Sun King, was a mere stripling. The Rives de l'Anc, also known as le Vieux Canal for obvious reasons, survives as a backwater, the main route now inboard of the opposite bank heading for Briare aqueduct.

The fortress-like grey stonework of the lock walls was relieved somewhat by troughs of jaunty pink flowers attached to the saltire-patterned balustrades of the lock footbridge. On the lower walls to the right of the gates we could see a 19th-century winch for hauling the barges on their perilous tow from lock to lock. We suspected it was not in its original location and a mere historical ornament. Sobered by the scale of all this, we rowed on downstream, the current neutralised by the upstream wind so Richard had little time with oars shipped. The sky was still cloudless and soon the spire of Briare church hove into view. On the left bank a sunken boat lay in the shallows, a fisherman making

use of the eddies stirred up by the wreck, elegantly clad in vest, shorts and bright green wellington boots, his keep net lively with his catch.

By now the Briare viaduct was fully in sight, bright sunlight picking out crisp horizontal channelled joints on the warm buff stone piers above their cutwater plinths. These piers supported the iron canal trough, painted a cheery municipal green. There was no doubt that it was the aqueduct as a cabin cruiser was making a stately way across. The pier nearest the Briare bank had trapped a vast amount of river-borne debris, a giant swan's nest.

We had always intended to land at Briare, to continue our industrial-history themed day and I spotted a small stone-setted slipway beyond the bridge and conveniently on the Briare bank. It also had the virtue of being somewhat screened by riverside grasses and dense foliage, so I steered towards it and we landed at about 11.00. The breeze had kept us cool on the river, but stepping onto dry land it was much hotter. Four and a half miles rowed and not run aground once.

*****

Emerging at the top of a tree-lined embankment, to the slightly startled gaze of arm-in-arm promenaders, we saw a canal running along its inner side. Passing under the later aqueduct, it is of course the Rives de l'Anc canal heading for the very much older Canal de Briare's terminus basin and river lock half a mile further downstream. Needless to say, the Briare aqueduct suffered in World War II. There is a contemporary photograph showing one span sitting in the river, looking as if it had been neatly lowered, a clue that it had been deliberately blown up rather than bombed.

Naturally, we intended to walk across the viaduct which looked even more impressive from dry land with its ornate and elaborate piers surmounted by obelisks adorned with dark green ironwork lamps carried by the bow ends of ancient Greek oared galleys. Squat versions emerged from the outer sides of the plinths, like those half-ships that adorned Roman columns celebrating naval victories. In truth, though, these Briare versions looked more like Viking longships, particularly those at the foot of the plinths with fierce-looking dragon figureheads. Great fun, the foundries having had a field day of late Victorian excess.

We spotted a cast-iron plaque commemorating a grand opening on 16th September 1896, listing government ministers, engineers and

others involved. Below, under *'Entrepreneurs'* (obviously its original meaning here) a famous name sprang out: Eiffel, the architect of the eponymous Paris landmark. Here, though, he was only responsible for the admittedly high-quality stonework. The design work was done by Mazoyer and Sigault, although the latter didn't make it onto the plaque: no doubt crowded out by government ministers keen to attend the formal opening.

The aqueduct is certainly impressive with wide towpaths on each side of the canal in its steel channel. We walked its downstream towpath, finding the cast-iron lamp posts curiously urban. Just below the gunwales on the westward-facing plinths' half-boats were cast the words *'Fourchambault 1895'*, the iron and steel town we had visited a couple of days earlier, and the name of the actual ironworks: *'Fonderies Magnard Cie'*. All this cast-iron work had come down the canal and presumably made the awkward Loire crossing at Châtillon-sur-Loire.

Such is the nature of the Loire with ever-moving sandbanks and islets occupying much of the area between its putative riverbanks that the bulk of the aqueduct is over a sandy waste: only three of Monsieur Gustave Eiffel's fourteen stone piers have their feet in the river. Everyone seemed jolly and relaxed as this was 'le weekend'.

There was a café in a former canal building on the Briare side looking out across the Quai Mazoyer so we ordered a coffee and a beer, a good mix for the heat. Settling down under the shade of a white awning, we watched a load of bikers park nearby, revving Harley Davidsons to let us know they had arrived. More noise to our left as a cabin cruiser, clearly on hire, hove noisily into view. Bikini-clad young women (a hen party?) squawked and yelled, wine glasses and bottles in hand, the boat bouncing along hitting both canal banks to hysterical gales of on-board laughter. A passenger boat's skipper expressed his views forcibly to the giggling women who had to give way, bobbing drunkenly alongside the bank as his boat headed onto the aqueduct, centimetres clearance on each side. The girls raised their glasses cheerily and noisily before eventually moving on. Good entertainment for the café clientele, and the girls knew it.

Falling into conversation with a British couple who were cycling along the banks of the Loire, they asked us what we knew about Briare's great enamel and mosaic works as I patted the café's dog. The answer, I'm ashamed to write, was nothing at all. Apparently, a mid-19th-century entrepreneur had taken advantage of Briare as a canal and river hub and his new factory produced enamelled buttons and cultured pearls, Briare becoming known as la Cité des Perles.

Suitably refreshed (and informed), we headed across the old canal and back onto the embankment. Relaunching, I rowed on towards the next town, Gien. As we headed steadily north-west, we passed several fly-fishermen standing away from the riverbanks in waders. It was getting very hot and Richard was thinking of a swim, his eyes darting backwards and forwards seeking a landing place. After an hour he spotted a suitable beach and steered us towards it. On landing we sent up a cloud of flies and churning mud as we got out of the boat. The Robinson brow furrowed and we relaunched, crossing to the north bank where we ran up onto a firm, yellow sanded beach. It was good as we could now contemplate Gien beyond its bypass bridge. Richard dived into the river but I kept the deep gashes on my right foot dry for today.

At about two o'clock we set off again, Richard considerably cooler than me, and rowed towards the 1980 bridge, the water smooth and calm. Beyond, the riverside town, apparently dozing in the early afternoon sun, opened up. We were looking from the same viewpoint as had Hornblower (except Forester named the town Briare). Forester had muddled the Briare's aqueduct with the ancient bridge at Gien besides giving Hornblower an unfeasibly long day's row.

Strikingly, both riverbanks were lined with double rows of neatly trimmed plane trees. Above them on the north bank reared the château, its slate roofs flanked by clusters of pinnacled towers, turrets and chimneys and what looked like the largest of them all beyond, in fact the pyramidal spire of the church of St-Jeanne-d'Arc in line with the château roofs. The old bridge was ahead of us, the stone work of its numerous cutwaters picked out in strong sunshine. Beyond this idyll of a medieval town loomed a discordant note: the thoroughly modern cooling towers of the Dampierre nuclear power station further downstream.

Ghosting along the glass-smooth river, only occasional swirls and ripples disturbing its surface in thirty-degree sunshine, we started looking for a landing place on the town side of the river. Much of the bank seemed to be occupied by a park, narrowing as it neared the town centre. In Gien there would be cafés aplenty for lunch, but there seemed little between Gien and Sully-sur-Loire some twelve miles or more downstream: in this heat something of a stretch. Richard steered us towards a slipway ramp by the end of the park, near which were moored several Loire barges, one of which did not look as if it was going anywhere, being full of river, its port gunwales barely above water. We landed and pulled the boat into the lee of the embankment to make it less conspicuous.

# 27

## Caillard's Revenge

Following the embankment's Quai Maréchal Joffre with its neat plane trees, we continued along the riverbank. Beyond the bridge the Quai Lenoir had numerous riverside cafés. It was immediately apparent that the town had been rebuilt in a range of traditionally inspired designs in the 1940s and 1950s but more later: we were thirsty and hungry. In the Restaurant l'Escale, we ordered beers and *moules-frites*, then discussed what we should do next. I felt we could not comfortably row on to Sully-sur-Loire in what remained of a very hot day. Languidly, Richard agreed and any urgency in our mission dissipated in the bright sunshine.

We mused on how much more enjoyable our *moules-frites* had been than Hornblower's boat rations: a pound of bread each per day, sacks of potatoes and peas, thin, hard and dry Arles sausages and the sailor's staple of dried cod augmented by some bacon, all provided by the Comte de Graçay. No doubt it gave Brown as ad hoc cook challenges, but even so probably better than his usual shipboard rations.

As we were not going to row on, Richard's eye had been caught by a modern hotel on the opposite bank which I had been staring at in an unfocused way, the Sanotel, its cream render and bright orange panels seeking our attention.

The entry in Murray's 1844 guide was not as long or as enthusiastic as for La Charité-sur-Loire, perhaps the author had been diddled by a Gien innkeeper. The preamble is not encouraging; '*The scenery of the course of the Loire* [hereabouts] *is not particularly interesting'*. The entry for the town is brief. *'Its old church St. Etienne* [now Ste-Jeanne-d'Arc], *has been injured by repairs. Nearby is a portion of the ancient Castle, now turned into the Prefecture. It was at Gien that the Maid of Orléans crossed the Loire on her way from her native village, to announce her divine mission to "Charles the Dauphin", at Chinon'*.

I had taken the Michelin guide out of my pack and read its Gien entry to Richard over lunch. It even includes a small street map and is a generally informative first edition, far more so than more up-to-date, zappier editions. The guide told us that Anne de Beaujeu, eldest daughter of Louis XI, King of France, was given the County of Gien by him in 1481 when she was only twenty years of age. Michelin quotes Louis' faint praise for his eldest: *'She is the least silly woman in France; I do not know of a wise one'*. Make of that what you will but she was certainly active, rebuilding the bridge and the château (to a Renaissance taste), and building or expanding the town's churches and convents. The château now houses the Musée International de la Chasse and Ste-Jeanne's church only retains the fine tower and spire from that built by Anne.

After lunch we climbed the Escalier Saint-Laurent, the steps leading from the Place Jean Jaurès, then being repaved, up to the plateau where the church and château dominate the town below. The church retains its tall and ruggedly elegant medieval tower but the rest of the building is modern brick. Inside the reason for the new church was obvious in a display of photographs from World War II. The French retreat in June 1940 had attempted to hold the river as a defensive line and the town suffered horrific damage, leaving most of the church flattened and the château a roofless, gutted shell. The German bombers, aiming at the bridge, destroyed many houses and the resulting fires did the rest. Elsewhere along the river many towns had sustained considerable damage but that to Gien seemed exceptional. The bridge itself was blown up by the retreating French, the nearby railway bridge having been bombed flat the day before.

Gien's tribulations were not over for there were other bombing raids and retreating Germans blew up the bridge again in 1944. Interpretation boards with wartime photographs were in various parts of the town and we were impressed by the determinedly high quality of the town's rebuilding. The church is a good case in point, the outside with tall triangular-headed lancets, and inside the building a tour de force, a 1950s version of a great Romanesque basilica, all in brick with immensely tall soaring brick columns. No more sightseeing for the moment, so we crossed the bridge for the first of many times and booked into the Sanotel without difficulty. Back across the bridge we headed to the boat, the town ramp now a hive of activity. A *fûtreau* was collecting a family with two children, poling off from the bank, all apart from the crew in bright orange life jackets.

On the ramp was a splendid wooden Canadian-style canoe with a man and woman in the characteristic pose that we no doubt adopted on many occasions: crouching bent-backed and rummaging into packs, bags, etc. Both French, he had a splendid set of Dundreary whiskers. Sadly, I have forgotten their names but they told us that they had left their respective husband and wife at home, uninterested in the great outdoors, to spend months together in their beautiful canoe, on this occasion kayaking the Loire down to Nantes. We photographed each other and a merry time was had by all. We agreed to look out for them downstream and perhaps have a meal together on dry land. Off they paddled with waves and '*Au revoirs*'.

*****

We launched the boat to row across river to the Sanotel in Gien's transpontine suburb. I took the oars and managed to get through the bridge close to the south bank. Unfortunately, there were great rocks which were unavoidable just beyond and we stuck fast. Richard leapt out, worked us free and hauled the boat on shore, although still some 150 yards from the embankment due to gravel ridges, sandbanks and dry shingle. We dragged the boat into reeds and grasses but it was very exposed, the aluminium bright in late-afternoon sunshine. Hefting the packs, we headed to the hotel, and collected our room key, the woman at the reception friendly, ample and casual. We changed into (slightly) smarter clothes and headed back onto the bridge, noting at the Sanotel end a stone pillar with a bronze shield inscribed '*Aux defenseurs de*

*Gien, Juin 1940'* with a representation of a castle on fire: a permanent reminder of the destruction wrought on a fine town.

An information board at the town end of the bridge boasts it as one of the town's most ancient monuments, being mid-13th century. Well, *up to a point, Lord Topper*. The major reconstruction for Anne de Beaujeu followed destruction by a 'brutal flood' in 1458. Another flood in 1733 resulted in a second total rebuild. The old adage of 'Caesar's Axe' came to mind. Another information board had a print of the bridge in 1700 with three houses on it. More interestingly, it also showed medieval town walls and a gatehouse at the north end of the bridge, all in decay. Forester describes Hornblower sliding under the bridge with a rush, amid barges loading or manoeuvring. Our boat still basked in sunlight, but no matter: we had rowed the River Severn and sixty-five miles of the Loire without incident.

Walking around the town we found ourselves in a park east of the old core, still on the plateau above the river. We crossed Ruelle des Remparts, following the line of the old town walls. Here was a 12th-century stone  ruin with an arcade of three round arches, a Hôtel Dieu located as usual beyond the town walls. Most towns and cities had them as early hospitals, tended by monks and nuns. Back in town, the riverside west of the bridge was still lively. In L'Antre Amis beers, wine and tagliatelle carbonara set us up well. Worryingly, the boat glinted in the evening sun, but another glass of wine and I relaxed.

At about ten o'clock we set off back across the bridge and to our horror saw kids mucking about throwing our oars around. I bellowed in my most authoritative voice '*Arrêtez!*' and '*Allez-vous en*' and the kids scampered away across the beach. I was quite impressed with my intervention but to be on the safe side we went down to the boat and retrieved the oars and rowlocks, taking them to our room for safekeeping. If only we'd taken the boat as well! We retired to our beds, recalling that Hornblower and his crew two centuries ago had camped far less comfortably on a nettle-infested islet downstream.

\*\*\*\*\*

Our room on the first floor at the Sanotel faced away from the river, looking over its car park and garden. As we headed downstairs to breakfast we tried to glimpse the boat but reeds, scrub and grasses would in any case have obscured it. During breakfast it occurred to me that it might be a good idea to get some bread and cheese as on a Sunday we might not find anything in the twelve miles to the next town, Sully-sur-Loire with its great château. I headed off to find a *boulangerie* or mini-market. Reaching the bridge, I could not see the boat where it should have been. You hope against hope that you might have forgotten exactly where a thing was and your memory is playing tricks. I walked up and down the bridge, squinting into the reeds and scrub, initially in the hope that it had been hidden as a hilarious jape. Back to the hotel, I entered our room, the oars now poignantly purposeless against the wall.

'The boat's gone. It's been stolen.' I blurted out for there seemed no other way to put it or sugar the pill. Even so, I felt curiously calm and slightly detached. Years ago, I would have been utterly crushed: our trip in ashes after such a wonderful day on the river yesterday. Was this some kind of French revenge for Hornblower having stolen a rowing boat after overpowering Caillard? A facetious thought and clearly nonsensical.

Richard was calm too. We immediately left the hotel to search the reeds, scrub and the river's shingle and coarse sand margins. We peered at the opposite bank. It was not in an inlet near the town's campsite, nor as far as I could tell was it trapped against the piers of the railway bridge beyond. We both assumed that our boat had been chucked into the river by the same teenagers we had chased off the previous evening, returning to make mischief. I don't know why we assumed this: it could just as likely have been stolen by adult thieves, carried off and spirited away.

Obviously, in hindsight we should have moved the boat into the hotel car park. After four days of sun-soaked adventure we had hit the buffers. This was particularly galling because the wind had changed and would have been behind us so the steering oar might have had a chance to come into its own.

Our hotel lady told us we should report the theft to the police. The gendarmerie was of course on the other side of town beyond the hospital. Arranging to leave our packs and the oars at the hotel we trudged off in the brilliant sunshine, the temperature already in the twenties. We crossed the Loire, now bereft of us but not showing any noticeable concern as its sparkling waters trundled past. From the bridge our eyes scoured the banks for our missing boat: a hopeless quest. Heading north we turned right to climb towards the large and very modern hospital.

Beyond it we found the gendarmerie and I rang the bell as you cannot just walk in. In French I explained our problem and a buzzer sounded to open the door. We entered a room with a table and a couple of chairs, recruitment posters and leaflets in racks. A sliding frosted-glass window opened and two gendarmes peered out in smart light-blue T-shirts. I started to explain in French what had happened and they buzzed us through into the office where we sat down and I continued. After a while the female gendarme asked whether it would help if we spoke English as both she and her colleague spoke good English. Tactfully put, I suppose, as I was outside my normal French vocabulary comfort zone.

It appeared that there was no crime classification code for small boat theft: it just never happens. Well, not entirely true of course as we stood before them in just such a situation. They said they would send a car to the barrage at Dampierre nuclear power station that afternoon to see if it had reached there. Given a copy of the crime report for our insurers, we promised we would let them know if we found the boat.

Pretty impressed with their friendliness and helpfulness, we set off for the station, seeking the shady side of the road beneath well-manicured pleached lime trees, intending to catch a train to Nevers and collect my car. I did not expect many trains to Nevers on a Sunday and I was right: the morning one had gone twenty minutes ago while we were still in the gendarmerie. The other of the two scheduled Sunday trains departed in the evening. This would get us to Nevers with a closed campsite office and vehicle exit and, as importantly, we would not get Richard's €250 deposit back.

I bought tickets from a machine for the morning, and we set off back into town and had a beer in the Rue Gambetta, a street parallel to the river and entirely rebuilt after 1940. The Sanotel was fully booked for the night but the receptionist phoned around and eventually booked us a room in the Mape Hôtel at Dampierre-en-Burly about ten miles west of Gien and two from the Loire. A complication, though: there are no taxis in Gien on a Sunday. '*Pas de problème, mon mari a son auto ici aujourd'hui.*' Before we knew it a white SUV parked at the hotel's rear doors. We loaded our kit and the three now-redundant oars and were driven to the hotel. We were now destined to be boatless and well away from the river and not how we had planned our Sunday.

# 28

## A Fruitless Search
## for a Lost Boat

Not sure how the Mape Hôtel got its two stars but reception was welcoming. There was no restaurant, the room pretty basic. *Le patron* warned us that no village restaurant would be open on a Sunday but we could get supplies at the mini-market near the roundabout until 6.00pm.

Named after the village of Dampierre, we thought it would be an idea to walk to the nuclear power station on the banks of the Loire to see if the boat had washed up or got caught at its barrage: we had nothing else to do. The hotel facilities would hardly fill the yawning oceans of time until we caught a train in the morning. On the map it didn't look too far to walk, although a bit of a stretch with the temperature hovering around thirty-five degrees.

In our heart of hearts, we still hoped we might spot the boat stranded or trapped in a cove or reeds somewhere downstream of Gien. We set off, me wearing almost new sandals on already sore and gashed feet, but only these, boat shoes of the neoprene type or flip-flops as options.

Reaching Dampierre village we bore right by the parish church and the château gatehouse and then into the countryside in sweltering heat. We could not miss our target as the power station's four cooling towers were now directly ahead. It was hot work as we headed due

south with no shade to reach the D953 road that passes alongside the nuclear power station's fences. I must say that the cooling towers looked enormous but of most excitement to us was that we could actually see where the main concrete walls of the cooling towers stopped some ten metres or so above ground, the whole structure above carried on a lattice of reinforced concrete struts. Within, water coursed to the ground and the whole thing was filled with swirling grey steam. We walked slowly past peering excitedly at the tower bases but not too slowly in case security thought we might be industrial spies or terrorists. I must say that the whole site looked remarkably open and devoid of heavy security and we wondered whether you could get this close to a similar facility in Britain.

Beyond the hamlet of Les Guérets we bore right but reaching the river was a big disappointment. The barrage was not a dam: more of a weir which would not have stopped our light shallow-draught boat. We scoured with our eyes as much as we could of the river but it was undeniably a severe setback, for if the boat had got this far it could have been swept downstream for who knew how many miles. Richard in his scientific way was on hand to produce a rough calculation based on a river current of two miles an hour. If the boat was thrown into the river around midnight the sixteen hours since would mean, all other things being equal, that it would have been swept some thirty-two miles, but here we stood a mere six or so downstream from Gien. However, he did agree that all things were very much not equal with reed-girt banks, sandbanks and bends offering constant checks and obstacles.

Somewhat deflated, we set off back on a different route, shaded for the last few hundred metres by a traditional avenue of plane trees. We bought supplies at the mini-market: bread, ham, cheese, beer and wine to cover all bases. It was a pretty close-run thing for the '*fermé*' sign went up as we left the shop, two laden carrier bags to the good. Back at the hotel I was glad to get my sandals off and the beers were most welcome. Nine miles in blazing sunshine was further than I had guessed from the map.

The Mape Hôtel served a surprisingly good breakfast with croissants freshly delivered from the local *boulangerie* and excellent coffee, all dispensed by *le patron* and his daughters at the relatively early hour of seven o'clock. We were welcome to leave our packs and oars at the hotel and, if closed when we got back from Nevers, we could knock on his door to collect our things. He also booked a taxi to Gien station.

This early train would give us more time to get back to Dampierre and search riverbanks for the rest of the day. Doubtless, a complete waste of time but we felt we had to give it our best shot. Somewhat absurdly, we felt our boat deserved the effort, having carried us down the Severn and some of the Loire. The train basically followed the Loire valley back the way we had rowed and with surprisingly few glimpses of the river. We emerged from Nevers station at twenty to ten and walked through the town centre, across the river and into the campsite. Relieved to see the car still parked, no doubt boiling hot inside after all the sunshine, we collected Richard's €250 deposit. There was nothing to pay for car parking and by a quarter past ten we were on the road back towards Gien, the roof bars thrumming in the breeze but sadly now redundant.

In Gien we were to report in to the gendarmerie to ask if the boat had been found but our timing was poor and the police station was on an extended traditional French lunch break. We made the best of a bad job and found ourselves back near the river in the Rue Gambetta. After a snack lunch and a beer, we headed uphill again to the gendarmerie, the same gendarmes slid open the glass hatch and we and they reported no sightings.

We drove to the Mape Hôtel to collect our things before searching as much of the riverbanks as possible between Gien and Sully-sur-Loire. Shaking hands, the patron wished us luck and we set off to pursue our probably futile search exercise. I will spare you the details of scouring both the banks, but suffice it to say that I was very footsore by the time we abandoned our blister-enhanced searches downstream as far as Sully.

There seemed little for it but to abandon the search and set off back home. I told Richard of a hotel in St-Benoît-sur-Loire that Jill and I had stayed in a couple of years ago to visit its fine abbey. He too had been there many years ago when he had regularly dragged his wife and daughters around France from Romanesque church to Romanesque church in their camper van.

We were, though, determined not to let the mere detail of having no boat deter us from our Hornblower emulation and we would return, a new boat on the car roof as soon as we could. After a night in the Hôtel Labrador we said farewell for the moment to the Loire valley and headed to the channel tunnel and home. This first phase of our row down the Loire was at an abrupt and premature end: Colonel Jean-Baptiste Caillard had indeed had his revenge for Hornblower's boat theft all those years ago.

_Orléans_

_Combleux_     Canal d'Orléans

Château de l'Isle     _Chécy_     _Châteauneuf-sur-Loire_

_St-Benoît-sur-Loire_

_Sandillon_

_Jargeau_     _Lazy_     Dampierre-en-Burly

Sully-sur-Loire

Centrale Nucléaire de Dampiere-en-Burly     _Les Guérets_

_Gien_

# Map 4: The Loire
# Between Gien and
# Orléans

# 29

# Back to Gien with a New Boat, October 2018

In a touch of déjà vu I found myself once again in Barnet Marine one warm October afternoon in 2017 collecting a boat identical to that stolen the previous June, this time without Richard. The new boat loaded onto my car's roof bars, I applied the ties: I had got into something of a rhythm over the past couple of years and could now do it with a mere couple of tension straps and a rope from bows to towing eye.

When we had returned from France Richard informed the Small Boat Register of the theft and they said they would immediately remove the boat from the said Register. A somewhat startled Richard queried this as there would be no way of connecting it to us in the admittedly unlikely event of it being found. Their casually dismissive attitude seemed poor 'customer care'. However, they had reckoned without Richard and after a desperate rearguard action they surrendered to an immovable force and the stolen boat remains an absent friend on the Register.

Unlike us, the hapless owner of the rowing boat Hornblower had stolen in December 1810 would have had no insurance cover but Richard had taken a policy out before we rowed, me assuming it might be useful if we hit a boat or a third party, little dreaming we would soon be claiming for the theft of *Flying Colours 70* itself. The list of policy exclusions included nuclear accidents, perhaps not so far-fetched with numerous nuclear power stations strung out along the Loire. Fortunately, the insurance company paid out and we got back about eighty per cent of the total cost of a new boat, now priced roughly twenty per cent higher than for *Flying Colours 70*. Apart from the minor element of deducting the £100 excess, the rest of the price increase was a direct result of the stark fall in the value of the pound against the euro following the 2016 referendum vote to leave the European Union. As the Marine 10 boat is made in the Czech Republic, the referendum reached out to punch a quick and sizable hole in our pockets.

Richard had big plans for the winter to augment the basic boat, buying more netting, cushions, brackets, and of course wheels to fix to the stern transom. He sent me the shopping list to assist me in paying my half of the costs. Unsurprisingly, there was a bit of a rethink on security and he bought a considerable length of sturdy chain and a much heavier anchor to replace the stolen tiddler. He placed the new name *Flying Colours 71* (we were a year older) on the stern along with the new Small Ships Register number and at the bows he added small French *tricolore* stickers to complement our red ensign at the stern. Technically, we should have flown the *tricolore* in flag form set above our red duster at the stern as a matter of courtesy. Richard pointed out this was not dissimilar to the fact that Hornblower was sent for his Paris show trial for flying false colours. While no doubt true, our 'crime' would be not flying a proper French flag and we were unlikely to face the firing squad.

The next thing to decide was when we should return to the Loire. May 2018 was agreed, but this fell through for various reasons and we ended up choosing early October, starting where we had left off, namely Gien and spending a night back in the Sanotel. This time the boat would stay strapped on the car roof in the safe seclusion of the hotel car park.

I should, however, add that Richard was a tad preoccupied for when I went to Devon to pick up him and the now-accessorised boat he had just received an email with grim photographs attached telling him that his Greek swimming pool had caught fire and burned down the previous evening. Apparently, his nearest neighbour had seen columns of smoke emerging above separating olive trees and their prompt action had prevented the flames spreading to the house. He had already arranged for the damage to be looked at, but as an ongoing process dealt with at a distance he was doomed to have his ears hot and sweaty from the mobile phone at what seemed like all hours of the day and night. He also had to deal with people who had made an offer to buy the Greek house and I think he had his Devon house under offer, but I can't be sure as it goes on and off the market like a defective torch.

\*\*\*\*\*

He didn't want to cancel the trip and we caught our first glimpse of the river at Chaumont-sur-Loire, and after lunching there headed to Gien to reach the Sanotel once again, at four thirty, the boat-crested car securely out of sight in the car park. Once again the Hornblower game was afoot.

Setting off for the town we passed again the bronze shield commemorating the 1940 battle dedicated '*aux defenseurs de Gien*', and on the river bridge we scouted a suitable arch to row under the next morning. Where to launch, though, was the issue: we did not fancy carrying the boat from the hotel to the river. I suggested the ramp upstream of the bridge where we had landed in 2017 and met the two French canoeists. The whole of the Quai Maréchal Joffre as far as the ramp was dug up so we would have to go all round the houses to get to the town ramp. While a complication, we decided running this obstacle course was easier than dragging the boat to the water from the Sanotel. If we could get the car close all would be well. That evening there were no diggers or other vehicles at this end of the Quai, so all might be well next day.

We retraced our steps beyond the bridge onto Quai Lenoir for a beer at one of the riverside tables at Le Winston (Churchill, presumably). As it was too early for supper, we went back to the hotel to fill time, transferring clothes and kit into our waterproof bags. At half past seven we were back on Quai Lenoir and further along the waterfront saw brand new stone steps and a stone-flagged piazza, the Place Jean Jaurés, still not complete but far more advanced than the all-dug-up and red-and-white-barriered building site it had been the previous year.

The road led to the Hôtel de Ville, a French Classical-style stone building of 1859 with a central pediment bedecked with French

tricolor flags looking towards the river down a long, narrow square, no doubt formed by demolishing numerous older houses to give the mayor a river view. This was also under restoration as part of the Coeur de Ville de Gien project. All very impressive and no doubt costly but at eight o'clock it was almost completely dark so we headed off to find supper.

Toing and froing a bit we finally settled upon L'Escale once again, where we had *moules-frites* and talked to an American and her daughter. Originally from Bordeaux, she now lived in San Diego but her grandparents were still in Gien in a house up near the château. More to the point her grandparents endured the June 1940 bombardments which destroyed their shop selling local faience ware. After the war they opened a new shop in rebuilt premises but that building no longer exists either.

Afterwards, we walked back across the river to the hotel, noting pretty lively water through all the arches. Close to the bridge terns, gulls and cormorants swirled and swooped, competing shrilly for roosting places on the cutwaters and under the arches.

\*\*\*\*\*

I woke before Richard and lay thinking that the boat theft could have drawn a heavy line through our ambitions. Yet here we were with an identical boat preparing to set off once again on our Hornblower quest, and I could not help sneaking a glance through the window to check the boat on the car roof.

After another good Sanotel breakfast we put our surplus luggage and overnight cases in the car and checked with the hotel that we could leave the car there for 'a few days' while we headed downstream. '*Pas de problème,*' was the laid-back response. There was no mention of a fee and we set off to try to reach our selected launch pad on the opposite bank of the Loire via a pretty substantial diversion.

Across the river we again passed the hospital, the gendarmerie and the ruins of the Hôtel Dieu to weave through suburban streets to the river near the launch ramp. Things did not look too good as access to the ramp was thoroughly blocked by a digger and lorry. The simplicity of the option of rolling the boat on its stern transom wheels vanished. We scouted around the park but there was no other vehicle access.

We waited around until the lorry had been filled with rubble and road diggings, expecting it to toil off. It did move to park nearby while the driver, the digger operative and other workers gathered round for a leisurely break and a smoke. There was just about room to ease the boat past the stationary digger but there were piles of rubble, etc, so we would have to carry the boat to the foot of the ramp. We removed it from the car roof and unloaded the oars, our packs and anchor and chain. I must say that Richard had gone 'overboard', the heavy anchor chain more suited to restraining a wild bull and the anchor a cabin cruiser.

Crossing one of the rubble piles carrying the boat I slipped on loose stuff and the boat's stern fell heavily on my right knee as I went down. The pain was considerable. I was only bruised but had a decided limp for a day or two. Richard seeing it thought that our voyage might be over before we had started. Following lots of rubbing and flexing of my knee I picked up the stern again and we got the boat to the water's edge, me cursing freely.

After a few minutes I set off back to the car over the rubble and spoil heaps, to drive slowly back to the hotel as the lorry, now full of rubble and spoil, pulled out as I approached and navigated agonisingly slowly through the tortuous diversion back to the town centre. Leaving the Sanotel car park on foot, I looked across the river towards the château ridge and there was a long extending crane at the left of St-Jeanne-d'Arc's church tower working on its cupola, a large number of disturbed pigeons, rooks and the odd tern wheeling angrily about the crane. Yesterday's bright blue sky had disappeared: it was grey and overcast and frankly pretty chilly.

Back at the foot of the ramp Richard had completed the boat organisation, the red duster fluttering at the stern. This was a significant moment after 2017's serious setback, overcoming Caillard's revenge we were ready to resume the Hornblower voyage. Had we been very considerably younger we might have exchanged high-fives but I merely took the oars for the first stint, the church bells ringing out for ten o'clock as Richard steered us below the bridge's cross dedicated to St Nicholas, the patron saint of sailors: we hoped he would shower benisons on our voyage.

It soon became apparent that the low river levels of October were going to make for tricky navigation with numerous rocks of all sizes lurking in the shallows. They either broke the surface in which case we could steer to avoid or lurked just beneath with tail swirls as a clue or no disturbance at all. Tricky stuff and we ran aground for the first of many times well short of Gien's 1893 railway bridge and still in sight of the Sanotel. Not a good omen, we felt.

Passing beneath the lattice-girder railway bridge, the stone piers with miniature copses growing on the cutwaters, white heron seemed very numerous on both banks and on islets along with grey heron and the near ubiquitous terns. Looking at these Richard took his eye off the river and we ran aground again a mere two minutes beyond the railway bridge but managed to fend off without having to get out of the boat. A little further along a heronry in the riverbank trees had numerous white heron circling it. Lapwing rootled around in the shallows, mingling with oystercatchers with their white bibs and orange beaks. At some point we must have passed the supposed location of Hornblower's campsite.

At ten to eleven the cooling towers of Dampierre nuclear power station came into view once again while upstream we could still see Gien railway bridge, the church spire on the plateau above the town at last almost hidden. As Richard's eyes were watering with the cold I said, Ranulph Fiennes-like: 'We'll need an electric saw to cut off your frostbitten fingers.'

As we rowed on past the cooling towers we had first seen in June 2017, columns of steam rose at forty-five degree angles into the sky, driven by a strong breeze. The river bore gently north-west and Gien disappeared from view and after an hour and a quarter's rowing we passed beneath electricity pylons and then on the left bank L'Ormet, a quite grand 19th-century house in simple Arts and Crafts style, all rendered elevations, louvred shutters and steeply pitched tiled roofs.

The power station buildings somewhat dwarfed by the four cooling towers were now in full view. We had consulted Souchard to remind ourselves how to get past the barrage at Dampierre and an inset map showed that there was a *'passe à canoës et kayaks à son extrémité gauche, le long de la berge'*. It also suggested approaching even

this with caution, so we did and landed on a reed-girt beach to survey the scene. The bypass, a concrete ramp, descended with a mere inch of water cascading down its weedy-slippery surface. We certainly could not row down it at this time of year so we lowered the stern wheels to walk the boat down the ramp. The strain of this was too much for Richard's almost new Karrimor sandals and a strap broke. 'Not to worry,' I said, 'we'll find a shop in Sully to get a new pair.' Richard was unconvinced as well as unhappy at such rapid product failure.

The ramp dumped us in a pool girt about by rocks and shingle banks, so we had to manhandle the boat across another barrier reef into deeper water. The sky was now a much more attractive proposition, the clouds lightening and breaking up. For the next hour or so there was much grounding, banging into half-hidden rocks and leaping out of the boat to haul it free. After this we heard the sounds of a weir, seemingly formed by rocks across the whole width of the river. They turned out to be rapids over which the river roared noisily and we ran them for about a kilometre, spectacular rocks roaring up to the water surface or just below, most just about passing beneath our flying and already battered keel.

Eventually, in calmer water we actually saw a boat in motion on the river: a green metal punt that briefly launched as we approached before mooring to fish. We rowed on, the clouds wholly dissipated and the river teeming with birdlife. At one point the shore appeared lined with small white rocks but as we approached the rocks rose into the air: egrets and hundreds of them. Approaching Sully there seemed innumerable cormorants, heron, terns, gulls and egrets, all clustered for a kind of fishing rush hour on two long, narrow islets. After further brushes with rocks and shingle banks, we rounded the last bend and ahead were the road bridge at Sully-sur-Loire and the towers of its château.

# 30

# Sully, St Benoît-sur-Loire and on to Jargeau

Upstream of the bridge and in front of the château at Sully-sur-Loire, we grounded (deliberately) onto an ocean of soft sand recently bulldozed clear of scrub. Across it we paused to empty our sandals of sand and to admire the château in its moat. Our trusty Murray's guide told us that in 1844 the town was *'possessing a wire suspension bridge (since 1836) and an old Castle, resting its front upon the Loire, and separated on the other side from the town by a deep ditch.'* Quaintly phrased but since the 17th century the château has been separated from the river by the

embankment erected by the Duc de Sully. He had plenty of time (and accumulated wealth) on his hands having been dismissed as 'prime minister' in 1610 after his master King Henry IV had been assassinated. Sully also created the wide moats around the castle by the simple expedient of diverting a stream.

The first suspension bridge referred to by Murray was replaced by a grander one in

1859 which, for once, survived World War II before collapsing in 1985 after a sudden cable rupture, the present one utilising 1859's landward stone abutments. Murray also adds that the château '*is now going to decay, and is no longer inhabited: in one corner a few bits of tapestry, old portraits, &c have been brought together; also a statue of Sully.*' The building is now in fine fettle and the magnificent great hall's timber roof is a quite stunning survival, its chestnut timbers actually dated to 1363. This classic 14th-century castle with corner drum towers was given a thorough going over by Sully whose work made it one of the finest 'Châteaux of the Loire'.

After the château we walked into town hoping to find replacements for Richard's snapped sandals and with great good luck a *chaussure* was open where he bought a pair of Australian (!) walking sandals. Greatly relieved on the footwear front, we headed off for a beer and a coffee. By our table outside La Navage bar, quoins were marked for the great floods in 1856 and 1866: they remember these things around here. We mulled over whether to stay in Sully or press on to St Benoît-sur-Loire where we had stayed last year after abandoning our search for *Flying Colours 70*. It was five o'clock and we reckoned we could row the seven miles or so before dark. A room duly booked at the Hôtel du Labrador in St Benoît-sur-Loire, we set off back to the boat.

*****

Rowing beneath the road bridge proved hazardous and we flashed through scraping along the side of particularly aggressive rocks. The railway bridge beyond bore pockmarks from World War II action. Next we passed the tall needle spire of St-Germain church, about 125 feet high, and then a c1900 abattoir, the word proudly cast into its main gable.

The autumn colours on the riverside trees were gloriously bright in low evening sun, exactly mirrored in the smoother water we now rowed through. The calm before the storm, though: I steered us into a dead-end channel and it proved difficult work getting off its glutinous mud back to the main river. Amid painful bruising of shins from clashes with the oars getting in and out of the boat and with rocks, we finally made it.

After an hour we ran aground again very firmly, apparently in mid-channel, and again I heaved myself out to push us off into deeper water, but the gravel shelving steeply, I found myself up to my waist in river. Hastily, I managed to pull the boat back and climb aboard. As Richard marked time on the oars, I checked my phone: it still worked. Good: next I checked the waterproof pouch; my wallet and passport were dry. I use the phone as a camera so of course it was not cocooned in the sensible pouch.

We ran aground again and this time it took five minutes to get free and around us dusk gathered. There was still a fair way to go to St-Benoît-sur-Loire and we did not fancy rowing in the dark on a river where you could run aground so frequently. A quick scan of the map in the gloom showed a village on the bank called Lazy and, after a few feeble jokes comparing our rowing to the village name, we landed just beyond a great drift of yellow spearwort on the river's edge, a beacon in the gloom.

It seemed a long walk to St-Benoît blundering around in the dark with our packs and it took nearly an hour to get to the hotel. Checked in, we headed into town and found a restaurant, La Madeleine, still open: delicious pork medallions, followed by an array of local cheeses and a good Muscadet. En route back we paused in the great early-11th-century westwork of the abbey church to inspect its superb floodlit capitals.

*****

The next morning after breakfast as we stood with our packs in front of the remarkable two-storey 'westwerke' of the Abbey of St Benoît, our Murray's guide informed us that the church had been *'attached to a monastery, destroyed in 1792. Its tower* [the westwerke] *was lowered in consequence of a revolt of the monks against the royal authority of Francis I'* in 1527. It was magnificent enough even in its two-storey survival, the ground-floor bays and their columns supporting a taller upper storey that had contained three altars, in effect private chapels for the builder Abbot Gauzlin.

Inside all is cool off-white, cream and white limestone and a further wealth of superb carved capitals, the whole building stone-vaulted. The choir and transepts date from the second half of the 11th century, the nave, rebuilt from about 1150 to

1218. Fortunately, the westwork was not rebuilt and remained intact until King Francis I's time. According to a life of Abbot Gauzlin the stone came on barges from the Nevers region where our Hornblower voyage had begun. Originally named Fleury, the abbey and the town changed their names to St-Benoît when the bones of St Benedict, the founder of the Benedictine Order of monks, were stolen in the late 7th century from Monte Cassino's great monastery to 'protect' them from Lombard raiders. His remains of course attracted pilgrims in their thousands, along with great wealth for the abbey.

Reluctantly, we moved on and sought what we hoped would be a less circuitous route back to the boat, following a Velo or cycle track past the hotel that curved towards the river at Port-St-Benoît. Here there were several older houses and no doubt where the Nevernais stone for the abbey had been landed. At the river two teachers and twenty pupils, all dressed in white tabards, busied about with a nature project of some sort.

We continued along the path which eventually merged with the one we had followed in the dark last night, so it was no less circuitous or quicker a route than last night. I rowed to the middle of the river to find deepish and less rock-strewn waters. As we rounded the first bend the woods to our left gave way and we saw a bottle kiln atop the high embankment along which runs a road. It was a 19th-century kiln of a square plan type but we could not see its other buildings from our lowly river position. A group of half a dozen walkers emerged onto the embankment, keeping pace for a while until I upped my stroke and we drew away.

Several Loire barges were moored off Port-St-Benoît and the white-tabarded schoolchildren were still foraging the riverbank when we at last rowed past. For a mile or so we could also see the towers of the abbey, the church itself hidden by the river embankment. There were other things to preoccupy us, though, as we ran aground several more times on the next stretch of river, out of the boat on several occasions to drag it in frequent shallows.

The sun broke through soon after midday and maybe this brought out our first kingfisher of the trip that dashed enthusiastically along the bank. Passing Sigloy we saw numerous swans swimming in pairs that took off as we approached, a spectacular noise produced by hundreds of wings beating, but scores of lapwing on a nearby islet remained unmoved.

We decided to land at Châteauneuf-sur-Loire to find some lunch. Now in sight to Richard at least, I asked him how far to the landing ramp he had spotted. 'It's only a couple of hundred yards.' The distance did not noticeably diminish and it was nearer a mile pulling alongside unpollarded limes on the embankment of the Promenade du Chastaing. Out of the boat after eight and a half miles of rowing, we tied the painter to a mooring ring on the ramp and paused to look more closely at yet another suspension bridge across the Loire with added horizontal cabling between the towers. It dates from 1935 and replaced a mid-19th-century one, again retaining the stone piers.

Along the sloping stone embankment towards the bridge there were some giant mooring rings and frequent flights of stone steps down to the grassy and reedy sloping banks to the river itself. Disappointingly, there were no cafés on the riverfront, only one near the bridge, sadly closed while the square in front was repaved. We decided to head into town and turned left at a T-junction, having spotted a church tower in the distance, hoping for a better church than the one at Fourchambault.

Ominously, the town was quiet with few people in the streets as we passed a market hall on our right, one of those splendidly ornate sub-Art Nouveau iron and steel ones found all over France. This one was dated 1903 and had a central 'nave' and flanking aisles, scrolly spandrels and a bell cote at the gable. At the end of the road we found a modest square at the gates of the château. Murray's guide informed us that the town has '*the remains of a fine château*'. Mostly demolished in 1803, a pedimented archway in an entrance lodge survives as the west side of the square and a vista closer for the road along which we had just walked. Behind it are fine formal gardens, now public, service buildings and a domed rotunda, formerly the town hall but now a river museum, according to our Michelin guide.

We however had our sights set on a beer and a bar opposite the 12th and 13th-century parish church of St-Martial. The church is an extraordinary sight for the nave had been adapted as a portico to a market hall beyond by knocking down the aisles. The west tower remains attached while the east arm and transepts serve as the parish church. We thought unfairly that the French Revolution had something to do with it but it had been heavily damaged during the war.

This earlier market hall had its hipped slated roof carried on three rows of eight timber columns, these and the crossbeams white-painted and on one beam was painted '*Cie Gale des Remorqueuers*' in what looked like earlier 19th-century typography. A hasty consultation with Larousse on my phone told me that it translated as the *general tugboat company*, presumably the barge-towing boats of the Loire but why a presence in the market hall? Perhaps they hired boatmen here and why two market halls?

I had plenty of time to contemplate this and the church as I drank my *pression*, for Richard was again crouched over his mobile phone. The pool fire and selling his houses was increasingly impinging on the voyage, mini-crisis following mini-crisis. We decided we would stop rowing for the day at Jargeau so, keeping his mobile phone to hand, he booked a hotel room there. We visited the church which has a splendid Baroque monument of 1681 beautifully restored after bomb damage and thought about lunch. We did not see a café that we fancied so we bought a lardon brioche and an apricot viennoiserie from a *boulangerie*. So delicious that by the time we got to the boat only crumbs remained.

*****

It was a little after three o'clock when we relaunched, Richard taking a turn on the oars, and as we passed beneath the pretty modern suspension bridge a dozen swans flew noisily overhead. As the river bore south-west we survived a crunching collision with a rocky pillar that almost reached the surface in deepish water. It almost capsized our spectacularly rocking boat and I got a painful cramp in my left leg as I grabbed the gunwales to steady us. Richard magnanimously accepted that the rock was invisible until it was too late to do anything about it.

We rowed on for a mile and, as it was now hot and sunny, Richard who was doing the physical work wanted a swim to cool off. I steered to a bankside beach, although I did not swim. Back on the water, eye off the ball, we ran aground again so thoroughly that I had to get out of the boat to lighten it and push it off the sandbank.

After another grounding, Jargeau's bridge and church tower came into view. I decided to head across river to land upstream of the bridge. It was a difficult row, bumping across a fairly shallow river strewn with rocks, both hidden and visible. Close to the shore and I got out to haul the boat through the rocks as it seemed the only way of getting to the bank. Unhappily, in releasing the boat from a stubborn rock it surged free and knocked me over. I was left lying in the river, covered in water and embarrassment. Scrambling to my feet I hastily checked my phone (OK) but my passport and wallet case proved no longer fully waterproof.

We finally landed at ten past five, Richard chaining the boat to an immovable boulder just in the water, the boat grounded in the shallows. I got the packs out of the boat onto the grassy bank and dripped river water. I hoped my clothes would dry quickly as we headed for our hotel. The sloping embankment had just been mown and my soaking trousers and sandals acted as magnets for the cuttings which liberally bedecked me, Richard making a feeble quip about Green Men as we scrambled up the embankment towards the bridge.

# 31

# Joan of Arc at Jargeau and the Canal d'Orléans

Jargeau's bridge and approaches were traffic-choked, the rush hour fully underway. This modern bridge of 1988 replaced yet another 1830s Loire suspension bridge destroyed in the war. The current one is aligned on the Boulevard Carnot some sixty-five metres upstream of the town's Grande Rue. We turned left into the Boulevard, built along the course of medieval town walls demolished in the 19th century. However, we would look at the town after we had checked in at our hotel, Le Cheval Blanc: more of a pub with rooms than a hotel, where I could change into dry clothes.

Apparently, our room had a terrace but this turned out to be a Juliet balcony. It faced west and I spread my soaking clothes on the balustrade to dry in the setting sun which flooded the room. We headed out to look at the town which had been besieged by the French under Joan of Arc in 1429, at that time held by the English. One of her semi-miracles had seen her hit on the helmet by a massive stone hurled from the battlements. She in effect shook her head and carried on thus discombobulating the besieged garrison who soon surrendered. Murray adds that '*almost all the garrison* [were] *put to the sword, in spite of the endeavours of the Maid to prevent the shedding of blood*'. I couldn't help feeling there was a bit of reputation management at play here.

Jargeau receives little attention in guidebooks but is a delightful old town with narrow, winding cobbled streets, a mix of 16th-century timber-framed houses and 17th and 18th-century stone and rendered ones. At its heart is the parish church which, Murray informed us *'though injured by the Huguenots in 1562, is still a fine building'*. Immediately south of it is another cast-iron market hall which looks to be designed by the same architect as that upstream at Châteauneuf-sur-Loire and of a similar c1900 vintage. We walked as far as the riverbank where, at the end of the Grand Rue is the abutment of the lost suspension bridge, its counterpart on the opposite bank. It forms a kind of viewing platform and is not surprisingly named Le Belvédère.

This gave us a chance to look at the water hurtling between the surviving pier foundations of the old bridge. It looked a tricky passage for the next morning with violent water and numerous large rocks between all but one of the pairs of piers. We walked out on the bridge to get a closer look and this rather confirmed the only possible route. Pensively, we walked back through the town noting commemorative

plaques to Joan of Arc and the ubiquitous flood marks inscribed on buildings. We stopped in the bar/*tabac* Le Narval. Looking up from my much-needed Ricard, I idly glanced at a British red telephone box in the Rue Gambetta, alien here and in use as a free library, rather like many redundant K6 kiosks in Britain.

Richard meanwhile had left me to my drink and contemplation and was striding up and down the Rue Gambetta on his mobile phone for twenty-five minutes dealing with domestic crises. After this we decided there was nowhere we fancied for supper in the town and we dined at Le Cheval Blanc. Rather wet soufflé starters were followed by andouillettes for me and a pikeperch for Richard, served by a young, rather absent-minded waitress requiring frequent reminders for wine and other things.

\*\*\*\*\*

Over a moderate breakfast Richard said he had slept badly, lying awake thinking of different ways to get past the old bridge remains as well as the problems of his swimming pool fire and house-selling mini-crises: I slept through it all. The sun was shining through fluffy altocumulus clouds as we left the hotel and the autumn reds of the maple trees behind the market hall and church were bathed in intense low morning sun. By the time we reached the river, the clouds had moved off south leaving a clear blue sky. To Richard the route through the old bridge remnants still looked difficult enough for him to suggest we remove our glasses and make all secure before launching: dramatic steps indeed.

At about ten o'clock we pulled the boat between the worst of the inshore rocks and over the sandbanks. Reaching deeper water, we clambered back in and I rowed hard across the current towards the

north bank before Richard steered me beneath the modern bridge and towards the racing waters between the old bridge pier remains. He aimed us with care, I shipped oars and we raced through, narrowly missing two massive rocks on our right and I mean narrowly missing: it was only the speed and power of the water surging along their sides that kept us bounding along. All very exciting but it probably only took ten seconds or so before we were in calmer but still rock-strewn waters.

Again, it was tricky finding a route and I was not filled with confidence as Richard said: 'We are following swans now and I haven't seen them run aground yet.' North-west of Darvoy, about six miles downstream from Jargeau, we deliberately ran the boat aground on an islet for a 'comfort break' as we had shipped too much coffee at breakfast.

Back on the water and some way downstream we ran aground on a serious rock, again one rearing up in deeper water without telltale swirls. This was a bit of a challenge: Richard was out of his depth and getting back in the boat was a desperate, floundering scramble.

As we rounded a long bend opposite Sandillon a vast white shape swam towards the boat's stern, inspected it and glided away before I could get my camera out. It was big enough to be a shark but Richard thought a giant catfish. I am sure he was right for back home a few moments research confirmed that catfish were a noted feature of the Loire, the record length being not far shy of nine feet. Ours was easily six feet long and I don't think that a fisherman's exaggeration.

The river now turned northwards and the sky began to cloud over as we saw the church tower at Chécy, white and bright against its backdrop of trees. There was yet more teeming birdlife and Richard remarked that: 'Each day we see more heron, egrets, etc, than ever before in our lives,' just as I was thinking the same thing. On the left bank the breeze was singing in the poplars lining the bank and there was more evidence of autumn turning the willows and alders golden in the returned sunshine, the clouds dissipating as we rowed on.

Richard decided that he had finally worked out 'river craft' by letting the boat choose its route through the current, assisted by tweaking the steering oar. I liked this idea as I could ship the oars and look around. It meant slower progress than continuous rowing but on the plus side it meant we would collide less forcefully with rocks. Richard's hunch was that as often as not the current would guide us into a safe course through the rapids and shoals, resulting we hoped in fewer groundings. Time would tell but we did not run aground again that day.

Passing Chécy with its houses close to the river, spectacular cascades of Michaelmas daisies clothed the sloping embankment. Shortly before we reached Combleux we were puzzled by what looked like a tower beyond the high embankments on the south bank. From our position in the water we could not see the lower parts of whatever

it was. Was it a church? As we came abreast, I saw that it was the ruins of a château, not a church, and we were looking at two towers, one with two walls missing. It appeared to be built in brick and did not enthuse our guidebooks: all eyes on Combleux on the opposite bank. Looking it up, these are the remains of the Château de l'Isle built in the 1530s for the then Bailli of Orléans Jacques Groslot. He also built the city's Hôtel de Ville in the same brick and stone. After various vicissitudes three-quarters of the château was demolished in the 1860s to make way for a new river embankment. An ignominious end, but this interesting fragment was at least left by the demolition gangs as a minor footnote amid the grand sweep of Loire Châteaux. Then Richard pointed and said, 'Three men in a boat, well, a powered punt.' I looked and there was actually for once a boat moored out on the water with three men fishing.

We had seen from the map that the Canal d'Orléans has a spur giving access to the Loire upstream of the city and ahead of us were massive well-cut grey stone walls flanking the lock. The same stone had been used for the side walls to the main canal that continued alongside all the way to Orléans. We drifted past the lock entrance

and headed for shore amid moored Loire sailing barges, an attractive smell of tar paint in the air. A man painting his barge waved his brush and we exchanged greetings as we nosed into a gap behind a barge.

We tied up and landed well set for a beer and maybe lunch. Who knew what we would find in Combleux? Beside the lock was just the place: La Marine hotel, bar and restaurant, a charming building with white-painted window shutters set off against weathered yellow ochre render. Tables were set by the lock beneath spreading lime trees but little happened. Eventually, a waiter appeared and came over to state rather forcefully that the kitchen was now closed. *'Seulement un pression peut-être, s'il vous plaît?'* He melted somewhat and a beer appeared quickly but at the same time he whisked away the cutlery, glasses and tablecloth so we could be in no doubt a drink was all we would get. He thawed further and we managed to extract an espresso and a smile. It was a wonderful location sitting by the lock in the bright sunshine, the nearby lock bridge railings adorned with troughs and profusions of bright red and white flowers.

We moved on and crossed the lock bridge to look at a cast-iron signboard giving distances along the Loire from Combleux, no doubt for bargees and boatmen. Nevers was not in the list but Gien was at sixty-six

| DISTANCES SUIVANT LA RIVE DROITE DE LA LOIRE DE COMBLEUX À | | | |
|---|---|---|---|
| BRIARE | 75.690 | CANDES | 177.086 |
| GIEN | 66.518 | SAUMUR | 190.384 |
| SULLY | 45.093 | LES ROSIERS | 205.595 |
| CHATEAUNEUF | 32.892 | ST-MATHURIN | 215.776 |
| JARGEAU | 14.561 | PONTS-DE-CÉ | 252.185 |
| ORLEANS | 6.322 | LA POINTE | 250.479 |
| MEUNG | 24.576 | CHALONNES | 252.573 |
| BEAUGENCY | 32.549 | MONTJEAN | 261.078 |
| MER | 48.318 | INGRANDES | 266.216 |
| BLOIS | 66.642 | ST FLORENT | 274.564 |
| AMBOISE | 101.148 | ANCENIS | 287.559 |
| MONT-LOUIS | 113.926 | OUDON | 296.495 |
| TOURS | 126.797 | NANTES | 322.560 |
| CINQ-MARS | 142.466 | INDRET | 352.506 |
| LANGEAIS | 148.915 | PAIMBOEUF | 362.914 |
| PORT-BOULET | 170.346 | ST NAZAIRE | 380.596 |

kilometres and Sully at forty-three kilometres. Orléans was a mere six kilometres but it was still over 300 kilometres to Nantes. This short canal arm appears unused and we decided to walk along it to the Canal d'Orléans, which headed west from the spur to Orléans while in the opposite direction it headed north east-ish to join the Canal de Briare at Buges. It opened in 1692 so a very early French canal and fell out of commercial use in the 1950s but we understood from locals that restoration was in hand. Beyond a disused swing bridge was a stop lock with its timbers in place.

We carried on to a lock where children were collecting litter (admirable project) and their teachers asked whether the children could ask us questions as Richard and I were fiddling about with the redundant lock-gate opening mechanisms. I explained to the children that we were students of historic architecture and answered their technical questions in French but they also wanted to know what two Britons were doing in France looking at such machinery so we explained about the boat and our trip down the Loire. I felt elaborating on Hornblower would tax them and my French too far. After effusive farewells and a lot of handshaking we set off back to the boat for the last leg of the day's rowing.

# 32

## The Maid at Orléans

A quarter of an hour after Richard rowed away from Combleux we perforce landed briefly for Richard to take another comfort break, blaming the beer and coffee just consumed. Alongside us was the towering wall that carried the Canal d'Orléans alongside the river, in effect the riverbank all the way to the city.

We soon got our first sight of the bridges of Orléans ahead, its railway bridge in the foreground. Gulls swirled about in the strong wind that had blown up since lunchtime and all the way along the foot of the canal wall fishermen were congregated along the river's bushy and grass-clad margins. Banks of cloud were now rolling up, no doubt hastened by the strong wind and at a quarter to five it started raining. We peered across the river where ruinous stone walls and floodable embankments separated the navigable from the unnavigable. Beyond were *étangs* or large lakes, so navigation was possible only along the north bank. As we approached the first two bridges, I could not see which arches to aim for, only frothing water and rocks beneath all of them. I steered towards a set of stone steps leading up to the canal so we could recce the bridge on foot.

Climbing to the canal towpath high above the river, we walked beneath the bridges which are close to each other, the railway one the Pont Vierzon and the road one the Pont René Thinat, the former rebuilt after the war in reinforced concrete, an elegant version of its stone predecessor. The Pont René Thinat is also concrete and spans

the Loire in five long arches, the river 'navigable' only beneath the northernmost. This Loire bridge, its northern approaches following the course of long-demolished 17th-century city walls, avoided war damage by the simple expedient of not being built until 1977.

We walked as far as the Canal d'Orléans' last lock where it joins the Loire. Here there had evidently been considerable expenditure to restore it and its surroundings, so the locals who had told us about bringing the canal back into use were right. The lock itself had no water and the canal behind it was heavy with sandy mud, so dredging was evidently still awaited. We turned back towards the bridges and decided that there was only one route through the railway bridge arches, albeit a difficult one: white water and a narrow, wild channel. It looked difficult, turbulent but was the only option so Richard said we should once again batten down the hatches and take off our glasses.

Back in the boat we set off, Richard once again at the steering oar and me rowing, my back to the bridges. Promenade strollers paused to watch as he aimed us into the heart of the 'V'. I shipped oars and we were tossed through the rapids. Ahead beyond the canal lock was a river access ramp and a pontoon with boats of various sorts moored along each side, some the ubiquitous Loire sailing barges. Richard chose to tuck in between the pontoon and the embankment wall, at its foot a concrete walkway. It was now raining hard as we landed and tied the painter to a big iron mooring ring, a somewhat neglected and rusty fishing boat between us and the pontoon. It was half past five and we had rowed a somewhat leisurely twelve miles in the day.

*****

The embankment where we had landed sloped up to the Quai du Fort Alleaume, the road beyond a wide boulevard with a line of magnificent mature plane trees. Hefting our packs, we headed into town aiming, not surprisingly, towards the great cathedral of St-Croix  where Joan of Arc, the Maid of Orléans, had prayed in April 1429 while leading the defence of the city against the English. During the fighting she was wounded in the shoulder and had the arrow plucked out so she could carry on. Some versions say she pulled it out with her own hands, picked up her banner immediately and charged on. Whatever the truth, the apparent miracle demoralised the English who soon surrendered.

The stuff of legend but the city she saw has long gone and indeed of the cathedral she entered only the ambulatory chapels of the choir completed in 1329 survive. Most of what we saw dates from the 17th century and is a deliberately archaic Gothic insisted upon by Louis XIV, following near total destruction in 1567 by Huguenots during the Wars of Religion. The west front and towers are even later, mid-18th century. Amazing really for from a distance it looks decidedly late-medieval Gothic, but I'm not sure it is a lovable building.

We headed to a bar/restaurant, Le Lutetia, facing a cathedral bathed in autumn evening sunshine, for the rain had stopped and the clouds parted. While we drank a Ricard and a coffee, I booked a town centre hotel, the Charles Sanglier in the road of the same name, Richard on his phone dealing with domestic crises. The hotel was off the somewhat grandiose and sombre Rue Jeanne d'Arc which in the 1840s had been cavalierly cut through the old city to give a long view of the cathedral's west façade. The author of Murray's 1844 guide was clearly incensed by this and other changes, writing '*Orléans is … deficient in tangible historical memorials, chiefly owing to the cacoethes of pulling down for the sake of what is called improvement, which has prevailed to a most destructive extent during the last 50 years in the town council. The town gates and walls have been destroyed, several of the latter since 1830, and above all, nearly every memorial of the heroine of Orléans, Joan of Arc, has been swept away*'. I certainly haven't seen 'cacoethes' used in any modern guidebook. It was also apparent to us that World War II bombing had done great damage to the city and there was considerable reconstruction, much of it replicating what had been lost, but things are better than in 1844. Murray again: '*Owing to the excessive filth and bad pavements of the older streets of Orléans, the stranger will do well not to trust himself to thread their labyrinths*'.

Having booked in we asked the helpful receptionist, Georges, to suggest a few restaurants and he named three, so we set off. The recommended restaurants did not fit the bill and Richard was also unhappy with our boat merely tied to the mooring ring by the rope painter. We returned to the embankment promenade and wielded the heavy anchor chain, then he could relax. At five past seven the sun was setting spectacularly beyond the next bridge down, the Pont George V, as we left the riverside and headed back into the city. After a bit of a tour we settled on Le Volpone which was full and very good. Kir royale aperitifs for a change were followed by eggs mayonnaise, excellent spaghetti carbonara with lardons, wine and Calvados as a digestif, then back to the hotel.

*****

The next morning over a breakfast brought to our room (not sybaritic luxury: the hotel has no dining room) we discussed our next move. Through no fault of his own, Richard was not entirely on board, if you will forgive the expression, and beset by bureaucratic nonsense. For example, his wife, Vicky, sent documents electronically to one of our hotels. He printed them off and signed them and I signed as a witness. Unacceptable apparently because we had used blue ink: an absurd hangover from early days when blue ink did not register on fax machines (remember them?). I'm only surprised they didn't require us to procure a quill pen. Anyway, enough of this, but it did cast a shadow of near-permanent worry over the Robinson brow and, heaven forfend, he was on occasion quite snippy with his oldest friend.

In short, the pressure of selling two houses together with the swimming pool fire were increasingly telling on Richard and to be frank we were weary after three days of constant struggle to find a way through rocks and over sandbanks, etc: our enthusiasm for the Hornblower project waning somewhat. We discussed all this and decided we had no real choice but abandon the Loire for a while so Richard could get home and deal with the problems directly: our supper had been interspersed with long phone calls involving remote crisis management.

Richard had a light-bulb moment and said we should hire a car to get back to Gien to collect my car as there seemed no feasible rail route from Orléans. We'd leave the boat in Orléans and ask Georges where we could hire a car. Near the station was the answer but before we headed there, I walked down to the river to check the boat. All looked fine with men angling near it and I watched dozens of cormorants fishing and diving close to the embankment, others apparently watching this aerial display with interest from the opposite bank.

Back at the hotel we loaded up and set off for the station where we hired a car with no problem, apart from Richard having to prove his address in England, the passport and driving licence apparently insufficient for insurance purposes. The problem resolved and in the smallest car we could hire, we drove to Gien.

Back at the Sanotel, we collected the car and back to Orléans, put the boat on the roof and headed north to catch the ferry back to England the following day. We were mellowing on the Loire project the further we got away from its rock-strewn shallows and frequent groundings. Bit by bit we started thinking about the next stage, heading downstream from where we had landed in Orléans. The stretch between Orléans and Tours and possibly on to Saumur looked more interesting for there were towns like Amboise and Beaugency en route, the latter seen in a memorable photograph sent me by Ludwig Heuse of the CS Forester Society.

On a more positive note to end this second phase of the Hornblower voyage down the Loire we had added a further forty-six miles to the first jaunt so suddenly curtailed by the boat theft and thus a grand total of 111 miles rowed. Chaps like statistics and we wondered how many more miles would we row when we came back to Orléans in 2019.

Orléans

St-Ay

Meung-sur-Loire

Beaugency

Centre Nucléaire de St-Laurent-des-Eaux

Menars

Muides-sur-Loire

Blois

St-Dyé-sur-Loire

Chaumont

Château de Chambord

Le Beuvron

Amboise

Map 5: The Loire from Orléans to Amboise

# 33

# The Happy Return, May 2019

Our return to the Loire took place in early May of the following year, 2019, when we hoped there might be more water under our keel than in October. I drove to Devon to load the boat on a different car, a Toyota hybrid this time. We took the overnight ferry from Portsmouth to Caen and drove to Beaugency where I had booked a hotel for the night, some seventeen miles downstream from Orléans. It seemed a reasonable day's row from Orléans, and we would moor the boat overnight in the city, return to Beaugency and take the train back to Orléans the next morning. I was rather pleased with this idea, preferring not to leave my car overnight in a big city if it could be avoided, perhaps scarred by the boat theft in Gien.

From the hotel, Le Beaugency, we headed into Orléans, arriving about lunchtime and managing to park near where we had landed the previous October. Walking along the Quai du Fort Alleaume we headed for the Canal d'Orléans exit lock that had been under restoration and it seemed work had finished as both it and the canal beyond were full of water. We also got a reminder of the teeming birdlife on the river with large numbers of heron in and by the river. It was good to be back on the banks of the Loire, the trials and tribulations of previous days amid the rocks and sandbanks having faded with the passage of time.

We headed away from the river to find some lunch and afterwards returned to the car. There was a gap in the promenade railings for vehicles, provided one took care not to collide with innumerable heedless pedestrians. I drove across it and down the launch ramp to the water's edge, passing a number of CRS police vans. We exchanged waves with the CRS who seemed to be doing little other than talking and smoking, apart from one of their number whizzing up and down the river on a small bright red speedboat. At the foot of the ramp I got into conversation with two Frenchmen who were launching a Loire sailing barge as we unloaded the boat from my car roof. I seem to recall there were several jokes and much chaffing.

The boat launched with Richard on board, I towed it alongside the concrete pathway at the foot of the embankment wall. He climbed out and tied and chained the boat to the very same mooring ring that we had used a year ago using our industrial-grade anchor chain. The three oars were joined to each other and to the boat by another sturdy wire and padlock. Once he was satisfied, we drove back up the ramp and across the boulevard to head towards Beaugency, the roof now boatless.

The D2152 follows the Loire westwards and looking at the map we decided to investigate a rather intriguing item marked in St-Ay nine miles from Orléans: the Fontaine de Rabelais. Apparently, François Rabelais had been a frequent visitor to the now-demolished Château des Voisins. He was the author of 16th-century novels *Gargantua* and *Pantagruel*, father and son giants whose hilarious adventures were regarded as outrageous, scatological, obscene and heretical. In the 1960s as a teenager I ordered the Penguin Classics version in WHSmith, undergoing something of a cross examination by a prim shop assistant who obviously thought it highly unsuitable. I scuttled from the shop clutching my book and did not have the nerve to point out that the so-called crudity was used to a purpose and refrained from a pompous teenage lecture on Aristotle. We would see

more examples of what might seem offensive to the rather prurient modernist mindset when we visited Blois further downstream.

However, before this, we parked in St-Ay's village square and looked at the parish church, a slate-clad spire and tower peeping out from a lane at its south-west corner. The church appears late 12th or early 13th century and the château beyond it has cylindrical stone gate piers topped by 13th-century crocketed capitals that you find all over France (but usually *inside* a church). Presumably removed at some stage from the church, they have found a new life in the open air. There was no sign of the Fontaine de Rabelais hereabouts, so back on the main road we shortly spotted a sign to it and turned onto a leafy country lane. This turned out to be the name of a large and beautifully landscaped riverside campsite, set in a nature reserve and named after St-Ay's illustrious visitor from the 1540s. We bumped along tracks and across narrow bridges at the ends of a lake but found nothing Rabelaisian. Disappointed, we gave up looking and headed back to the main road.

Back in Beaugency we parked on a pavement (legitimately, I should add, and our hotel had no car park) and explored the town. Particularly impressive and stark is the donjon keep of the town's castle which is, according to
Murray's guide, 115 feet (thirty-five metres) high. Built in the late 11th century by the barons of Landry, it is square in plan and rises six storeys but you can see sky through its upper windows so appears to be roofless (since a fire as long ago as 1568, we subsequently learned). Locally known as the Tour de César, adjacent to it is the substantial late-11th-century church of Notre-Dame, once part of an Augustinian abbey, its former abbey buildings between it and the river now the Grand Hôtel de l'Abbaye. To the north-west of the church with its ambulatory and radiating chapels is the 15th-century château built by John, Count of Dunois, a companion of Joan of Arc. The church does not get a mention in Murray but he does say that *'Beaugency gives its name to one of the best wines of the Orléanois'* so the guide had its priorities in good order. The church was complete by 1152 when it hosted the Council of Beaugency that annulled the marriage of the redoubtable Eleanor of Aquitaine to Louis VII. She next married England's Henry II and he got hold of her huge estates, including of course Aquitaine.

The mention of wine led us to seek dinner and we chose Le Relais du Château nearby in the Rue du Pont, a restaurant of *'cuisine traditionelle'*. We dined in solitary splendour from a sophisticated menu served by an ancient but solicitous waitress, Richard chose foie gras followed by sturgeon, a fish not often seen on a menu, and I had a velouté, then veal, and we both had an excellent unctuous tarte tatin. All was washed down with good wine and very content we headed off to the station to inspect its timetable and opted for the 8.22am train to Orléans.

*****

During the night the heavens opened and I lay listening to the rain crashing onto verandah roofs and overflowing onto garden beds and paths beneath. I must have dozed off and the alarm I had set for 7.00am failed to go off. Fortunately, I woke at 7.35 so we had just enough time for a hasty breakfast and a dash to the station. We caught the train by the skin of our teeth but would have missed it had we been weighed down by our packs (they had been left at the hotel).

We got the last two seats in the commuter train and from Orléans station walked down through the city to the river and our boat. Here we found the river had risen about six inches and was slopping onto  the embankment walkway which had been dry the previous afternoon. Looking at the river, it was wild and choppy, the wind ferocious enough to give many of the waves white, foaming crests. Moreover, the wind was blowing upstream so we would be rowing, in our waterproofs, into the teeth of the gale. The rain itself was now lighter but we did wonder whether we would be able to make much headway downstream. The weather undoubtedly made our 'Happy Return' a wet and windy one as we finally launched at about ten o'clock: we were back on the Loire following Hornblower's escape.

# 34

# Rowing Back to Beaugency

Once out on the river away from any shoreline shelter the going was tough, the sky grey with racing clouds and rain coming in fitful scuts. The water was very choppy all through the Orléans bridges, the first one being the Pont Georges V. This replaced the one Joan of Arc rode over in 1429 and was formerly the Pont Royal, rebuilt in the 1750s. It was renamed in the British king's honour in 1914, largely destroyed during World War II but rebuilt soon after. For us it produced the most turbulent passage of all the Orléans bridges. After an hour's strenuous rowing to achieve any downstream momentum we passed beneath the last bridge, a modern one carrying the A71 motorway.

The wind-battering not only made rowing hard work but whipped up the water sufficiently for us to crash into troughs and cut through foam-topped waves. It made steering difficult for Richard with the stern oar leaving the water as we pitched and tossed. I dare say it was pretty trivial compared with the open sea but in our light metal boat it was quite excitingly strenuous work.

Behind us the cathedral's great and complex west towers were still in sight: what a landmark! Around us swallows swooped to hunt close to the rough water while the swifts swirled in the wind high above. There seemed to be hundreds of swans swimming or being shoved upstream and numerous heron, geese, terns, sandpipers, dippers and sand martins buffeted about all along the river. Perhaps they knew this stretch was a nature reserve, that of the cumbersomely named

Ile de Saint-Pryvé-Saint-Mesmin. Mind you, the weather was so unpleasant that Richard, his waterproof jacket's hood tight around his face, was an absolute picture of misery.

It was a long hard row as we passed St-Ay where we had fruitlessly searched for the well of Rabelais the previous day and we felt pretty storm-battered by wind-raised waves trying to shove us back upstream. Reaching Meung-sur-Loire we landed at the foot of a concrete slipway at a quarter to three after a strenuous ten-and-a-half-mile row. This ramp was upstream of rapids formed by the remnants of former bridge piers, just as we had encountered at Jargeau. Amazingly, the noise of these rapids had been carried on the wind to our ears for nearly a mile, giving us either an indication of the power of the rapids or of the wind (or possibly both). We clearly needed to land to recce the situation and choose a route through the old bridge remains or, in extremis, to portage.

We walked past the riverbank's Le Relais Louis XI, clearly an old building and trading on Joan of Arc's connection with Meung (she had captured the old bridge in June 1429 in a daring attack on her way to besiege Orléans). There is a stone plaque of 1829 to this effect on the building installed on the 400th anniversary of the siege. We looked out at the bridge remains for possible routes through. All but one of the cutwater piers seemed present, except that nearest the Meung bank where the bridge's abutments were just below the water surface. There was certainly no archaeological doubting the location of the old bridge, but about 400 metres downstream we could see its successor, a suspension bridge built in 1834, rebuilt in 1929 and destroyed (no surprise here) in 1940. The current one opened in 1948 utilised (again no surprise) the 19th-century piers. Mind you, life would have been easier through several towns during our voyage had

the ruined piers of predecessor bridges been cleared away. We selected what seemed the least turbulent: an arrow of fast, clear water heading towards the rock-strewn rapids.

More intermittent squally showers whipped up the river but all that could wait as we continued along the Quai Jeanne d'Arc on a grassy path between a double avenue of trees towards the town which is now focused on its collegiate church and château. By the time we reached the Rue du Pont the rain had stopped, the uniform gloom diminished and even very small patches of blue sky appeared.

Crossing onto the Quai du Mail we passed a pillar with a St James conch shell informing us Santiago de Compostela was still 1584 kilometres away. We were back on the Chemin de Compostelle, the pilgrimage route heading towards the Pyrenees via Orléans. There were two former watermills, one on each side of the road powered by the Les Mauves streams, as they headed towards the main river. In fact, a town map showed there were once fifteen watermills along this stream, mostly flour, paper or tanning. The town must have smelled grim from the tanning mills. We turned left by a covered market hall to head to the church and castle.

Murray is brief and laconic ('*It has a Romanesque church and a red ruined Castle close beside it, partly concealed by trees, and backed by a hill*'). The collegiate church of Saint-Liphard, a 6th-century saint, is rib-vaulted in stone throughout, aisled and has semicircular apsidal transepts and chancel. Much of the church seems 12th and early 13th century and it is no surprise that the church was a grand one, as the adjacent château was a principal residence of the Bishop of Orléans until confiscated during the French Revolution. A curious feature is the 11th-century tower, the Tour Manassès de Garlande, like a medieval castle attached to the church's west tower which is also in part 11th century. The poet and general rapscallion François Villon had been imprisoned by the bishop and tortured in the tower in 1461, although presumably the cleric did not personally wield the thumbscrews. The château itself, a little south of the church and its attached castle tower, is partly 13th century but much enlarged by the bishops in the 18th and set in well-treed parkland. Unfortunately for us it was closed but we could get into the church and admire its elegant Gothic interior.

At the gates of the château in the Place du Martroi we sat outside the Café du Commerce for a Ricard and a *grande crème*. We moved on and bought pies for a very late lunch at a charcuterie nearby before heading back to the boat, one pie each eaten en route, following up with a pork and bacon pasty on the boat. Not a health-giving lunch, we agreed, but in our defence it was cold and grey and the rowing from Orléans had been hard work against the wind with many calories consumed by the oarsman (me), the helmsman miserably inert and getting the full brunt of the headwind.

With me rowing and Richard the great helmsman, we rushed the rapids formed by the medieval bridge remains. No doubt he was streaming Mark Twain's *Life on the Mississippi* and reading the water for hidden obstacles, not trusting me to steer a safe course through rapids and rocks. The modern bridge passed, Richard decided to assess my rowing stroke rate and produce some rough calculations, ever the scientist. At forty per minute this would give 2400 per hour and in a six-hour shift a grand total of 14400 pulls on the oars. It sounded quite impressive.

The river wound on with numerous islets, channel splits, etc, but we did not run aground once. Beaugency bridge came into view, a leaflet we had picked up the previous evening claiming it as both the longest on the Loire at 435 metres and the oldest surviving. Its twenty-three arches are certainly of various periods, some medieval pointed arches, some 16th and some 18th-century round ones. There is a story that the Devil built the bridge in the 12th century and would claim the soul of the first person to cross it in payment. He was tricked when the townspeople thrust a hapless cat onto the new bridge and the Devil retired in disarray. Do cats have souls? Anyway, James Joyce wrote a children's story, *The Cat and the Devil*, about it: not his normal output. We had prospected the bridge already and decided the wide arch nearest the town bank, flanked by narrower medieval spans both in and out of the river, was the one. Particularly as it was also the one Ludwig Heuse and C S Forester had both used. We shot through, landing alongside the Quai de l'Abbaye, tying the boat to a grille covering a drainage outflow, the concrete flanked a little bizarrely by fig scrub. I assumed this was the result of figs consumed in the town and seeds emerging from the drain.

Unfortunately, as I got out of the boat I fell backwards onto a rock concealed in the long grass and bankside scrub: more pain and in due course a lurid bruise but of course no sympathy from my co-voyager. Emerging from the bank, seventeen miles rowed in the day, we got talking to a young Frenchman who seemed astonished by three things: we were in a rowing boat, we had rowed all the way from Orléans in a day, and had started in Nevers. Looking across the river we saw a huge colony of black-headed gulls on the sandbanks to add to innumerable swallows, swifts, sand martins, terns, cormorants, egrets, ducks, geese and a few heron.

We walked back to the hotel alongside the town's medieval west wall, the Petit, then the Grand Mail. Reaching the Avenue de Blois we turned right and I saw that my car was still where I had left it. In the evening we looked again at the town, including its other medieval church, the 11th-century St-Etienne which was a dependency of Vendôme Abbey. Less costly and much simpler than the Augustinian Abbey

church of Nôtre-Dame we had visited the previous day. It is also a cruciform church but on a smaller scale and now used as an arts centre. Next to it is a 16th-century stone well head housing with an ogee roof, all built against the gable of a house. We continued into the Place du Dr Hyvernaud to admire the Hôtel de Ville, a splendid Renaissance-style building of 1525 by the celebrated architect Charles Viard. From here we descended northwards to the Rue du Pont and had a Ricard in a bar before heading back to the hotel where we had dinner, an enjoyable meal (and wine). We returned to our room well-contented.

# 35

# Nuclear Portage and Madame de Pompadour

Over a much less rushed breakfast than the previous day and with an overcast sky we again walked down the Grand and Petit Mails back to the river. Launching at 9.15 accompanied by the screeching of innumerable gulls on the opposite sandbanks, we headed downriver, a heron flapping slowly across ahead. More than one cuckoo was calling from somewhere in the riverbank trees. As usual with that elusive bird we could not see it and to complete unlocatable sounds we could hear a woodpecker tap-tapping at another riverside tree.

The straggling multi-arched Beaugency bridge gradually receded as Richard pointed out: 'A ragged skein of terns.' Surely 'skein' normally related to geese? The river was glassy smooth and trout were jumping all around us but we were struck by the absence of swifts. Up ahead I saw more nuclear power station cooling towers, this time only two with the further one emitting grey steam into grey clouds. The towers belong to the grandly named Centrale Nucléaire de St-Laurent-des-Eaux but we still had a few miles to row before reaching them.

Beyond Tavers we headed to the middle of the river to pass by a shingle bank that for once conformed exactly in size and location to that shown on the map in our Souchard guide, apparently a rare stability since publication in 2011. Rain came as we rowed past a warning sign on the left bank with a hunched figure carrying a kayak on his back confirming that we would have to portage past the nuclear power station's barrage. Our Souchard guide had already made this clear with a skull and crossbones on a red lozenge: *débarquement* in this case clearly the only option. As the rain eased, a watery sun emerged and we heard another cuckoo in the distance. Richard rowed steadily towards the power station, whose two huge reactor houses partially occupy gigantic steel frames. We saw the barrage signpost and headed for the portage. I steered us alongside the ramp but its foot was at least half a metre above the river's current level, so we climbed out and hauled the boat alongside and up onto the mud and grass.

Once on the ramp we lowered the stern wheels and set off. There were various signs and bright orange spray-painted marks to make matters clear to casual passers-by with a fishing rod, that this was a '*Réserve du Pêche*'. Standing beside a sign to this effect we looked down on the water surging over the barrage, a two-step continuous weir. No way across that in a rowing boat. The Nucléaire had opened in 1969 and we noted that it had suffered one of France's worst nuclear power

accidents in 1980 when the cooling system failed and a graphite core melted; French insouciance promptly denying any plutonium leaks into the Loire.

Down the opposite ramp we relaunched, accompanied by the surprisingly loud noise made by condensing steam within the active cooling tower. We had crossed from one *département* into another near the power station, from Loiret into Loir-et-Cher, and it occurred to us that here was another complication for Hornblower's escape voyage. Each post-Revolutionary *département* would have had zealous customs officials in newly minted uniforms collecting tolls and regulating river traffic at its boundary. Perhaps C S Forester assumed a rowing boat would not have attracted the attention of these officers, but who knows. Discussion of all this occupied us until the cooling towers disappeared from sight. After two hours of rowing Richard suggested we land at Muides-sur-Loire for lunch, a large village for once on the left bank.

I rowed onto a sort of beach just upstream of Muides' road bridge, an attractive and graceful concrete tied-arched one of 1931, replacing, as usual, a suspension bridge built in 1843. It has four spans, each a shallow arch with reinforced concrete stays supporting the road deck: a modern version of Thomas Telford's 1796 cast-iron Buildwas Bridge. Landing, I took the opportunity to jettison my neoprene boat shoes whose soles had wholly disintegrated and in places left my feet exposed. We walked into Muides to find lunch and replete with croque-monsieurs, frites and salad we walked round this delightful village with its early 16th-century parish church, carefully restored, its stone bright with fresh pale-ochre limewash, the tower with a tall, slender slate-clad spire.

Back at the boat, Richard took over the oars and rowed us through the bridge, following the left channel. After what seemed well over a mile we rejoined the main river, amazingly having not run aground in the shallows and sandbanks of my ill-chosen channel. The next riverside village is St-Dyé-sur-Loire which was a river port, thriving during the building of Francois I's magnificent château of Chambord some four miles inland, the stone, timber and other building materials unloaded at the wharves of what was then a walled town. Begun in 1519 the château was by no means complete in 1547 when Francois I died. Work continued sporadically, no doubt to the delight and profit of St-Dyé's boat owners and wharfingers. I'm ashamed to report that we had no intention of landing and heading to the château: perhaps another day and in better weather.

A flèche came into view above the riverbank trees. It belonged to a former grand Gothic collegiate church whose income was augmented by feeding and accommodating pilgrims on the Chemin de Compostelle. It also had the pilgrim-attracting relics of St-Dyé given by Louis XI in the 14th century. Much rebuilt, the church has a massive but truncated west tower in full Renaissance style, rising no higher than the nave  and with a utilitarian pitched roof, so evidently money or will ran out.

Accompanied by swallows, house martins and swifts that had been strangely absent all morning, we rowed on, miserable rain returning. Eventually, easing round a bend, we saw beyond walled parkland the château at Cour-sur-Loire built for Louis XII's 15th-century treasurer, Jacques Hurault, its scale somewhat overwhelmed by the adjacent 16th-century parish church. Another long stretch of stone

park wall indicated we were approaching Menars and its much larger château. As it was now five o'clock we felt it was time to call it a day after sixteen miles of often strenuous rowing. From our lowly riverine position the upper parts of the hundred-metre-long riverfront of the château emerged behind its parterres and ramps. Beyond, we selected a spot to run the boat into the shore and landed, now near the south-west lodge and gates to the château.

We hefted our packs and walked into the village of Menars. The locked church at the gates of the château was started in 1629, in effect the chapel at the château gates. We peered through modern gates towards exceptionally fine 18th-century iron ones at the end of a horse-chestnut-lined avenue. These gates frame a prodigiously long rectangular courtyard surrounded by wings and pavilions built for Madame de Pompadour, Louis XV's mistress. The château itself dates from the 1640s, its grounds laid out by Le Nôtre in the 1670s. Now in excellent nick, unlike when Murray's visited in the 1840s and described it as a *'well-built but ill-kept château which belonged to Madame de Pompadour, and under Louis XVIII to the Duc de Bellune'*. We asked a local about a hotel in Menars. No, but there was a *chambre d'hôte* in the Rue des Grèves, a turning off the main road. Fortunately, they had a room, so our night's rest was sorted.

# 36

# Entre Deux Châteaux: Menars to Chaumont-sur-Loire

We woke to rain but after breakfast it was replaced by clouds and some bright blue sky, and amid the puddles the road shone a deep metallic slate blue. We walked back to the river by a different route, passing a restored communal wash place with a slate roof carried on timber posts. It was apparently built by the brother of Madame de Pompadour utilising a stream from within the château's grounds.

We launched back onto the river a little after nine o'clock, the rain holding off contrary to a doom-laden TV forecast watched over breakfast. Swifts swooped low over the water, and we saw another kingfisher, and then two stone piers of a former railway bridge sitting in the river as useful spots for gulls to perch and survey the scene.

This bridge, just beyond St-Denis-sur-Loire, was another casualty of World War II, having been bombed by the Allies in 1944 and never rebuilt.

Beyond, we rowed past a grim and now rather dated Modernist/Brutalist campsite/restaurant HQ of Lac de Loire camping and leisure: all grime-streaked concrete, angular roofs and massive concrete cantilevered terraces. In front on the bank was a very dead tree which seemed a suitable reaction to this monstrosity. Ahead, we could see a modern river bridge carrying the D174 and in effect Blois' eastern bypass, the Pont Charles de Gaulle, but before reaching it there were concrete towers and piers rising from the river. Part of a continuous weir? As we got nearer it seemed politic to land to assess the problem of getting past what seemed a fairly comprehensive barrier. We headed to the pontoon of a boat club that occupies part of the Parc des Mées, a riverside leisure park for Blois. I stumbled on landing over a boat cable: not a dignified arrival.

There were seven of these concrete structures in the river which we thought initially to be some hangover from the war, but the rowing instructors told us they were fifty years old and similar to our

London Thames Barrier, so were flood defences of some sort, water coursing over barrage weirs between each tower. According to one of the instructors they had been left to decay as they prevented salmon migrating upstream. We discussed the best route through with the oarsmen and women who were preparing to launch four-seater sculls. All agreed the channel closest to the bank was feasible, if turbulent. As we watched, the sculls filled with young people and set off rowing upstream. Rowing upstream!

Back in the boat we rushed the narrow channel nearest the bank (quite exciting), rowed beneath the modern road bridge and saw the graceful and many-arched stone Pont Gabriel but not yet the city of Blois. We ran aground in full sight of Blois in the shallows on the south-east side of the river. Richard had to get out of the boat to free us before I could row gingerly across the shallows eventually reaching deeper water. Landing at eleven o'clock on a grassy beach/ sandbank, we saw sand martins nesting in holes in the quayside embankment walls above. We were about 250 yards upstream of the eleven arches of the Pont Gabriel. Rising to a higher central arch, the parapet surmounted by a tall, bulbous obelisk with royal arms on a cartouche below, the bridge was originally built between 1717 and 1724 to replace one swept away when exceptionally thick river ice broke up in 1716. J M W Turner painted a watercolour view of Pont Gabriel bridge in 1826 and, almost needless to report, the bridge was destroyed in World War II and then rebuilt.

We had more practical concerns and walked out onto Pont Gabriel to assess which arch to row through and settled on the second one from the Blois bank, although there seemed to be another barrier reef about fifty metres downstream to navigate. Over a coffee we discussed whether we would stay in Blois for the day but we had only rowed

five miles which seemed an inadequate day's work. We decided to row on, probably as far as Chaumont-sur-Loire, Amboise looking a bit overambitious in a day. In any case we would return to Blois, probably on our way home from however far we got downstream.

Decisions taken, we bought provisions for a picnic lunch and another coffee, this time a take-away, and headed back to the boat, passing again a dead swan amid the riverside weed. As we had a tricky bridge to row through, Richard took his position at the steering oar, leaving the crew to respond to his orders and getting through was indeed pretty lively, followed by finding a route amid downstream rocky turbulence. Richard was getting pretty good at picking the right line. Looking back to the city centre, the former Benedictine monastery church of St-Nicholas with its twin west towers capped by tall spires looked more interesting than the cathedral and we made a mental note to make sure we visited it when we returned. Murray agreed that it '*is a fine Gothic edifice, chiefly belonging to the 12th century*'. Soon, we passed under another presidential commemorative bridge, the 1994 Pont Francois Mitterand. As I rowed steadily away from Blois, Richard ate his lunchtime feast: a paté pie, a potato cake, crisps and water.

At 12.50 he took over the oars while I ate my boat picnic, the weather warm at last, although heavy with cloud. Opposite Chouzy-sur-Cisse as the river bore south-west we were amused by two picnickers who had driven out to the country, parked on the embankment and set up folding chairs next to their open car boot. Blois under heavy rain clouds fell out of view but at last we were rowing in sunshine, the heavily forested ridge behind Candé-sur-Beuvron ahead. Incidentally, it is time to report a curious phenomenon that we observed; namely, when pulling the oars nature sees a grand opportunity to cover a head in itches. These can be ignored (with difficulty) or the rowing rhythm disrupted for a frantic scratch. The converse of this is that the steersman never gets these itches: it is only when the oars are taken up and both hands are occupied.

Just before the Beuvron, a small river, joined the Loire, the lush green pastures behind tall riverbank willows and poplars were full of sheep. They were grazing the Loire bank, some in the shade of the trees, others in the sunshine. We had heard them for a while as they bleated vigorously, presumably telling each about lush and tasty fresh grass. The general cheeriness was slightly dented by an obviously dead sheep lying on the riverbank a few yards beyond.

Rowing in sunshine had warmed Richard so he took off his jacket, a signal for the sun to vanish behind heavy cloud. The sun soon reappeared, greeted by the croaking of frogs on an island to our left. As we emerged from a long, quite shallow bend the bridge at Chaumont hove into view, a modern one with five steel box-girder spans on concrete piers.

Through the bridge we had to dodge between the remains of piers belonging to an old suspension bridge destroyed (of course) in World War II. In various states of survival, the pier remnants project above the water and are covered in low-set vegetation. We got past them without difficulty and looked up at the great château on the ridge high above and dominating the little town. Or as Murray's guide put it: '*The Château de Chaumont, a conspicuous building picturesquely situated on a height, with machicolated towers, forming 3 sides of a square. It was the residence of Cath*[erine] *de Medicis, whose chamber is shown, and who here spent her time plotting and reading the stars until the death of her husband Henry II* [in 1559]'. We ghosted alongside the town, a single street sandwiched between the cliff-like ridge and a long, narrow riverside meadow. We headed for a solitary riverbank willow directly in line with the château, slightly upstream of a number of moored Loire *fûtreaux*.

We pulled the boat onto the grass beside the willow, a mastless punt on the grass beyond it. Richard looped our substantial anchor chain around the tree as I looked around. While the greenery had looked like meadows from the boat, it was now clear this was a naturalised sandbank cum beach, the riverbank proper nearer the

houses, although an access road had since been laid along the foot of the old embankment. Now three o'clock, we had rowed about fifteen miles and our minds turned to finding somewhere to sleep. We headed up to the main street, Rue du Maréchal de Lattre de Tassigny, named in honour of a general involved in the 1940 defence of the Loire who then escaped to join the Free French under de Gaulle, so a worthy man to commemorate. The church looked a typical skinny 19th-century effort that did not detain us for more than a few moments and we continued to the Hostellerie du Château which looked fine: three 19th-century storeys, the third partly within hipped roofs, the upper two with planted timber-framing to give a medieval or Swiss chalet character. They had a first-floor room at the rear overlooking the river available so our night's sleep secured and dinner booked we set off to look around Chaumont and the riverside.

We walked to the river bridge and crossed it, pausing to look at the river just beyond the bridge with the regular green-clad islet remnants of the old bridge piers. On the north bank by the D952 crossroads was a sculpture group celebrating the local wine Vignoble Touraine-Mesland, with stainless-steel figures set in a miniature vineyard. I can't report that we felt it a masterpiece of modern art, the figures unconvincing, but at least it was different and the vines were real.

Later, back at the hotel we dined well starting with local asparagus from a farm just across the Loire, then duck confit with beans, all washed down with a bottles of local red and white wines. I hope I don't give the impression that food is the be-all and end-all of our trips, but nevertheless if you can't mention the food in France where can you?

# 37

# Royal Amboise

When we got up the sun was shining from a virtually cloudless sky so we could abandon our foul weather gear. But that was not the best of it, for ghosting along fifty feet or so above the river, mist still rising from it, were four hot-air balloons, their exuberant colours aglow in early morning sunlight. After breakfast we headed back to the boat where some of the half-dozen *fûtreaux* were moving about preparing for the day, one with a large, alert dog proudly guarding the stern and all looking like Victorian photographs of the river.

As we readied the boat we agreed we were uneasy about going as far as Tours and leaving the boat tied up in what looked to be a very large city indeed. More to the point, it was at least twenty miles away with Amboise a more reasonable hot-day distance of eleven miles, so we decided to head there instead with its royal château and Leonardo da Vinci connections. That decided to our satisfaction, we launched at about a quarter past nine. I rowed and Richard relaxed, his elbows on the transom, leaning back contentedly.

Opposite les Caves near Artigny we swapped roles and soon I saw beyond Richard the eastern bypass bridge that indicated we were nearing Amboise. It is an elegant reinforced concrete box girder bridge opened in 1981, the piers tapering from river to deck, all pretty stylish. We agreed it was civil engineering at its best. Richard rowed on, the left or south bank a shelving beach pushing us towards the other bank. Ahead there seemed to be various unsatisfactory-looking channels to choose to get through the bridge but the most feasible seemed under the two arches nearest the north bank.

An island engulfing the pier at the left side of the channel was invisible beneath a vast colony of black-headed gulls idly watching us. Passing this audience as near mid-channel as possible took us towards the north channel, the river dividing either side of the Île-St-Jean or Île d'Or. For once this was a genuine island complete with a chapel and streets of houses: radically different from all the uninhabitable shifting sandbank islands we had seen downstream from La-Charité; the river there and at Amboise crossed by two bridges that meet on a central island.

As we approached it seemed that the river channel to the right of Île-St-Jean resembled more a shallow weir than a riverine highway. Not surprisingly, we opted for the left channel, gingerly picked our way across the narrow (and shallow) channel between Black-Headed Gull Island and Île-St-Jean to the Amboise side of the river. Banks of deposited sand and gravel kept the water away from the embankment and we rowed for about half a mile before the water finally reached its foot. To our right we saw the Île-St-Jean protected from Loire floods by a continuous levée or embankment: very necessary, no doubt.

Looking for a place to land, I guided us to a spot that looked promising with a flight of heavily overgrown steps climbing to the top of the embankment, in fact too overgrown. We relaunched and edged further along the riverbank, finally landing as the city's bells rang out for midday. It was a rather tricky landing point with a similar long flight of stone steps up to the road, foliage and scrub near the river, but clearer beyond. More to the point there were saplings aplenty to secure the boat's painter.

The stone steps led onto the Quai Charles Guinot, Amboise's former royal château towering above us. The walls, perched on the north edge of the limestone ridge, looked truncated and battlement-free on our side of the enormous Tour des Minimes nearer the river bridge. Murray's guide is pretty dismissive of the château, stating that the '*late possessor*', King Louis Philippe no less, had so '*improved*' it that '*in the interior there is nothing worth seeing. The improvements … had pierced holes as big as embrasures of a battery in its old and massive walls, to admit broad day into vaults once perhaps cachots or oubliettes, but now, by the aid of whitewash, ventilation and stoves, converted to kitchens, larders, pantries, and cellars; while the upper rooms, papered, polished, and filled with cast-off furniture from the Palais Royal, preserve no trace of antiquity*'. The palace buildings have been '*reduced to a small portion of their original extent, [and] occupy the platform of a lofty rock*'. Not promising.

After Amboise was confiscated in 1434 by Charles VII from its lord, it became a royal palace. Most of the rebuilding and enlargement was undertaken by Louis XI and Charles VIII who after invading Italy in 1494 brought Italian designers and craftsmen to labour mightily (170 masons and seventy hod-carriers on site continuously). Unfortunately, en route to a game of real tennis in the moat Charles banged his head on a stone door lintel. Shaking it off, he watched the game but soon afterwards fell into a coma. Placed on a bag of straw (not exactly a royal feather mattress), he died nine hours later.

He never saw his great project completed but it remained a royal residence until 1560. I should add that the château is now in excellent nick, having been restored by Louis Philippe's descendent the Count de Paris after bomb damage from German planes in 1940.

Although much was demolished soon after 1800 at least the range overlooking the river, the Logis du Roi or the king's apartments, survive, the Tour des Minimes to its left. It is this range with its row of distinctive crocketed dormers and Renaissance styling that makes the whole composition so memorable. The Tour de Minimes and the Tour Hurtault (on the south side of the ridge) are spectacularly large in circumference, for as Murray points out they each '*contain 2 winding, inclined planes of so gradual a slope that horses and even carriages can ascend them to the summit of the rock*'.

Ahead was the main Loire bridge crossing to the Île-St-Jean, its eight arches looking remarkably fresh, with elegant reinforced concrete spans, the outer faces dressed with stone arches. Once again it is a post-war structure built on the restored piers of an 1846 one blown up in 1940 to slow the German advance. Old paintings and prints of the 16th-century predecessor, setting aside the artist's depiction of picturesque decay, show a massive gatehouse on the last span defending the town and château. This bridge was washed away in January 1789, again by an exceptionally harsh winter's ice breaking up.

From where we were it seemed a difficult bridge for a boat, so we consulted our Souchard guide which showed portage at each end through the outer arches, on our side using the riverside walk. Souchard seemed to indicate all arches could be kayaked through, portages '*si besoin*'. Today it looked tricky but that decision could wait, as we wanted to head into the town and visit the château where the great Leonardo da Vinci lived from 1516 until his death in May 1519.

He had been invited to the French court by Francis I who, as every schoolboy knows, had met our Henry VIII at the Field of the Cloth of Gold in 1520. Francis was a true Renaissance prince and counted it something of a coup enticing Leonardo to Amboise, indeed a feather in his elegant cap. It is also, incidentally, how the Mona Lisa came to France as Leonardo brought her with him.

Francis settled him in the Clos Lucé, a substantial villa in an expansive park uphill and about 300 metres south-east of the royal château. To get there we followed the Rue Victor Hugo (obviously not its medieval name) which ran at the foot of the château's towering south walls before climbing towards Clos Lucé. We were amazed to see atop one of the projections from the defensive walls not battlements but a fully fledged Gothic church. I muttered the Durham tag, 'Half house of God, half castle against the Scots,' for it looked wholly incongruous atop a castle mural tower. It is in fact the cruciform Chapelle St-Hubert, a perfect cathedral in miniature

with transepts and an ornate stone central flèche spire, described in Murray's guide as '*one of the most exquisite morsels of profusely florid Gothic in France*'. It was finished in 1493 specifically for the Queen, Anne of Brittany, and is a delightful essay in Flamboyant Gothic.

Beyond the Tour Hurtault, the road climbed towards Clos Lucé but the queue to enter what might be termed the Leonardo Experience stretched far downhill. We contented ourselves with peering into the crowded courtyard of the 15th-century mansion, its red brick and immaculately restored pale-cream limestone gleaming in the warm early-afternoon sunshine. Perhaps as it was the 500th anniversary year of Leonardo's death the queues were understandably long.

Back down the curving Rue Victor Hugo we lunched at Le Comptoir Amboisien on the Place Quai de Charles de Gaulle to the west of the river bridge. The tables were set in a long narrow rear yard and I was intrigued by the menu item Burger du Moment. It turned out to be a perfectly routine burger but no complaints about quality and washed down with two welcome cold beers. Over lunch, we discussed our next move, as we had begun to think of finishing this particular leg of the voyage at Amboise. Richard again had property sale problems crowding in and was increasingly feeling he needed to be on hand in England to deal with them.

If we abandoned ship we agreed we should do full justice to Blois. We had whizzed through the town doing little more than buy a coffee and a picnic but we knew it had good historic architecture and was a fine town, so we decided to set off for Blois and home the next morning. First we would take the Loire-side railway back to Beaugency to collect the car, returning to spend the night in Amboise with both car and boat in close proximity once again.

Leaving the café we saw a modern sculptural group fountain by Max Ernst erected in 1967, the very necessary interpretation board in French and, remarkably, Braille. Its title is a suitably pretentious and opaque '*Au cracheurs, aux drôles, aux genies*' but its fountain and pool were dry and lifeless. Suitably mystified by Surrealist playfulness, we crossed the river, briefly diverting to look at the houses on Île-St-Jean in the middle of the river. The Gare d'Amboise is in the north bank suburb and it was just as well we didn't dawdle on the island for we would have missed the 14:22 to Blois.

We had to change at Blois station to a different line back to Beaugency where the car was, we hoped, patiently waiting for us. The station forecourt was filled with young people heading to a pop concert somewhere near the city. They queued for coaches, all remarkably orderly, while others got into taxis. Richard had suggested, rather extravagantly, I felt, taking a taxi to Beaugency as the next train was in a couple of hours. Fortunately, the taxis were reserved solely to ferry non-bus festival goers. We had a beer in the station café watching the coaches arrive, fill up and go: there must have been thirty at least running as a shuttle service while the elite were whisked away in the pre-booked taxis.

After the beer we had some time left and decided to head towards the edge of the plateau, thinking we could get some good views of the river below. That certainly worked but on the way we stumbled by chance upon what looked like a compact but rather grand pinnacled and turreted Loire château. It turned out to be the residence of Victor Auguste Poulain built for himself in the 1860s next to his chocolate factory. The factory was rebuilt in more fitting arcaded market hall style soon after. To Frenchmen, '*Chocolat Poulain*' has both a chocolatey and a cycling aura, for Poulain sponsored mountain sections of the Tour de France for many years (the Polka-Dot Jersey). The Château de la Villette is now converted to flats and the factory has moved elsewhere, but it was an interesting interlude that enjoyably occupied the time between the beer and the train to Beaugency.

By the time the Beaugency (and Orlèans) train arrived in the station the crowds had thinned and Richard muttered that if we had waited we could have actually gone by taxi, the rank now freed of its concert obligations. I pointed out that we would still have had to wait just as long and we had at least enjoyed a beer, people-watching and a brush with one of France's favourite chocolate bars, even if we had not eaten one. The journey to Beaugency was initially mostly through miles of Blois suburbs and commerce and industry before reaching open country, still with no views of the river well to the south. The car was where I had left it in Beaugency and we drove back towards Amboise, having worked our way through Blois and its suburbs. We crossed the river at Chaumont to follow the road along the south bank of the river as we were interested in seeing the wine *caves* cut into the chalk cliffs.

Reaching Amboise, we parked on the Quai Charles Guinot at the foot of the château's river-facing ramparts. Descending the steps down the embankment back to the boat, we relaunched and rowed the 150 metres to the foot of a boat-launching ramp that descends to the river from the bridge-side car park. We dragged the boat onto the ramp and I reversed the car down the ramp (with some difficulty due to my poor reversing skills). The boat loading and strapping completed, we found a space in the car park.

Richard had booked a hotel on his phone earlier, so we walked to it via a riverbank path alive with Sunday strollers. The path passed beneath the bridge and we climbed a set of steps up the embankment, a central divide marked in metres all the way up to measure flood levels. Our hotel, the Hôtel Le Français, was near where we had had lunch, our room looking out onto the Quai General de Gaulle.

We had a beer in the Café Jules below our window and again walked around the town, before watching the sun set spectacularly behind the opposite riverbank's higher ground. The river was a golden glow, within which were dark silhouettes, one a moored *fûtreau* and another a character seemingly straight from a Caspar David Friedrich painting staring out across the river.

Over a leisurely dinner in Le Lion d'Or restaurant, we discussed the highlights of this section of the voyage, our recollections getting rosier and more fanciful with glasses of wine and with the prospect of time in Blois to delay the departure from the river Loire.

# 38

# Doing Justice to Blois

The next morning we breakfasted and returned to the car, the Loire glistening in the sunshine. A momentary twinge at deserting the river, we drove along the north bank towards Blois, increasingly distracted by high-pitched vibrations and thumping from the car roof. We suspected some strap ends had become detached but I hoped we could survive the din until we got to Blois. Richard was less sure and painted a picture of the boat dislodging and flying through the windscreen of the lorry following unnecessarily close to our rear bumper. So we pulled off into a lay-by and Richard sprang out and fiddled and adjusted and when we set off again the thrumming and slapping had gone.

Reaching Blois I parked on the Quai de Foix. We walked slightly inland to visit St Nicholas, once a Benedictine abbey church and whose dark-slated twin spires had been a prominent feature when Richard rowed away from the city. It sits on the flat land between the Loire and the château whose walls and towers loom from the plateau above. We approached

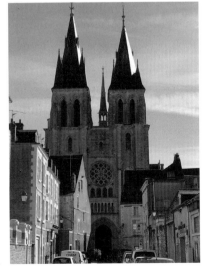

directly along picturesque narrow lanes, the west front of the abbey church revealing itself seemingly reluctantly. The abbey church is a remarkably intact 12th-century one, Gothic pointed arches but a feeling of Romanesque solidity. Admittedly, the west part of the nave and the west towers are a bit later and more influenced by the great Gothic cathedral of Chartres. The abbey buildings however were not so fortunate: largely devastated in the religious wars that wracked 16th-century France, they are mostly 18th century and now a hospital. In a way I suppose a use that continues medieval monastic tradition. A helpful information board outside refers to a 9th-century northern French foundation that relocated to Blois, the monks escaping the Vikings and carrying with them the relics of St Laumer, the original dedication saint of the abbey church. I could not find any information or reason for changing to a dedication to St Nicholas but presumably this took place after the French Revolution when the monks were given their marching orders.

Entering through the west doors the upper parts of the nave have an ethereal character, as though heavenly clouds occupy the space above the main arcades. In truth and much more mundane these are fine-gauge nets, presumably connected to a repair campaign or as Richard suggested to catch falling stone fragments and bat droppings. It's a splendid church, though; a view shared by our Murray's guide, noting it '*is a fine Gothic edifice, chiefly belonging to the 12th century … The manner in which the capitals are executed, and the regularity of the arches, deserve notice*'.

Many of the capitals are what one would expect of the period but we wondered whether our guide was being a touch delicate, for I have never seen so many capitals atop columns with bare-buttocked crouching figures appearing brazenly contemptuous of the monks

and pilgrims below. You can find these capitals of defecating men all over the Romanesque and Gothic world, even on misericords that supported the most respectable clerical posteriors. Weirdly to our modern eyes such capitals can have a biblical scene or an Annunciation on an adjacent capital and one authority takes the view that, as they only occur in male abbey churches and cathedrals, etc, they are demonstrations of masculine dominance. Who knows: the carpenters and sculptors are not around to ask. In case a reader thinks of such earthiness as typically French, a visit to Norwich Cathedral's 14th-century cloister walks will show just such defecating men on roof bosses, one immediately by the Bishop's Door. Rough humour, no doubt, but also a reminder to clergymen not to vaunt themselves too high: we are all human beings. In the church all the defecating capitals were in the eastern parts of the church that was built between 1138 and 1186 and no doubt within sight of the monks in their choir, not to mention pilgrims visiting St Laumer's shrine. I counted five before a return to contemplating the rest of the church's architecture.

Although much of the city around the great Loire river bridge was destroyed in June 1940 by German bombers (but well-rebuilt after) much of the old city survived around St Nicholas, particularly in the Rue St-Lubin and the Rue des Trois Merchands. Along them and in the lanes off are numerous tall timber-framed houses of the 16th and early 17th centuries. Quite a few have a distinctive and striking criss-cross pattern of timbers in the panels. Blois seems yet another city and town along the Loire to have had Coventry levels of destruction during World War II. Sufficient of what Murray's guide described survives to keep the description recognisable: '*numerous streets of stairs running up the hill, and winding narrow lanes lined with picturesque old houses*'.

From the Rue St Lubin we turned left up the steps of le Petit Degrés, which wound up to emerge in Place du Château with views of its east front of red brick and pristine white limestone bathed in warm morning sunlight. The Place is a fine irregular space, widest by the château which is dominated by an equestrian statue of Louis XII in an elaborate late Gothic architectural frame encrusted with cusps and pinnacles. As one guidebook laconically puts it, the statue that replaced the original destroyed during the French Revolution '*does not altogether resemble the original as seen in old engravings*'. In fact, the château was in a poor way by 1845, according to Murray's guide, having been used as a barracks and *allowed to go to ruin* until *with laudable zeal restored to its pristine splendour*. It certainly has that and looks today, recently cleaned and refurbished, as if it had been built yesterday rather than in the early 16th century. Following on from the earlier defecating capitals, there is another odd conjunction. The label stop to the ground-floor window immediately left of the grandiloquent statue of the king has a spectacular woman lifting her skirts and baring her nether regions towards a man on the opposite label stop. Was the sculptor, we wondered, cocking a snook at his superiors and the great adjacent equestrian statue of Louis XII?

We peered into the great courtyard with its snowy-white limestone elevations to see one of those characteristic French Renaissance staircase towers that set up a contrary rhythm to careful regularity by having the staircase expressed by the balustrades climbing with the staircase. We contemplated the stairs and wondered whether they were used by those involved in the treacherous murder of the Duke of Lorraine in 1588 by the then king, Henry III. Murray's guide dwells on the details in which Henry *distributed with his own hand the daggers to his 45 gentlemen in waiting who were to rid him of his rival*. Forty stab wounds later the king emerged and having kicked the corpse in the face *ordered it to be burnt, and the ashes thrown into the river*.

Turning aside we paused to admire the fine views over the river and adjourned to sit in a café on the north side of the Place. Sipping a coffee in Le Marignan café, suddenly the windows of a building on the east side of the square swung open and giant gilded dragons' heads emerged. They moved about and roared spectacularly before vanishing back into the building, the shutters closing. A few minutes later they reappeared, an art installation at the Maison de la Magie that occupies the building. Apparently, inside there are magic shows in mime, that particular French art that tends to pass over the heads of the British: think Marcel Marceau and the invisible sheet of plate glass. Anyway, a curious and surprising accompaniment to our coffee in the sunshine.

We could see the cathedral further to the east but it did not appeal, having been rebuilt after a whirlwind struck it in 1678. Descending from Place du Château into the city parts rebuilt after 1940 bombing we passed the 15th-century Fontaine Louis XII which survived the buildings abutting it having been demolished in 1825. In a late Gothic style and designed by Pierre de Valence it is a remarkable survival.

From here we walked back along the Quai Abbé Grégoire past the former abbey buildings, the church towers above them, back to the car and once again drove away from the Loire and back to England via Vendôme and Le Mans, planning to return in October to continue rowing past Tours and (who knows) as far as Saumur.

# 39

# A Happy Return Postponed

As Richard's selling of properties was still under way we agreed an intended October 2019 date for wetting the keel in the Loire would be problematic. We rescheduled the next voyage for May 2020 with a final trip if needed in October the same year. We had hopes of getting much further in a full week in May, perhaps to Saumur or beyond. Optimistic as it subsequently turned out. Things were still looking promising as, to the relief of all, the sales of both the Greek and Devon houses went through. As far as rowing-related matters were concerned, the boat would go with Richard to his new home near Bath and enter an unexpectedly prolonged period of storage in its grounds. Nearer to Buckinghamshire than Devonshire, we would be in a better location for logistics purposes, halving the distance between our respective homes. So all to the good. We looked forward in an optimistic frame of mind to resuming the Hornblower project in 2020.

However, I am getting ahead of myself but at least Richard and Vicky managed to complete their move to Bath on All Fools' Day 2020, via a couple of months 'sofa surfing' at their younger daughter's house. For some reason Richard saw the date as of some symbolic significance. The alert reader will have spotted that this was after England went into Covid-19 lockdown towards the end of March 2020, so they were fortunate to manage the move. The measures taken to deal with the Covid pandemic put an end to any hopes for a '*calm sea and prosperous voyage*' for the whole of 2020, joining other causes of postponement that included my wife's gallstone operation. On the positive side, property selling would no longer distract the Great Helmsman, although our project along the Loire was beginning to be as long-winded as the construction of a French medieval cathedral.

It seemed we would have to wait for a resumption until 2021 with luck, as we intend to carry on rowing downstream in the wake of Horatio Hornblower who had not had a pandemic to get in the way of his escape. If he had taken as long as us, the Napoleonic Wars would have been long over. We had started out on the River Severn in May 2016, hoping to complete our rowing of the two rivers in two or at the most three years. We rowed down the Severn from the Welsh border to beyond Tewkesbury in two goes in a single year and on the Loire from Nevers down to Amboise in three tranches over three years, the first abruptly terminated by the theft of the boat in Gien.

What remained to row in Hornblower's watery wake? Well, we had rowed well over half the total to date, 170 miles from Nevers. As we looked downstream from the river bridge at Amboise in October 2019 towards the obviously invisible Nantes, 137 miles of rowing remained. Add in the Severn and we had achieved a pretty creditable (we think) 275 miles of rowing. Downstream of Amboise lie three superb towns for the architectural historian, namely Tours, Saumur and Angers with many minor accents such as Langeais. Admittedly, there were fairly long lacunae described in our Souchard guide as '*mers de sable*'. Neither C S Forester nor Northcote Parkinson dwell on the lower Loire sections, saving their verbal firepower for Hornblower's daring recapture of the ten-gun cutter *Witch of Endor* in Nantes and their escape out to sea and the British blockading fleet.

Obviously, we wanted to complete the voyage as we were aiming to replicate Hornblower's escape in full but Richard and I had had a splendid series of voyages on two great rivers and seen towns, cities and villages in a completely different way from the usual road or rail-borne ways. There is something immensely satisfying in approaching a place slowly. First seen in the far distance, on occasion its presence revealed by a church tower, gradually a place emerges, assuming character and presence as you get nearer, first buildings, riverside trees, embankments and moored boats, then people until finally you arrive.

It is a 'slow-reveal' that gives more insight into the nature of a settlement and its physical character than you could ever get driving in by road, or even arriving at a town-centre railway station, usually through amorphous suburbs. It demonstrates in a way no other mode of transport can the reasons for the settlement and the overwhelming significance of a river and its bridges to a town's story. It is similar approaching a port from the sea: a smudge on the horizon gradually becomes distant buildings, then human bustle as you get nearer. On a cross-channel ferry the upper decks are always lined by people delighting in this gradual revelation: it's little different on a river.

We have had a truly revelatory experience, and another reminder of the astonishing wealth of our medieval architectural heritage. France and England have a rich raiment of medieval churches still in use and cherished down the years by succeeding generations. We also saw the dramatic effects of the Dissolution of the Monasteries under Henry VIII in England and the French Revolution in France. Ruins, such as Buildwas Abbey, and traces of Western Europe's rich monastic past are equally evocative. Who could forget the view from the river of Worcester Cathedral or La Charité-sur-Loire? Or of the châteaux of Chaumont or Amboise? Fine historic towns and villages, exciting bridges such as the Iron Bridge or the Pont Gabriel at Blois. The architectural and historical riches we had rowed through will

remain vivid in our memories for years to come. The title of Paul Binski's authoritative and magnificent book seems apposite, *Gothic Wonder*, to which we would add 'Romanesque Wonder'.

On the Loire we rowed through towns, villages and above all bridges that had been bitterly fought over in both 1940 by retreating French forces and in 1944 by retreating Germans. The scale of devastation was staggering and some strategic towns such as Gien and Blois had suffered massive destruction. As for the Loire bridges and the occasional aqueduct virtually all were destroyed or severely damaged, many in both 1940 and 1944 and much of this is discussed in the book. The grainy photograph taken in 1940 shows the Pont Neuf at Orléans.

Our voyage was also a revelation of how strongly the French defended the Loire front and at what human and material cost. We had both recently read a book about the Fall of France which was another eye-opener as in British history the 1940 focus is very much on Dunkirk (*Case Red: The Collapse of France* by Robert Forczyk). The French fought like tigers and although with very few superior tanks and dreadfully stretched resources in men and equipment inflicted very heavy losses on the Germans. Had Weygand not decided on giving up while the army and heavily depleted air force were still fighting courageously, things might have been very different. We saw for ourselves the results of French heroism and commend the book to all who subscribe to myths about 'cheese-eating surrender monkeys': a gross calumny on a brave people.

Much of my aim in writing this book has been to a great extent met and the rowing of two rivers provided us with unforgettable experiences. In discussion we agreed that publishing our voyages to date was fully justifiable. In due course we could produce an expanded second edition adding further chapters following our intended return to the Loire. We had seen sufficient of all we had wished, apart from the lower Loire and Nantes, and what I have written can stand on its own. After all we had achieved rather more than Jerome K Jerome who only got as far as Oxford. I did toy briefly with publishing the Severn sections as Part One, with the Loire when completed as Part Two. Richard and I concluded that the two go together like oars and rowlocks so this 'first edition' therefore covers both rivers.

We certainly did not appreciate as we left our hotel in Amboise to head for Blois, then England, that we would not be back afloat for a least eighteen months, Covid writing off 2020. We pondered what Hornblower would have made of our decision to publish before we had reached Nantes. C S Forester himself, in the *Annie Marble*, appeared not to have motored all the watery way from Nevers to Nantes. From our researches he did not go down the Loire from Gien to Orlèans, so we could advance that in our defence to a possibly disappointed shade of Horatio Hornblower. One somewhat unexpected benefit of our voyage was a greater insight into the creative workings of C S Forester's mind and his use of his own experiences to provide plot elements and these greatly enriched his books. The first day on the Loire downstream from Nevers and the canal and river-borne dash

down from Gloucester to London were transformed by these direct experiences, even if they took place long after Hornblower's exploits.

Another grainy photo shows the Foresters in their powered punt passing through the bridge at Beaugency in 1928. I reread the relevant pages in Forester's *The Hornblower Companion* (pages 126-34) for a further authorial confessional and enlightenment. Our fathers had of course 'lived in the moment', reading the books as they were published, producing an immediacy and excitement that we could not have, but we had both been infected with their Hornblower enthusiasms. In a way, we felt that Forester was with us in the boat as much as Hornblower, Bush and Brown.

Furthermore, our voyage had demonstrated several issues for Forester fans to ponder apart from the well-known one concerning the whereabouts of the Château de Graçay: the impossibly long first day's row of the escape, the Canal Latéral à la Loire not having been built until decades after the escape and confusing Briare's aqueduct with the bridge at Gien. Northcote Parkinson gives the dates of the voyage as starting on 17th April 1811 and reaching Nantes on 3rd May, a total of sixteen days, an average daily row of about twenty-three miles and well within feasibility limits. Our average thirteen miles a day was fine as we were not trying to escape France and were intent on visiting and revelling in France's great historic architecture. We hope our enthusiasm will encourage others to get onto the Severn and the Loire and if they have as much fun on their adventures we will be delighted. Our abiding memories will undoubtedly be of the joy of rowing rivers with challenges to a small rowing boat, an abundance of birds of all sorts, even the odd otter and giant catfish, and of course the scenery. Also medieval and later historic architecture seen from a riverine perspective: the history of communities writ large in stone.

When we next return to the Loire we will be older and wiser (?) and possibly have to rename the boat *Flying Colours 75*. In the meantime, we renew the boat insurance in case of another Gien, ready to get on our way to the Loire. So, I conclude with a photograph of the sun setting at La Charité-sur-Loire. After all the sun always rises over the river and will do so again for us.

# A Selection of the Books Referred to and Used in this Book

**The River Severn**

*The Buildings of England, Yale University Press*

Brooks, Alan & Pevsner, Nikolaus, *Worcestershire* (2nd Edition 2007)

Newman, John & Pevsner, Nikolaus, *Shropshire* (2nd Edition 2006)

Verey, David & Brooks, Alan, *Gloucestershire 2: The Vale and the Forest of Dean* (Third Edition, 2002)

*British Regional Geology, Institute of Geological Science, London*

Hains, B A, *Central England* (1975 Edition) HMSO

Smith, Bernard & George, T Neville, *North Wales* (1961 Edition) HMSO

*Other titles*

Forester C S, *The Hornblower Companion* (1964) Pinnacle Paperback Edition, 1975

*Hornblower and the Atropos* (1953) Little Brown

Fort, Tom, *Downstream: Across England in a Punt* (2008) Century

Glover, Julian, *Man of Iron: Thomas Telford and the Building of Britain* (2017) Bloomsbury

Jeremiah, Josephine, *The River Severn: A Pictorial History* (1998) Phillimore

Jerome, Jerome K, *Three Men In A Boat* (1889) Penguin edition 1957
   *Three Men on the Bummel* (1900) Penguin edition 1994
Richardson, Linsdall, *The River Severn between Upper Arley (Worcs.)
   and Gloucester* (1964) Published by the Author
Waters, Brian, *Severn Tide* (1947) and *Severn Stream* (1949) London,
   J M Dent

**The River Loire**

Forczyk, Robert, *Case Red: The Collapse of France* (2017) Osprey
Forester C S, *Flying Colours* (1938) Michael Joseph
   *Lord Hornblower* (1946) Michael Joseph
   *The Voyage of the Annie Marble* (1929) The Bodley Head
Murray, John (ed), *A Hand-book for Travellers in France* (1844,
   regularly updated) John Murray
Parkinson, C Northcote, *The Life and Times of Horatio Hornblower*
   (1970) Michael Joseph
Souchard, Jean-François, *La Loire Vue du Fleuve – Guide de
   Randonnée Nautique* (2011) Le Canotier Éditions

# The award-winning Slow Travel series from Bradt Guides

Over 20 regional guides across Britain.
See the full list at bradtguides.com/slowtravel.